Open Wide the Doors

A Memoir of Faith, Hope and Freedom in Iran

MAHVASH SABET

*Translated and edited from the original Persian
by A. Mottahedeh and B. Nakhjavani*

ONEWORLD

A Oneworld Book

First published by Oneworld Publications Ltd in 2026

ISBN 978-1-83643-223-4
eISBN 978-1-83643-222-7

Typeset by Geethik Technologies
Printed and bound in Great Britain by Clays Ltd, Elcograf S.p.A.

The authorised representative in the EEA is eucomply OU, Pärnu mnt 139b–14, 11317 Tallinn, Estonia
(email: hello@eucompliancepartner.com / phone: +33757690241)

Oneworld Publications Ltd
10 Bloomsbury Street
London WC1B 3SR
England

Stay up to date with the latest books,
special offers, and exclusive content from
Oneworld with our newsletter

Sign up on our website
oneworld.co.uk

shining example of dignified defiance shows us the path to a glorious future for Iran in which power and prosperity is derived from the noble potentialities inherent in human beings.'

Payam Akhavan, Professor of International
Law and former UN Prosecutor at The Hague

'In this deeply moving book, first-hand insights are shared about how to survive prolonged injustice and pain with profound dignity and strength. Mahvash Sabet's love shines throughout – love for family, colleagues and friends, for co-detainees with various records of criminality, and even the very prison and intelligence officials who preside over her suffering, solitary confinement, torture, isolation and threats. In this book she demonstrates how delicate personal and artistic sensibilities can not only survive but also be finessed in such ugly settings and, in that, she demonstrates lessons for us all.'

Nazila Ghanea, Professor of Law, University of Oxford,
UN Special Rapporteur on freedom of religion or belief

'Mahvash Sabet, a prisoner of conscience in Iran, invokes doors – iron doors, doors with double chains and locks, doors with knobs on only one side – again and again in her heart-wrenching account of injustice, violence, and prejudice. Yet faith, conviction, grace and dignity cannot be locked away. They move beyond enclosures, beyond the reach of tyranny. No door – no machinery of repression – can bar their power or their passage. *Open Wide the Doors*, edited and exquisitely translated by Bahiyyih Nakhjavani and Azita Mottahedeh, is an eloquent testimony to that truth.'

Farzaneh Milani, author of *Veils and Words*

CONTENTS

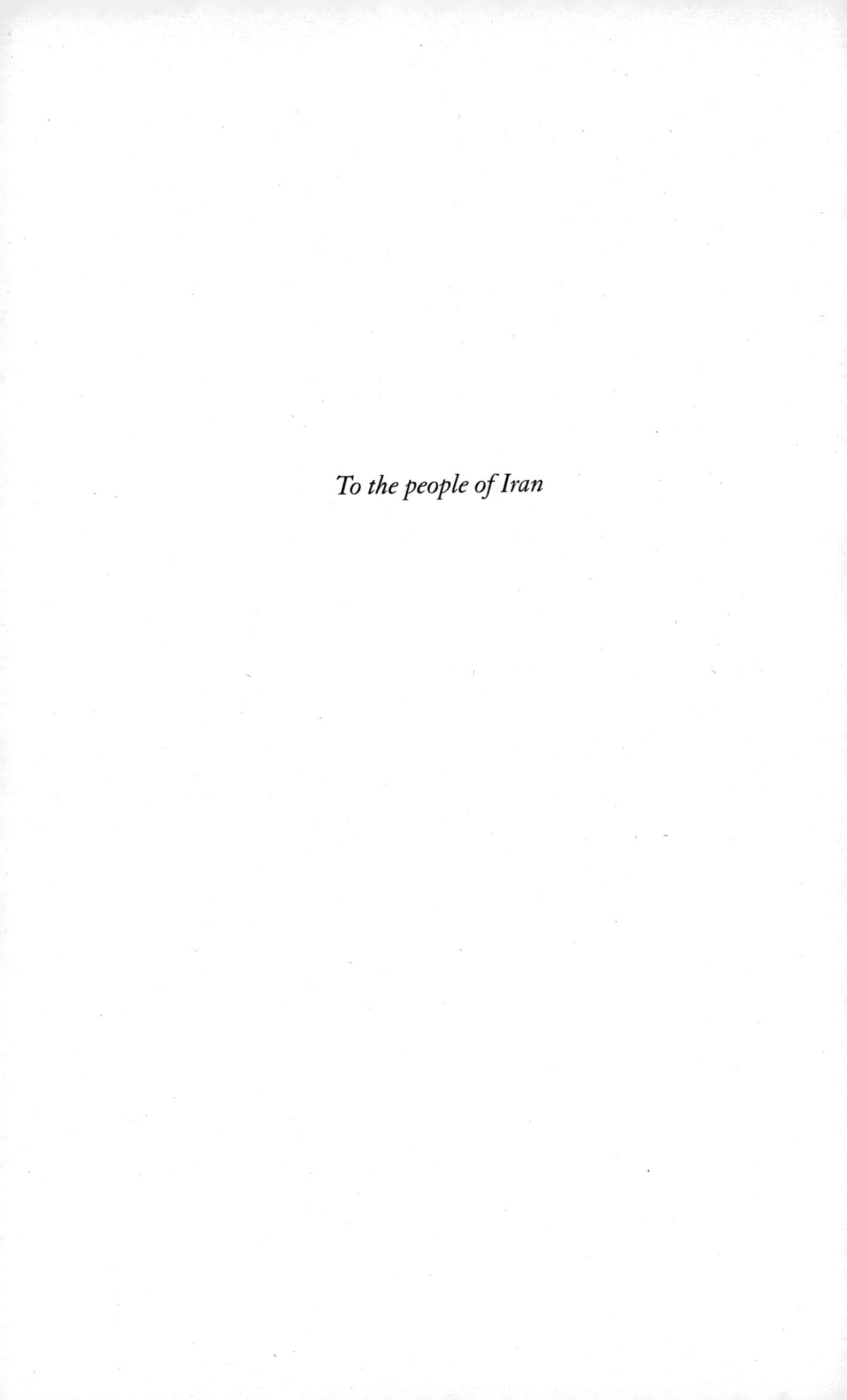

To the people of Iran

Why stay in prison when the door's wide open?

Rumi

INTRODUCTION

Mahvash Sabet is a prisoner of conscience in Iran, condemned for being a follower of the Bahá'í Faith. Over the past twenty years, she has been incarcerated in four Iranian prisons, arrested on three separate occasions and held for thirty months without trial. She has twice been given ten-year sentences because of her beliefs, the first time in 2008 and most recently in 2022. In May 2025, there was a call at the European Parliament for her unconditional release, on humanitarian grounds.[1] It has, until now, been ignored.

Born in Ardestan on 4 February 1952, Mahvash grew up in the provincial town of Zavareh, where she was first exposed to fanaticism and prejudice against the Bahá'í Faith as a child. When she was about ten years old, her family moved from the provinces to the capital, enabling her to continue her education in Tehran. A bright student with a flair for poetry, she later received a bachelor's degree in social sciences from Reyhan University,[2] and embarked on a teaching career soon after her marriage to Siyávash Sabet on 21 May 1973. After several years, she became the principal of 21 Farvardín, a prestigious school in District 13 of Tehran, and later directed the school of Tehran's Air Force Base personnel. She was also invited to serve on the National Literacy Committee of Iran, as a respected education professional.

But everything changed, for Mahvash and many others, when the Islamic Republic came to power in 1979. It changed catastrophically for the 350,000 Bahá'ís, members of the largest religious minority in the country.

When the Bahá'í Faith first emerged in Persia in the middle of the nineteenth century, its message of social justice and religious renewal swept through the land like wildfire, causing consternation at court and a crisis among the clergy. The mullahs, their authority already weakened, felt threatened by the claim that religious truth was relative, not absolute. The newly crowned Qajar monarch Naser al-Din Shah feared insurrection and the loss of power, as his people protested against corruption. So from the mid-1840s onward a campaign of persecution was launched against this Faith, killing over 10,000 adherents in the last half of the nineteenth century alone, and double that number by the beginning of the twentieth. The Báb, the young forerunner of the Bahá'í Faith, was repeatedly imprisoned before being shot in Tabríz in 1850. Bahá'u'lláh, its founder, was banished to Baghdad in 1852, and later exiled for life to the fortress of St Jean d'Acre in Palestine, a penal colony of the Ottoman Empire. After Bahá'u'lláh passed away in 1892, the remains of the Báb were brought to rest on the slopes of Mt Carmel, making the twin cities of Haifa and Akka a focus of prayer, pilgrimage and the point of adoration for the Bahá'í community, long before the state of Israel was established in 1948.

Over the course of the twentieth century, the Bahá'í Faith continued to be persecuted in the land of its birth. Bahá'í properties and lives were ravaged in towns and villages under both Pahlavi governments. Anti-Bahá'í propaganda was unleashed on radio programmes by radical clerics during the 1950s, and the National Bahá'í Centre in the capital was occupied by the military and partially destroyed in 1955. But throughout the same period, the Faith grew to become the second most widespread religion in the world, with some seven million members in more than 230 countries and adherents from many cultures, races and spiritual backgrounds. Its internal governance depends not on individuals but on institutions, voted for by secret ballot, locally and nationally. At the head of this essentially spiritual system of administration is the Universal House of Justice, elected every five years to guide and govern the affairs of the Bahá'í world from its seat in Haifa.

However, within months of Khomeini assuming power, the new Iranian theocracy branded this entity as 'political'. And despite the Faith's roots in Persia, its world centre in present day Israel gave the regime a spurious reason to accuse Bahá'ís of being 'foreign spies'. From 1979 on, their persecution became systematic. From one day to the next, Bahá'ís were 'disqualified'[3] from civic life and denied the protections extended to other religious minorities in Iran's constitution. Bahá'í professionals lost their jobs; Bahá'í-owned businesses had permits withheld and ultimately confiscated by the state; Bahá'í children were harassed and hounded from schools; Bahá'í students were expelled from and denied access to university; Bahá'í cemeteries were destroyed and sacred Bahá'í sites were razed to the ground. And, along with thousands of other Bahá'ís, Mahvash was fired from her teaching position and permanently barred from working in the public sector.

During the so-called Iranian 'Cultural Revolution' which followed, the Bahá'í Administrative Order was specifically targeted, and its institutions duly decimated by the government. Between 1980 and 1983, all nine members of the

National Spiritual Assembly of the Bahá'ís of Iran were abducted, never to be seen again, eight members of a newly elected National Assembly were executed without trial, and scores of Local Assembly members across Iran were similarly taken into custody and killed. Finally, when a legal ban was officially announced against their administration on 29 August 1983, the Bahá'ís dissolved all elected institutions in the country, in compliance with their principles.

From then on, and with the tacit approval of the authorities, an *ad hoc* group of first three, then five, and finally seven individuals was appointed to be community caretakers. The Yárán-i-Iran, or Friends of Iran, were responsible for registering births, marriages and deaths as well as providing financial and medical support, counselling services and training programmes to help the oppressed community. Among the many services they developed was the Bahá'í Institute of Higher Education (BIHE), a remarkable project founded in 1987 to ensure university education for students. Until recently it offered more than fifty-six academic courses in the sciences, engineering, business management, social sciences and humanities, which are recognised by 115 universities worldwide. Mahvash became its first director and served in this capacity for fifteen years. In 2005, she was also appointed to be one of the 'Bahá'í Seven' – as the last group of the Yárán came to be known – and was the group's secretary for three years. Imprisoned in the notorious Section 209 of Evin Prison in Tehran that same year, she was released after thirty-four days, then arrested again on 5 March 2008.

And that is when this story begins.

Covering ten months of Mahvash's incarceration – from March to December 2008 – this memoir describes the beginning of her first ten-year prison sentence. It was a gruelling time of unmitigated solitude. She was unable to communicate with anyone while in the detention centre of Mashhad, and friends and family were kept in ignorance of her fate for the many weeks she was holed up in the public prison of Vakilabad. Eight months would go by before anyone was allowed to visit her in Evin Prison and she was also separated for most of this time from her fellow members of the Yárán. Only at the very end of this period was she finally reunited with her dear friend and colleague, Faribá Kamalábádí, who was condemned like Mahvash to another decade of incarceration.

This is an intensely personal story. Written in unvarnished prose, the writer's honesty is palpable and her self-doubt as well as her faith sincerely shared. She describes her fellow prisoners with unwavering compassion, while depicting her own experiences without a trace of self-pity. She records the attacks against her beliefs as well as her defence of them without exaggeration, and endures her isolation with a biting wit. Her characteristic irony is as much a survival mechanism as a literary device.

The events described in these pages were compiled by Mahvash more than three years after they occurred, and edited and translated with her approval almost a decade later. Real first names are used when permission has been granted or individuals are already in the public domain, and pseudonyms are given to officials associated with the regime. Days and months have been identified according to the Persian calendar, with Gregorian equivalents in parentheses.[4] Mahvash was able to answer questions about her writing during her brief years of freedom, but once imprisoned again, it was impossible to reach her. Any blame for infelicities or inaccuracies in these pages must therefore be laid at the translators' doors.

The third and most recent arrest of Mahvash Sabet took place on 31 July 2022, while she was recuperating from Covid-19 with her husband in the north of the country. She had to undergo four more months of solitary confinement, interrogation and physical abuse before being condemned to a second decade-long sentence. But we are dealing with that rare, almost mythic creature in this story: a reliable narrator. Mahvash may be a captive behind prison walls, but the truth she tells defies them. Her memoir was born of harsh injustice, but it bears witness to the endurance of love, the resilience of hope. She refuses to be bound. Her voice is free, her words ring true, and her story opens the doors of the heart.

The translators

1

ABDUCTION

'You're late,' spat the judge, with a jerk of his head.

He was a grim-faced, sullen-looking man in his mid-fifties, and had evidently been expecting me for some time. He ordered me curtly to fill out a form. Name. Address. Husband's name and profession. Number of children. Specific duties in the Bahá'í community. He already knew that I was a member of the Yárán-i-Iran; he also knew I served as secretary of the group. He glanced at the completed form, cursorily, without saying a word and then turned to leave, indicating with a wave of his hand that I should remain behind.

'Wait here,' he barked over his shoulder. 'You'll need to answer more questions.'

The door slammed shut.

I waited. Ten minutes. A quarter of an hour. No one came. The place was deserted. The offices had closed at noon and everyone, including the judge, I suppose, had gone home for lunch. There I was, all alone in one of the departmental offices on the second floor of the Revolutionary Court in the city of Mashhad, thinking about a corpse.

I had taken a flight from Tehran early that morning because of this corpse. Originally from Bushehr on the Gulf, the dead man had recently been buried in the Bahá'í cemetery of Mashhad. Soon after, the Intelligence Bureau of Mashhad had launched a lawsuit against the Yárán-i-Iran, claiming the dead man should have been buried in the Muslim cemetery. He had recanted his faith as a Bahá'í and returned to Islam years ago, according to the Bureau, and the Bahá'ís had no right to bury him with all of their other 'apostates'. The Yárán had investigated the matter and ascertained that even though this person had withdrawn from Bahá'í activities at the start of the Islamic Revolution, he had never formally resigned and never actually removed his name from the community list. Nor had he ever, as was customary, publicly announced in the press that he no longer wished to be considered a Bahá'í. Instead, he had quietly continued to be in touch with the Bahá'í community all these years and even attended gatherings from time to time. Finally, during his last illness, he had sent us a letter, signed also by his wife and children, requesting burial in the Bahá'í cemetery of Mashhad. And so his wishes had been respected, and he was laid to rest as a Bahá'í.

This, however, was unacceptable to the radicals who controlled the government in this province. Denunciation had been evaded while he was still living, but punishment was unavoidable now that he was dead. The form I had just filled out for the judge demanded to know, yet again, why permission had been granted to bury a Muslim according to Bahá'í rites, why he had been laid to rest in soil polluted by apostasy. Our formal response to the lawsuit, which already provided all the careful research of the case, was apparently not enough for this Intelligence Bureau. I had been obliged to travel to Mashhad in order to justify our actions to the judge in person, all over again.

If truth be told, I did not know the dead man. We had never actually met. But after repeatedly explaining, over and over,

who he was when alive and why and where he had been buried after his death, I was becoming intimately acquainted with
the poor soul. I was even beginning to feel slightly concerned
that all this red tape prevented him from resting in peace.
Unfortunately there was no space for humour on the form I
had just filled out, not even of the darkest kind, or I might
have been tempted to add that if the family had changed their
minds, they were more than welcome to dig up the body and
bury it elsewhere. We would not have minded, and I'm sure
the corpse would not have cared either.

Would you?

My query was respectful, but naturally, there was no
response. I glanced at my watch again and sighed. Half an
hour had passed. How long was I supposed to wait? I couldn't
call anyone because the security people had taken away my
phone at the entrance. I couldn't contact the kind friend who
had picked me up at the airport or the one who was waiting
outside to take me back there, his eyes no doubt awash with
concern. I was stuck in this room, wrapped in a black chador
borrowed from a neighbour, talking to a corpse in my head.

I sighed again.

Well, neither of us can do much about it, can we?

The stagnant air shifted around me, almost as if the dead
man, in his unquiet grave, were sighing too. So I counselled
myself to learn patience from him.

Finally, after an endless interval, two men entered the office.
Fear sliced through my heart at the sight of them. They had
rough, three-day beards and hostile faces. Their shirts hung
loosely over their crumpled trousers, and they looked for all
the world like thugs from some low-budget mafia movie. Who
were they? No word of introduction. They stood some

distance away from me, their eyes fixed on the floor. As if to avoid the contamination of my gaze. As if to illustrate the world of difference between us.

Then one of them spoke brusquely. 'Come along now!'

'Where?' I asked. 'Where are we going?'

The other echoed the judge's last words, with an unpleasant grin. 'More questions.'

I rose, trying to keep a brave face, heart pounding. They did not spare me another glance as I followed them into the car park. I was ordered to sit in the back of a waiting car and, after a few moments, the man beside the driver shoved a thick blindfold at me.

'Tie it tight,' he ordered, without turning around, 'and press your forehead against the back of the front seat.'

'Who are you?' I asked. 'Where are you taking me?'

'We already told you. You have a few more questions to answer.'

The car swung round, turned right, left, continued swinging round corners randomly for what seemed like an age, and finally stopped with a screech of brakes. The man beside the driver then told me to get out. I had no idea where I was. The blindfold was so thick and wide that I couldn't see a thing beneath it and I stumbled as I tried to find my feet on the pavement. Then the voice of another man rasped out orders.

'Watch it! There's a step! Be careful. Come here!'

He was walking just ahead of me, pulling at the corner of my chador to guide me, but I could not even see the backs of his heels, despite looking vertically down under the blindfold. I was lurching after an unseen man into the unknown.

A moment or two later, we seemed to have entered a building, because a suffocating silence surrounded me. No sight, no sound, but all my senses started to tingle. I walked round a corner, and a lingering scent of *attar* of roses or rosewater wafted towards me. Another corner, and the air felt warm, sour and close. From time to time, a fleeting current of air suggested someone walking swiftly past. I even thought I felt eyes on me, the silent weight of a gaze. Maybe the sense of being stared at made me straighten my back and hold my head high. Somehow I managed to avoid tripping.

After changing direction several more times, and walking a considerable distance, we turned a final corner and came to an abrupt halt. Peering down with vertical vision, I guessed we were in front of a door.

'Go in,' my guide grunted, as he opened it. 'Give me the blindfold and leave your chador in there.'

Behind the door was a narrow corridor with a hook on the wall. I turned to give the blindfold back to my guide and glimpsed him, just as he was closing the door. He was an old man. Who was he? Why had he brought me here? And where was I?

Half-blinded after the long, black walk, I looked about me. An empty grey cell?

Then the door burst open again, and I swung round to find a woman standing behind me. She had entered without warning, without knocking. Had she been following me all this time or just waiting outside this room? Her pale face chilled me to the bone. She was dressed like a bat, covered in black from head to foot in a full-length veil, with only her two hands visible and the severe circle of her face. She beckoned me forward, avoiding my eyes, and indicated, with an impatient gesture, that I should raise my arms above my head. Without warning and in total silence, she performed a full body search on me, probing every nook and cranny with two invasive fingers. When it was over, she removed my watch, snatched my handbag, and left the room without uttering a word, taking my breath along with her.

* * *

I stared around me, half-stunned. The cell was about ten metres square, with a basin and a shower stall in one corner and a pile of blankets in another. But I had hardly registered more than the dullness of the walls before there was a knock at the door again, and a shout.

'Get yourself ready!' The old man had come back.

That's when I noticed that the black chador I had borrowed from a neighbour was no longer hanging on the hook. Had the woman taken it away with her? In its place was a navy-blue chador speckled with tiny flowers, which stank. I put it on, overwhelmed with revulsion, and followed the old man down the corridor again, blindfolded and filled with mounting dread. Once more the long passages, once more the twists and turns through this labyrinth, until he brought me into – where?

The space seemed to widen into a room as I walked in.

A chair was pushed at me: I backed into it blindly. A piece of paper was lying on the armrest of the chair: I rolled up the lower edge of the blindfold an inch to see it. A logo was stamped at the top of the page: the Intelligence Ministry of Mashhad. Was I in the detention centre of the Khorasan Razavi Intelligence Bureau?[5] There was no knowing. I was handed a pen and a list of written questions. Not a word, not a single gesture, apart from sheet after sheet of paper placed on my armrest in rapid succession – all with the same questions on the same subject as before: the dead man.

I completed the last answer on the final form and was startled by a voice behind me.

'Take her away!'

What an icy tone. What an iron hard voice. It was not the old man. And it was certainly not the corpse in my head. Someone else had been in the room with me all this time, watching me write, handing me the pen, giving me the forms to fill.

The interrogator!

I stood up with a shudder and blundered after whoever was pulling me by the chador. Back we went, through the winding corridors to the same grey cell, and when I finally took the blindfold off and the door closed, I wasn't sure my eyes were actually seeing anything. I had been in the dark for hours. I was tired and longed for a shower. But even as I began washing my hands and face in the sink, I heard another sharp rap behind me.

'Get ready!'

It was the old man again and this time he flung the door wide open as he called for me. I was taken aback; it was just as well I hadn't had time to undress! And that's when I noticed for the first time there was no doorknob on the door.

How strange – a door that can only be opened from the outside?

'This way!' he ordered, as I put on the blindfold and stumbled into double-darkness again. 'That way!' The cold air pricked my skin. 'Mind the step!' A sharp smell of petrol. A car was waiting by the curbside, the engine throbbing. 'Watch your head!' I bent slightly as a door squeaked open and barely managed to be seated before it slammed shut behind me.

'Lean forward and place your forehead against the front seat.'

Someone else was giving the orders this time. A different thug. Another male voice, throwing words at me like bones. I could only hear him, not see him, but I sensed the violence. Same words, different man. After a drive of about twenty minutes, he spoke again.

'Take off your blindfold and put it under the seat.'

I blinked in the darkness and saw that we were parked at the back entrance of the Revolutionary Court, where I had been dropped off earlier that afternoon. With sight restored, it was easier to walk fast. I hurried through the front lobby, as instructed, and just as I reached the top of the stairs, my eyes fell on a worn old clock face on the wall.

Ten p.m. Eight whole hours had passed since my arrival in Mashhad!

Another judge was in the office I entered, seated behind a large desk. He was not the sour-faced man I had encountered earlier, but was younger, perhaps about forty, short, stocky and trimly dressed. Two other men were sitting side by side some distance away from him. I guessed from their tell-tale three-day beards and resolutely scruffy appearances that, like the previous gentlemen I had met, they too were agents of the Intelligence Bureau.

The judge called me forward and asked me again to verify my name, then placed a typed document before me. I read it, standing in front of him. An indictment. The charges were as stated: the unauthorised burial of a Muslim in the Bahá'í cemetery of Mashhad. I was guilty of a corpse being interred in the wrong bit of earth. As 'evidence' of this heinous crime, he handed me the letter from the Yárán granting admission to bury the dead man in our cemetery. It bore the signature of my aide, who assisted me with such routine matters.

'Is this your signature?' he demanded.

I told him it was written at my request and signed on my behalf.

'If you have a defence,' he said, 'you'd better write it now.'

Once again I took up the pen and scribbled as fast and as fully as six paragraphs and a margin would allow, repeating that the matter had been thoroughly investigated, that the dead man had never formally renounced his faith, that he had stayed in touch with our community, and that the burial had been arranged at his personal request, and with the written approval of his family. I signed my name at the bottom of the page, with a mental nod at the corpse.

Let's hope this will allow you to be left alone at last.

The judge skimmed the page perfunctorily and responded with measured sarcasm.

'Your reasons seem very convincing,' he drawled, with barely a glance in my direction. Then after a moment, he said, 'I rule 10 million *tumans* as bail. Can you pay that?'

'Yes, certainly,' I replied, feeling a dizzying surge of relief. 'Of course, yes indeed, the money can be sent at once, wherever you wish, with a single phone call, yes!'

Thank God! I thought. The worst is over. Bail. Ten million isn't that much. Some bail bonds amounted to three or four billion *tumans* (roughly $100,000). My arguments must have convinced this judge that the offence was not so severe. Perhaps I could go home now?

He scrawled on the page and then said dismissively, 'Call to arrange for bail.'

'Thank you, sir,' I babbled, my words tumbling over each other. 'Thank you very much indeed, sir.' I was so dazed with gratitude that I barely noticed the two agents had risen to their feet and were shambling over to stand on each side of me.

'Come along then,' said one.

'Let's go!' growled the other.

I was taken aback. But what about phoning for bail? I wanted to leave this place, but not with these men. I turned to the judge anxiously, earnestly. 'Please allow me to phone first, sir,' I urged. 'Please let me arrange for the money transfer directly from here.'

But he brushed off the request, as if I was just a fussy, melodramatic woman.

'What's your problem?' he said, with cool disdain. 'These gentlemen have mobile phones, you know. You can call from anywhere.'

I started to panic. If the phone call was not made then and there in front of this judge, or if the judge himself did not explicitly instruct these grim-looking men to phone on my behalf, I had no guarantee of anything. My case could be delayed interminably.

'Please, sir, please won't you order these gentlemen to make the call right now please, about the bail?' I insisted incoherently. It was more of a spill than a speech. I had become the very archetype of the hysteric the judge had dismissed me for being.

He disregarded me completely, swung round on his swivel chair and busied himself with paperwork. The two men shrugged and left the room. I could see them waiting outside the door and grew desperate. I appealed to the judge's humanity, still assuming that he could, would and surely *should* protect the innocent, still believing that he might, must, at least *try* to administer justice. But it was no use. He continued to ignore me, and after a few minutes, it was clear that he had no intention of doing otherwise. His papers were far more important and there was no alternative for me but to turn from his well-tailored back in dismay.

As soon as I stepped through the door, the two agents frog-marched me straight to the car. It was late. It was dark. The whole city seemed as suffocated as I was, in the back seat. But when the driver finally came to a halt and I removed the blind-folded, I could not believe my eyes. We were parked in front of Vakilabad – the public prison of Mashhad!

The agent next to the driver leapt to his feet and opened the back door of the car.

'Get out!' he hissed.

2

QARANTINEH

It was midnight when we entered the main lobby of the prison. The agent took a gun out of his breast pocket and handed it to the policeman on duty, and I took refuge on a black metal chair some distance away and watched. He walked up to the front desk and greeted the security guards with familiarity; they seemed to know him well. He pulled a folded document out of another pocket and one of the guards read it, ogling at me from time to time. I shrank inside the smelly chador and crossed my legs to defy his vulgar stare. After a brief exchange, the agent signed a ledger, retrieved his gun, and swaggered back into the night.

I was starting to feel tired, but the security guard was already calling me over and the business had to begin all over again. Personal details. Name. Address. Place of birth. And now, indictment. So the corpse also had to be registered this time, in another ledger, over my signature. After that, a soldier took me to the fingerprinting room and from there to the photo studio, where they gave me a card, with a number to hold against my chest with inky fingers. Only when the flash of the camera went off, for my full-face mug shot, did the horror of the situation finally hit me. I was a convict now? Officially registered in a public prison?

Back in the main lobby, a couple of young men were awaiting their turn at the front desk, each handcuffed to a soldier, so the guard ordered me into a separate room, set aside for women in custody. Two young girls were already seated on the floor, leaning against the wall. They were wearing layers of heavy make-up and ignored me completely, engrossed in whispers. When a female guard summoned me out, I was almost relieved to leave them.

She ushered me through the main lobby and conducted me across a vast, dimly lit courtyard towards the women's section of the prison. The darkness was oppressive out there, the shadows of the buildings forbidding, the female guard taciturn. Once indoors, however, another official entertained me pleasantly enough, for almost an hour, by registering all the same details about me into yet another ledger at a painstakingly slow pace. By the time everything had been noted about the corpse too – where he had lived, where he died, why he had been buried in a Bahá'í cemetery – I heartily wished the dead man could provide the answers for himself. But he didn't have that option. I imagined his embarrassed apologies.

*Never you mind. What's a little repetition between friend*s?

After my fingers were blackened one more time, another female guard in an equally black chador was summoned to take me to the *qarantineh* section, where I was told I would await bail.[6] I was greatly taken aback and said that I had already offered to pay bail with a single phone call. But my protestations were dismissed. In chilly silence, two more female guards, in government uniforms – jackets, trousers, navy-blue scarves – conducted the registration process, yet again. But the body-search was done by a couple of prisoners, who seemed more friendly and asked many questions, though I wished they would have kept their inquisitive fingers to themselves. By the time one of the female guards finally marched me to the stairs of the qarantineh section, I was exhausted and could not help reproaching the corpse, as we began to climb, step after step.

It's your fault I'm here, you know.

The weight of his embarrassment dragged at my heels. The guard told me to hurry.

But don't worry; no one will notice you in the wee hours of the night.

A second guard was waiting for us at the top of the stairs, in front of an iron door. The two of them exchanged a few hurried words and rattled their keys officiously.

They might even allow a dead man into the women's ward.

But after opening the door, they thrust me through, alone.

* * *

I found myself in a small antechamber with two tiny windows just below the ceiling and a row of rusty, triple bunk beds against the wall. They were all occupied, and someone in a lower bunk was just waking up as I stumbled in. I guessed she was the warden in charge, for she acknowledged the guards at the door with a sleepy wave, and beckoned me in.

As soon as the iron door clanged shut behind me, I was assaulted. A hysterical woman from a bunk bed in the far corner rushed at me, gabbling frantically.

'What do you think? What should I do? Can you help me?'

Then a woman in one of the top bunks began yelling, 'I'm dying, give me something, I swear by Abu'l-Fadl, I'm dying! Don't you have anything for me?'

The warden was not the least bit fazed by this cacophony. She pointed, with half-closed eyes, towards an open doorway at the far end of the room, indicating that I should go through.

I walked forwards a few steps, hesitated and turned back again. The warden flapped her hand at me, implying that I should keep going, further on.

'Into the hall,' she finally muttered, then rolled over, turning her back on me.

Beyond the open doorway, I could see a long, rectangular vestibule lined on each side with ten or twelve sets of the same rusted iron, triple-bunk beds, placed end to end. Dozens of women were lying on the floor so the space between the beds was crammed with bodies. Faint wails and moans rose and fell all around. The ceiling was relatively high in this long hall, but there was no ventilation; the air was stale, smelled fetid and stank of faeces. I was reluctant to go in and stood transfixed in the doorway.

All of a sudden, a woman in one of the top bunks leaned over abruptly and vomited onto the blankets of the sleepers below. Someone objected loudly and two more women half-raised their heads to see what was going on. Another ran to the far end of the hall and could be heard throwing up there. The rest simply covered their heads beneath their blankets and continued sleeping, as the groans continued, like a dreadful dirge.

Nausea overwhelmed me. I was paralysed. At that moment, another woman noticed me from a top bunk. She seemed as shocked to see me as I was to be there.

'Who the hell are you?' she called.

Her voice was strident and a few more heads turned towards me. For several minutes I was the object of dull scrutiny, but nothing more was said, and everyone soon looked away. It was unnerving. Since I had no idea what to do, I returned to the antechamber and went back to the warden's bed. She shifted position, saw me hovering, and gave me a hooded glare.

'What is it?' she slurred.

'Where,' I asked, timidly, 'am I supposed to sleep?'

'Find any corner,' she mumbled, shifting away again, 'and shut your eyes.'

'A blanket, perhaps?' I hazarded, after some hesitation.

'None left,' she muttered drowsily. 'Share.'

As she turned her back on me, a woman with a large birthmark on her face slid off another bunk and reeled past us. She stopped briefly in her tracks at the hall doorway, before staggering on over the prone bodies, whimpering weakly as she made her way towards the far end. Her helpless noises summed up the futility of further enquiry. The warden was already asleep by the time I stepped back into the hall.

'*Salaam*,' I announced to no one in particular.

No response. No empty beds. No space even on the floor. After a few moments, a large woman, lying beside the door, noticed me standing there and rolled her flabby body slowly over towards me. The poor creature lay humped under a soiled army blanket, helplessly obese; her cheeks were pale and puffy, her face lifeless. But what eyes she fixed on me! Her gaze seemed to rise from the depths of a fathomless need, as though she was searching for a sign, a hint, a hope of something in my very presence.

I slid slowly down beside her, blocking half the doorway, because there was literally nowhere else to be. And since she seemed not to care and soon withdrew her famished gaze, I slipped my freezing feet ever so carefully under her blanket. I only dared use a corner of it, but oh! what a relief it was to feel her blessed body heat. Then, just as the comforting warmth started to penetrate, just as my taut muscles began to relax, she rolled slowly and heavily over in the opposite direction, pulling the blanket away from me.

After that, there was no alternative. I just shut my eyes and shook in my shoes, and counselled myself to wait for dawn.

Surely you can cope for one night, and you'll be back home tomorrow.

It was then I remembered my husband's words that morning. When I told him I would be back in the evening, he had looked into my eyes for an unusually long time.

'How can you be so certain? What if you don't come back?' he had said.

'Of course I will,' I instantly retorted. 'I've paid for a return ticket, remember? I haven't even said goodbye to Negár and Fúrúd because I'll be home tonight.'

He smiled and deployed that generous catch-all phrase that covers all eventualities and allows for the slippage and uncertainty that so often attends human affairs.

'*Enshallah*,' he had murmured. 'Take care. Call me if you need anything.'

By now, news of my detention must have reached him and the rest of the family. Was our home going to be appropriated now that I was in prison, and if so, how were my precious husband and children coping with the situation? The worried faces of my daughter and son rose before my eyes; Negár and Fúrúd were young adults, and no longer children, but this abduction would stir dreadful memories of my previous arrest. I imagined the anguish of my father, my sister, my brother who would suffer on my account; would they be at risk now, too, because of me? But I was most concerned about my husband. Despite his Muslim background, Siyávash had not been much interested in religion when we first married. But as a Bahá'í, he was now a target for extremists. Was he under pressure? When I was leaving him that morning, I had lingered some minutes before getting into the car, just to watch his dear figure disappear down the 'alley of our eternal friendship.'[7] Síyávash was my soul mate.

His vulnerability led me to ponder the deteriorating conditions of our times. Violence had become endemic in our country. The rule of law seemed non-existent, corruption widespread. It was as if we had returned to the Qajar era, when punishment was harsh and arbitrary, inflicted at whim and utterly disproportionate to any crime. The basic values of civil society seemed utterly eroded, and no one's rights could be protected these days. Of course in theory, we all had the same constitutional rights, even the Bahá'ís, but in the present climate no one could guarantee these would be honoured. It was as if all Iranians shared the plight of the Bahá'ís now – at least to a limited degree.

As I sat, feeling wretched and worrying about Síyávash, I remembered the early years of the Islamic Revolution, when Bahá'í administrative bodies were officially disbanded by the government, in 1362 (1983). After they had first kidnapped and then killed the members of our elected institutions, we had to find ways to take care of the community's internal needs. And for twenty-three years, the Yárán had been able to do this; they had managed, with great difficulty but with wisdom, to maintain relations with government officials on behalf of the Bahá'í community. In a spirit of transparency, they had even shared communications with them from the administrative centre of the Bahá'í Faith, as proof of our non-political aims. But the situation had recently deteriorated. When the extremists came into power in 1385 (2006),[8] they shifted the emphasis of their repression from apostasy to political espionage, arresting us not only as heretics but as foreign agents, and accusing us of being spies for hostile governments,

Israel in particular. Although the Universal House of Justice respects all governments, including that of Israel, and calls upon Bahá'ís everywhere to do likewise and to obey the rule of law in their countries, its authority is purely spiritual and unrelated to either the foreign policies or the internal party politics of any nation. Nevertheless, this issue was now being used to hunt us down.

I remembered when the Yárán-i-Iran introduced themselves to Mr Aslání, our liaison with the regime. I remembered, with a shiver, his enigmatic response to the news of our appointment for that year.

'Well, congratulations to you all,' he had said, with an ironic smile. 'Now that you've stepped into the ring, you'd better be ready for a fight. If not, you'll be beaten down.'

A few months later, his mobile number was blocked and our sole means of communication with the government was lost; after that, no one gave us any information, no one offered us advocacy. From that day on, the Bahá'ís had no recourse to justice through the law and were automatically disqualified from legal permits and civic rights. And although other religious minorities were under the jurisdiction of the Ministry of the Interior, we were placed under the purview of the Ministry of Intelligence. These were the gentlemen who had detained me in Mashhad, a stronghold of extremism in the north. These were the ones who could order the arrest of my beloved husband at any time.

* * *

Suddenly, a woman screamed for a painkiller, and I lost my train of thought. Why was everyone so profoundly wretched in this place? The pain around me was devastating. Some of the women seemed dead to the world; others twisted and turned in agony, thumping their fists against the wall. A few kept begging for painkillers, though no one paid attention. Several spent the whole night running back and forth to the far end of the hall, where I realised there must be a toilet. Almost all looked desperately ill: pale, frail, forlorn women; helpless, hopeless, captive women; old and young, skinny and fat, with dark rings around their eyes and tattered clothes. Their hair was brittle and scruffy or simply falling out; some had shaved heads, covered in open sores. Their faces seemed abnormal too, partially bruised, blotched black and blue. And why were birthmarks so common among them?

It was like landing on another planet, encountering another species. But where in outer space were we? Lucky Little Prince to have landed where he did and found the love of a rose. And I began to ponder about parallel worlds, worlds that never meet, worlds forever divided as they roll towards infinity. The worlds of the haves and have nots, of the privileged and deprived. What immensities lie between us. What abysses. Who in the world of the affluent or comfortable in Tehran knew what was happening in this miserable world of the forgotten and forlorn in Mashhad? Had a thought about them ever crossed my mind?

Sleep fled from me that night. But it had nothing to do with being deprived of a bed. I had not been sleeping well since the Yárán started being harassed about the burial of the dead man. As secretary, it had been my responsibility to answer the Mashhad Bureau of Intelligence, and for days and nights my mind had been preoccupied with how to defend our position.

In addition, I had to wake up before dawn because I was… yes! Fasting.

Fasting in Vakilabad Prison?

I had completely forgotten about it. No wonder I was so hungry. The thought almost made me laugh out loud. How was it possible to forget the Bahá'í Fast?[9] For Bahá'ís, the spring equinox symbolises a spiritual awakening and during the period leading up to Naw-Rúz (New Year), we rise to breakfast at dawn and refrain from food and drink until sunset. I had not eaten for twenty-four hours.

By now it was morning. Women were beginning to move back and forth between the hall and the antechamber. I tried to shut them out, by closing my eyes, by trying to pray. But it was impossible. Voices were being raised, women were grumbling, chattering. I could not concentrate. And then the warden poked her head through the door.

'Sabet! Wake up. They're calling for you. Get ready.'

I scrambled to my feet. It was time to brave the fetid bathroom.

* * *

The so-called sanitary area of the qarantineh, which catered to at least a hundred women, contained two toilets and two showers. The place was lit by one dim lamp, but total darkness would have been preferable. The filth was appalling and the stench even worse. Piles of excrement and heaps of used menstruation pads reeking with stale blood lay all over the floor; balls of hair were scattered everywhere, seething and quivering in the faint light. The floor was slippery underfoot and the air so foul that I could hardly breathe.

I splashed my face with cold water over the muck of the washbasin. Even the tap water stank. I dried myself with my scarf to have the illusion of being clean, but there was no trace of perfume left in the cloth. Finally, after smoothing my hair and straightening my clothes as best as I could, I was ready.

The young female guard who had come to escort me could only repeat herself. 'Downstairs, go downstairs. Hurry, hurry, go down.'

'Where to?' I asked.

'Maximum security!' she replied. 'Criminal investigation. Hurry!'

My heart sank. Why was I being taken to the section of the prison reserved for murderers and felons? What crime had I committed? Hadn't I already been granted bail? But the female guard, who had the misfortune of being cross-eyed as well as repetitive, offered me no straight answers; she merely pulled her black chador over her head and mindlessly reiterated the same words, over and over again.

'Hurry! Hurry down! Go downstairs!'

3

THE DETENTION CENTRE

We ran down the stairs I had toiled up the previous night and walked along the same corridor to the entrance of the women's ward. Although I could see where I was going now, I stumbled behind the young woman in a haze of horrid body odour, wishing the chador did not smell so bad. It was a reminder, as if I needed it, of the corpse again.

I've fallen into your grave. Will I ever get out?

At the registration desk of the women's ward, a new escort was waiting for me, a middle-aged man whom I had not met before but instantly recognised, from his grim bearing and slovenly appearance, as one more agent of the Mashhad Intelligence Bureau. I did not acknowledge him but stood to one side until he finally came towards me, avoiding my gaze and gesturing to the door leading to the courtyard, as if to an animal.

'Get going,' he said rudely, and then walked two paces ahead of me across the courtyard, towards the main prison building on the other side.

Whatever happens, you must find a telephone as soon as possible and bail yourself out of this place. You can't stay trapped in here any longer.

'Where are you taking me?' I asked.

'Same place as yesterday.'

'So – not maximum security?'

'No.'

Was it wilful ignorance or calculation on the part of the cross-eyed girl to give me the wrong information? Or was she just as confused as they hoped to make me? We reached the main lobby of the prison, and the agent retrieved his gun from the policeman on duty at the front desk, placing it inside his jacket pocket, just like the man who had brought me here the night before. My heart skipped a beat.

All these men have guns.

When we passed through the main doors of Vakilabad Prison, the armed agent was rolling a sheet of paper in his hand like a bludgeon. I glanced hurriedly to the right and left, as we stepped out into the open. The entrance way was jam-packed with people.

Is someone there for me, someone to save me, someone I know?

Everyone was looking for someone. None of us was finding anyone. We were all seekers, wandering here and there, anxiously waiting, earnestly watching. For the One.

A Peugeot, light beige in colour, was parked some distance away. The gun-toting agent opened the back door for me and then settled himself next to the driver. The air inside the car was muggy and not exactly fragrant. We drove along for a few minutes before I had to go through the same blindfold routine. 'Wear this. Lean your head forward. Press against the back of the driver's seat.' I obeyed, lost sight of the world again, and was driven around for another twenty minutes in muffled silence. When the car finally drew to a halt, the agent opened the back door and instructed me not only where to walk but how. 'Watch the step. Keep going. Don't lift your head. Move it.' And then a few minutes later, a familiar bark.

'Follow me!'

It was the same old man, my guide from yesterday. Once again, he took hold of a corner of my chador and walked rapidly ahead of me. We stepped around a corner, and again I smelled the faint trace of rosewater in the air, again felt the momentary draught of someone walking by. A few yards on, and then to the right; several paces further and a dank, closed atmosphere on the left. I stumbled after him like a zombie all the way up to the same cell as the day before. And the minute I stepped inside, I remembered the shower stall.

You have to take a shower today, you must.

But there was no time. Before I could begin to consider how to go about it, there was another rap on the door. Already? Once, twice. It was the old man. Again.

'Ready for interrogation!' he snapped.

This time, when I stepped into the room, I tilted my head back as far as I dared to see from under the blindfold where I should sit. In the far corner of the room, facing the wall, was a chair with an armrest. I walked towards it carefully, sat down gingerly and pulled my chador forward over my face. Then I straightened my spine, lifted my chin high and tightened my empty stomach as much as I could. Hunger hurt.

The interrogator moved up behind me, speaking quietly, almost respectfully; the metallic chill of his voice was replaced by the insidious silk of a '*Salaam.*'

I salaamed him back, without enthusiasm, on my guard.

'Did you sleep well last night?'

Instead of replying, I raised the issue of bail.

'The judge agreed to ten million *tumans*. I've been waiting to phone for the money since last night. Can I call now, please.' I made it a statement not a question.

'Who do you want to call?' he asked, in the same smooth tone.

'A friend in Mashhad.'

'Fine. No problem. But first I must ask you a few questions.'

I told him to go ahead and ask his questions. I was eager to finish this stupid business, eager to find a phone, to call Siyávash. To get out of this place. I fidgeted in the chair. The interrogator cleared his throat but did not speak. Silence ensued. I waited some more. More silence. After several minutes had passed without any attempt on the part of my interlocutor to even engage me in conversation, I realised, with a sickening jolt, that he had no intention of finishing this business. These gentlemen of the Intelligence Bureau had abducted me for a reason. I was here for a purpose, in accordance with a preconceived plan. And with that realisation, all their past communications flashed through my mind.

Some time ago, the Intelligence Bureau in Mashhad had informed the Yárán-i-Iran, through the local Bahá'ís, that we had to work under their supervision. After consultation, the Yárán decided that, since we were responsible for the Bahá'ís nationally, we should not be supervised regionally, by a provincial office. We wrote a letter explaining our position and sent it to the Ministry of Intelligence in the capital. Although the letter came back by return post, by dint of patience and repeated visits, we were finally able to hand-deliver it; we even had it stamped and received a precious registration number – a small administrative victory for us, tantamount to an approval of our position. Although we discovered that the letter had been eventually forwarded to the gentlemen of Mashhad, the Ministry stamp and that registration number justified our right to ignore their subsequent demands. Now they were holding me hostage because they probably wanted to force compliance from us.

Having ostentatiously cleared his throat again, the interrogator started pacing behind my chair. He still did not speak but I could hear him huffing and puffing heavily behind me. The hair rose on the back of my neck each time he drew near. It was difficult not to be intimidated by those gusts from his mouth; they conveyed so much revulsion and disgust. And yet, when he spoke again, it was with restraint and the same innocuous questions.

'Did you sleep well last night?' he repeated softly.

'Thank you.'

He continued to pace back and forth behind me, still saying nothing, still inhaling and exhaling like a congested steam engine. So what about his so-called 'few questions'? Was he ever going to start? Each time he drew near, I dreaded the sensation of his snuffling breath against my skin. It was most unsettling. Then suddenly, when I least expected it, he reached over my shoulder and abruptly placed a piece of paper on my armrest.

I jerked away in surprise. Another questionnaire? I rolled up my blindfold just enough to see the same demands about my personal details and duties I had already replied to the previous evening and so I answered them all over again. Yes, I was the secretary of the Yárán-i-Iran. Yes, I had written the letter of permission for this burial. And yes, the dead man was obliged to meekly acknowledge his part in the affair at the bottom of the page.

How many times will they harangue you, my dear fellow, just to hold me hostage?

Hours passed. At lunchtime, I mentioned that I was fasting. The interrogator did not react in the slightest. The questioning proceeded slowly, and with difficulty, all through the afternoon, because I was attempting, within the limits of the law, to avoid replying to anything that was not directly related to the specific charges against me concerning the allegedly 'unauthorised burial.' The corpse became my shield against the interrogator.

But it was soon clear that the burial issue was just an excuse. Although the dead man was being dragged into the cross-examination at every turn, none of it was actually about him. The interrogator kept returning again and again to my role as secretary of the Yárán. In order to avoid self-incrimination as well as confrontation, I sometimes held my tongue and said nothing. At other times I replied as briefly as possible. On a few occasions, I even managed to deflect the question altogether and change the subject. It was a duel of sorts.

No doubt the interrogator was also appraising me, gauging my weaknesses with every thrust and parry. But it was an unequal contest, for while I sat exposed before him in the plain light of day, he remained hidden from my view, and not only because of the blindfold. I was ignorant of the methods of these gentlemen of Mashhad. I had no idea how to protect myself against their subtle techniques and was at the mercy of the doubts they planted in my mind. I felt hopelessly inadequate.

* * *

All through that day until nightfall, I sat in that chair, and due to my 'lack of cooperation,' was sent back to the prison after the evening meal had been served, so I remained hungry. But the warden was still awake and on this second occasion, at least, she welcomed me with a friendly smile. Since it wasn't so late, we spoke together a little. Her name was Parváneh, and she was quite beautiful; I guessed she was in her mid-thirties. She told me about the qarantineh ward and how most of the women here were on remand. She was a prisoner herself and had agreed to work as a warden because it reduced the length of her sentence. She did not mention her responsibilities, but I surmised that her position gave her some privileges.

In the course of our conversation, I noticed a young girl sitting on a box in the middle of the hall while another woman shaved off her tangled, matted hair. Lice, I was told. And then I remembered the seething balls of hair in the barely lit bathroom. I also asked about the unusual number of bruised women. What was the matter with them? Had they all been beaten up? Why were their faces so black and blue? Crack, I was told.

'Most are addicts,' Parváneh added, in an offhanded manner. 'Crack does that to skin. Some are going through withdrawal. Some get methadone.' And then she explained that the women were kept in qarantineh for 'as long as it took' to determine if they had ingested packets of heroin or crack. I did not pursue the matter further.

That evening, I noticed that one of the top bunk beds next to the sanitary area was empty, and Parváneh confirmed that I could use it. By then I was desperate to sleep but how was I supposed to climb up there? I hesitated, watching the other women haul themselves onto the iron bedsteads. In fact, none of the beds had ladders, so this was the only way to do it. The hall was still overcrowded, still filled with moaning and wailing, but a bed was preferable to the icy floor. So I seized the bedframe and heaved myself up like the others.

Once installed on my throne, I discovered there was nothing on the bed springs but a single military blanket instead of a mattress. No cover, and of course no pillow. But what a unique bounty to have a place to sleep! *Just sleep*, I counselled myself, *sleep*. If anything, the toilets smelled even worse from this height, but at least I was warm.

I sat on my bed for a while looking at the women below. Two of them were huddled close to each other on a bottom bunk. They had lowered their scarves and were leaning their heads together, sniffing some powder from the palms of their hands. Then one of them glanced up and saw me staring. Our eyes locked briefly before I drew back in fear at the threatening glare she gave, but perhaps she was equally frightened of me.

A few moments later, I noticed an emaciated body on the edge of a bottom bunk opposite. God help us! A young woman, in her thirties perhaps, but what had she done to herself? Skin and bones. A head like a prop for an anatomy class. Eyes set back in deep rings of darkness. Bones starkly prominent above hollow cheeks and thin, black lips stretched around a gaping, toothless mouth. She was rubbing her skeletal legs with skinny hands – the personification of poverty, loneliness and utter abandonment.

Suddenly, I found myself down beside her. I didn't stop to think, or wonder whether I was imposing, much less consider what I could do for her. I just sat gingerly on the edge of the bed and reached out my hand. She turned and gave me a look of pleading desperation.

'Are you in pain?' I whispered.

What a stupid question! She did not reply. How could she? This woman was not 'in' anything: she was pain itself, the embodiment of it, the incarnation of it. I was ashamed of even opening my mouth and appalled to be just sitting there, healthy and strong, beside her. I reached out instinctively to caress her shoulder – and had the shock of my life. You could have counted every bone in her body. It was terrifying. The embrace

I had been prepared to give her might have harmed the poor soul. She could have literally broken to pieces under my touch.

I don't know why, but my heart flooded with love for this young woman. All I could do was hold her hand, and as we sat there, side by side in silence, I saw her eyes moving with excruciating slowness, down towards the ground. She was trying to show me something, tell me something. Then I realised that she wanted me to look at her feet. So I did. They were tragic. Old wounds on the heel, oozing sores between the toes, huge fungi bursting out of the flesh, bleeding skin, protruding bones. And she was filthy. She might have had just one bath in her whole life, and that was when she was born. I slipped down to the floor and held her foot in the palm of my hands, conscious only of her suffering. My heart was breaking as I sat holding that festering foot. It was an attempt to cup life a little longer, to keep death at bay. How could she be kept here in this condition? What kind of place was this in which to house such suffering? This woman needed to be in a hospital, not a prison.

After sitting with her a while, I went to the bathroom to wash. The conditions in there were as ghastly as ever: the stench, the heaps of hair, the piles of menstruation pads, were staggering. In fact, such an abundance of excrement and contamination in a place of such scarcity and deprivation was a real paradox. I guessed most of the women began to bleed from the sheer stress of being locked up here. It was very dark, very difficult to see clearly or to breathe without gagging, so after looking around and trying to gauge the scale of the mess, I gave up. There was nothing to do but wash my hands and clamber back onto the bed.

But my thoughts were in turmoil. I was very tempted to clean that whole sanitary area, to scour it down. Could I try to rake up the worst of the filth, somehow? At the same time, I rebuked myself for being such a pious prig. Who did I think I was? Mother Teresa? And yet, if I didn't do it, who would? Who even could? Most of the women in this place were incapable of undertaking such a task. They were too sick, too weak. And then I remembered the story of an early Bahá'í[10] who had been asked to clean the room of a foul-smelling invalid whom she could hardly bear to approach at first, and who discovered that in performing this simple act, she overcame her disgust. That story galvanised me, renewed my determination. Within minutes, I was talking to Parváneh about my plan, telling her that I could certainly achieve it with some disinfectant and a few garbage bags.

It was not long before the bathroom was relatively clean that night, and it proved not too difficult to do, because Parváneh, together with another young girl and a few older women, worked with me. Parváneh even found a glove to wear while gathering up the mess and provided a large plastic sack in which to stuff the piles of waste. We scrubbed the grime away and threw water at the walls from top to bottom; we found a large round basin and mopped the floor from side to side. The result was something like a miracle.

I was the first to take a shower after that. I washed my clothes and, on Parváneh's advice, hung them to dry near the radiator on the bed railings next to hers. Afterwards, wrapped in an overall with the chador round my shoulders, I pulled myself up to my bunk opposite the now relatively clean toilets. Parváneh even gave me a glass of hot water and an extra blanket. I was still cold and hungry, but at least I slept in a bed that second night.

Of course, no real sleep was possible on the qarantineh ward. Everyone moved about the whole night, back and forth, back and forth. But lying under the ceiling with my mop of wet hair, my thoughts were as restless as the women pacing the hall. I was no longer thinking about access to a telephone or paying bail or even going home. I knew I could go nowhere until those gentlemen chose to release me. So I revisited all the questions asked by the interrogator that day, trying to understand his motives. What was he really after? What were these men of Mashhad trying to get out of me, by holding me hostage here?

When I articulated this question to myself, I came up with some grim answers. Apart from extorting compliance and forcing the Yárán to submit to their regional authority, they probably wanted to extract information from me, which they could use to attack the Bahá'í community at its very heart. They wanted to undermine the faith of the Bahá'ís all over Iran. They wanted to erode our trust in our institutions and fill us with doubt about our beliefs. And they were ready to resort to terror and intimidation to do it.

Suddenly, I began to tremble. Whether it was from the cold, or my wet head, or some dread too deep to articulate, I don't know, but I started shaking from top to toe. To calm down, I tried to remind myself that all of this was to be expected. It was, in a sense, 'normal.' This was how all autocracies, all totalitarian regimes behaved. No authoritarian government could tolerate people who thought or believed differently. They all tried to stifle and suppress those they could not govern through fear. It was not the first time this had occurred in history, and Iran was not the only country where it was happening.

Cheer up. There's nothing unique about your situation.

Even the corpse agreed with that conclusion, and so I began, gradually, to relax.

4

A CRUST OF BREAD

Early the next morning, someone called out my name.

'Get ready! Maximum security! Criminal investigation!'

By then I had guessed that the words 'criminal' and 'maximum security' were euphemisms for the Intelligence Bureau. I scrambled off the bed, screened myself off in a corner, and pulled on my still damp clothes, before running down the steps.

This time, without the blindfold, I was able to look at the courtyard as I hurried across it, see the lifeless flower beds scattered around, and notice the weeds beginning to sprout. It was the 17th of Esfand (7 March 2008), some weeks before Naw-Rúz, but spring was just round the corner. A tremor of joy ran through me at the thought, even though we were still trapped in winter, the nights bitter cold, the days chilly and filled with fear. But seeds of hope began to stir quietly in the heart of this incurable optimist. Somehow despite all my dark thoughts the night before, I was still able to believe that today, perhaps, the matter might be resolved; perhaps today, I might be released from prison, after all.

In the meantime, there I was, sitting in the interrogation chair again, struggling with hunger pangs. My pride did not allow me to protest such treatment. I suspected the interrogator was doing this intentionally, sending me back and forth before and after the scheduled mealtimes so I would have no chance to eat. He was deliberately punishing me, hoping to break my spirit by aggravating these interrogations with hunger, sleeplessness and the miseries of the qarantineh ward. This was 'normal', I reminded myself. These were the common tools of tyrants.

I pulled my stomach in tight and squared my shoulders. Posture conveys a clear message to the interrogator: it tells him whether you will break, or if you are inwardly strong. It also controls how confident or fatigued you feel during these prolonged sessions of inert misery. I set two rules for myself in the detention centre: to sit up straight and stay calm at all times, to be restrained, and remain courteous under all conditions. In addition, I refused to respond to any line of questioning outside the scope of the charges against me. As a result, the interrogator was becoming more and more infuriated with me.

If the second day's interrogation was any indication, there would be tough times ahead. Every question concerned the directives of the Yárán-i-Iran to the Bahá'í community and our engagement with society at large: Why were Bahá'ís allowed to take part in the election of the Islamic Parliament? Why had they participated in the campaign of One Million Signatures demanding change to the discriminatory laws against women?[11] Why were letters sent reinstating certain Bahá'ís into the community who had previously recanted their faith 'under pressure'? Why were the Bahá'ís in other countries appealing to the authorities in Iran about 'religious persecution'? Why did they collaborate with institutions abroad that were advocating for so-called human rights? Why did they associate themselves with the United Nations and other international organisations?

It went on and on and on. Dusk came and went and night fell. I had been sitting in that chair, blindfolded, since morning. I asked for a glass of water.

'We also have tea,' he said coolly.

I did not reply.

Silence.

After a few moments, he offered it again: 'Tea?'

The tempting proposition hung between us.

Well, tea won't compromise you; it's better than water and at least a little warmer than this man's voice. Perhaps there might even be sugar cubes?

I didn't usually take them but, 'Yes, thank you,' I said.

He took the interrogation sheet off the armrest, and it was replaced, minutes later, by an old red plastic teacup, together with a couple of sugar cubes, brought in by the old man.

I waited until I sensed that the interrogator had left the room before sipping the tea carefully, warming my hands around the tepid cup. I had lifted the blindfold slightly to write, so now I raised my head and turned warily around to look at the forbidden area behind me. The room was empty. Bare walls, bare floor. To the left of the door was a wooden table, with a pile of papers lying in a heap, next to a black Samsonite briefcase, open. The door was shut but I guessed a closed-circuit camera was probably watching me.

I took two or three sugar cubes and sipped the lukewarm tea through their dissolving sweetness. The tea smelled of plastic, but those sugar cubes tasted pretty good. My stomach cramps were more painful than ever; I told them not to make a fuss. But I was still struggling with hunger pangs when the interrogator came back. I wondered if he had needed a break himself and put the teacup on the floor as he slid another piece of paper onto the armrest.

'What are your ways of contacting the Universal House of Justice?' he demanded.

'I do not have to answer that question.'

'Why not?' he retorted, his voice mounting in irritation.

'Because it is unrelated to my present charges.'

A bellow of uncontrolled rage erupted behind me. 'It is related,' he shouted. 'Everything is related!'

I sat very still as his voice rose in wrath. Was he going to have a heart attack? He even stamped his foot on the floor and thumped his fist on the table. Might he kill me? He charged at me from behind, and I shrank away from the expected blow. When it ended with no more than the heat of his breath on my neck, my whole body was shaking. I crossed my legs and leaned slightly forward to escape the blasts issuing from his mouth.

'Everything is our business here,' he hollered in my ear. 'Do you understand? *Everything*!'

I held my head in my hands to block the stentorian reverberations of his voice, but I was still shaking after he stopped yelling. He wanted to frighten me, and he had succeeded. I had not intended to provoke him, but my response had evidently induced a tempest of fury. He finally left the room, slamming the door behind him. Now that I had seen it briefly, I could imagine the door shuddering, jolting, even splitting in its frame beneath the blow. I wondered if the whole thing might not crash down behind me, as his footsteps faded.

The room was immersed in silence. The plastic cup sat placidly on the floor by my feet. There was still a bit of cold black tea left at the bottom, and I drank it up. Some time passed before he returned, and by then the storm had mercifully subsided.

I had dodged the interrogator's questions for several hours, but there was one issue I wanted to address, if he raised it, one question I was determined to answer, if I could do so when the atmosphere was less turbulent and he was relatively calm. In fact, I had decided that if he brought up any more misconceptions about the Bahá'í Faith, then I had a responsibility to clarify these issues and answer him fully. And the question finally came.

'Which governments and foreign embassies are you in touch with?' the interrogator asked. 'Name each one and state the manner in which you communicate with them.'

I lifted my head with a ready nod. 'We have no relations with any foreign embassies or governments,' I answered cheerfully.

The interrogator erupted. He exploded. He was beside himself and hit me on the head several times with a roll of paper.

'Relations with no embassy?' he screamed. 'No embassy whatsoever?'

'Absolutely none,' I replied, as steadily as possible. 'No embassies at all.'

'You say something like that, and I'm supposed to believe it?' he thundered.

'As you wish.' I took a deep breath and spoke with all the restraint I could muster. 'You must have some basis for your opinion – some evidence, surely? None exists unless someone lied to you, and no Bahá'í would lie – it is against our principles to practise *taqqiya* and dissimulate our beliefs to save our lives – unless someone forces a person into making false confessions under fear and torture.'

Again, he hit me on the back of my head with the roll of paper and began to hiss and splutter curses behind my back. I felt myself becoming increasingly detached. I neither wished to breathe the air from his mouth nor listen to the words he was saying. Perhaps it was due to lack of food and sleep, but my calm composure was a surprise even to me. And it certainly upset the interrogator. My low unruffled tone must have galled him. This gentleman with his leonine temper was reduced to a state of frustrated impotence in the presence of a prisoner too physically weak to be other than dispassionate.

* * *

For the third consecutive night I was sent back to the qarantineh ward too late to eat. This time Parváneh received me with evident pleasure, her face wreathed in smiles. She even invited me to sleep in her antechamber rather than the main hallway.

'Come here and sit with us,' she offered kindly.

Three women were curled up on the floor of her room, sharing stories. It was late and I was exhausted, and longing to sleep, but I found a place and sat down beside them. One was quite young, with an attractive face and a witty turn of phrase. She was describing why she had gone straight back into drug-dealing after eight years in jail.

'What else could I do?' she was saying. 'I had no one to support me, and no other qualifications. What choice was there? And I had a certain reputation to maintain after all.'

I was bowled over by her pragmatism and her cool analysis of the situation.

'I'll probably get a heavy sentence this time round,' she sighed, with a dramatic roll of the eyes. 'But I'll soon get released, with the right bribes. And when I get out this time, I've decided: I'm going into personal relations.'

'Personal relations?' I asked Parváneh.

'Prostitution' was the terse reply.

'Honestly,' the young woman continued, unperturbed. 'What's the point of drug-dealing when the charges are so steep? In personal relations, the money's good, the sentences are much lighter, and I'll have some fun at least.'

Fun? I turned towards her then and we exchanged a long look. There wasn't a trace of embarrassment or irony in her gaze. She was simply stating the facts. Why should she be ashamed? Her honesty was a revelation to me. I remembered the two young girls sitting on the floor in the waiting area when I arrived that first night, their whispers, their cool demeanour under all that heavy make-up. So, this is what happens in a society ruled by a theocracy that claims to be executing the laws of God on earth?

Parváneh pointed to the top bunk of a bed near hers.

'You can sleep right here tonight,' she said.

I thanked her gratefully.

'There's a rolled-up carpet on the bed instead of a mattress. Will that bother you?'

Glancing up, I saw a khaki-coloured carpet tucked against the wall. I was so eager to get out of the stifling atmosphere of the main hall that I did not think twice about it. I merely asked if there were any blankets for the bed, and she told me to bring the one I had been using the night before. But when I went back into the main vestibule to retrieve it, the blanket was gone. There was no point in pursuing it.

It was more tranquil in Parváneh's room than in the terrible hall and the air was much easier to breathe up on the third bunk. She cursed fulsomely, however, whenever anyone tried to wake her in the middle of the night and I was glad she had not spoken to me like that on my arrival. Other than a predilection for florid swear words, she was generally quite unperturbed and level-headed and seemed a likeable, intelligent woman.

That night, as I struggled to find a comfortable position, I discovered a piece of dried bread in one corner of the top bunk. After several days of fasting, I was terribly tempted to eat it. At first, I counselled myself to forget about it. What a vile idea to eat a dirty piece of bread. How disgusting! Who knows who had touched it, where it had come from, how long it had been gathering dust up there? But I kept thinking about that revolting husk and gradually began to imagine its taste and texture in my mouth, to dream of chewing it, swallowing it. And before I knew it, I had eaten the whole thing. To be honest, I was starving.

I started to shiver after that. I was desperately tired but couldn't sleep for the cold. How to get warm? I was afraid I would disturb Parváneh sleeping below me each time I rolled over, but finally, on looking up, I discovered an open louver window near the ceiling. No wonder the antechamber was better ventilated! But unfortunately, I was immediately beneath it and no matter how hard I tried, I couldn't reach it. So, I did the only thing possible: I unrolled the carpet, stiff and heavy as it was, and crept beneath it. Ah, the relief. Now my stomach was full, and I was warm at last.

It was early morning when I awoke, and Parváneh was already out of bed. Half-dreaming, I saw her whispering to someone by the door. I had hoped they would come a little later for me today, so I might have breakfast. Fresh *barbari* bread, white cheese and tea. But even as I was thinking about food, Parváneh turned round and saw that I was awake. With a nod, she confirmed I had to go. Now. Immediately. Before breakfast.

By then I was so hungry that I was beginning to feel quite weak. But it helped to talk, even blindfolded, while I was in the car. So, on the way back to the detention centre, I told the agents from the Intelligence Bureau about the young woman who had shared her story the night before, about her lack of choices in life, about the difficult decisions she faced.

'Gentlemen,' I said, with my head pressed against the back of their seats, 'perhaps you can inform those who control the regulations about this woman's circumstances. Perhaps the policies that have led women into such dilemmas should be reviewed?'

The driver was a courteous man. I had noticed, from my previous rides in the car, that he always spoke with a certain old-fashioned decorum, and had seen, before putting on the blindfold, that he usually wore a mustard-coloured sport jacket with four pockets. He was the only person who spoke to me like a human being, instead of barking orders.

'It's true, Khánum,'[12] he said solemnly. 'You're right. Unfortunately, grave damage has befallen our society.'

We continued to talk about general matters until the car came to a stop and the man next to the driver told me to get out. From that day on, the courteous, antiquated agent in the mustard-coloured jacket became my regular transport person.

5

FOR THE SAKE OF GOD

On the fourth occasion I was questioned at the detention centre of the Intelligence Bureau in Khorasan Razavi, in sharp contrast to his violent reactions the evening before, the interrogator deployed smooth small talk again, asking how I was doing, how I was feeling, how I was coping in prison. To relieve the tension, I told him about the prisoners I had met.

'Why did you clean the toilets?' he interrupted curtly.

How had he heard about that?

'And how many people have you reformed so far?' he added, with a sneer.

I suppose he was referring to the brief conversations that I had shared with a few of the young women, while we were scouring the sanitary area together. I realised then that these gentlemen would receive a report of everything I said and did in prison, no doubt through Parváneh. She was friendly, but she had a job to do.

I was feeling dizzy from hunger that day. Since the mood of the interrogator seemed subdued, I asked him if I could please have a glass of water. I wished to inform him indirectly that I was not fasting. As a result, he began to quiz me on the subject.

'Why aren't you fasting today?' he queried.

'I'm just not,' I shrugged, trying to sound as indifferent as possible.

But he would not let the matter go. It was as if he had nothing better to talk about.

'No, seriously, why were you fasting the other days, and now you're not?'

He kept repeating the same question over and over, and I kept giving him the same answer, as courteously as possible, again and again. Fasting and prayer are private matters for Bahá'ís, performed for the sake of God, and are no one else's business.

'That's just how it is. I'm not fasting today,' I repeated. 'There's nothing more to it.'

This line of questioning, which continued for the rest of the morning, seemed both tiresome and rather infantile to me. I suppose he simply wanted to goad me.

Towards noon, he finally changed the subject and informed me, somewhat randomly, that I was the only female prisoner in the detention centre. Since I had to be kept there until the next day, and since there were no women guards available for the night shift, he'd been obliged to call in special assistance.

'Háj Khánum, please come in,' he then called out loudly.

Under my blindfold, I could not tell whom he was speaking to. The door behind me opened and closed. A shuffle of footsteps approached. Then, all of a sudden, someone close by me spoke, wheezing slightly, with a singsong Mashhadi lilt.

'So here we are,' she said, as if speaking to a child. 'Let's go then, shall we? You just come along with me.'

As she guided me out of the room, the interrogator continued speaking to this unknown lady, in a tone that was both flattering and patronising, unctuous and insincere.

'Háj Khánum, thank you very much indeed for coming all this way. Thank you, Háj Khánum, for making yourself free today. Háj Khánum, thank you for being available so that this wretched creature of God does not have to go back and forth to the prison.'

How nice, I thought. At least he considers me a creature of God. But his ingratiating manner towards this Háj Khánum upset me; he was clearly mocking her provincial accent.

To my immense relief I was given lunch in my cell that day – a delicious aubergine stew – which to humiliate the prisoners they served in a battered tin bowl, the kind used to feed a dog. But I was not eating the bowl, so I didn't care. In fact, I was so energised after the meal that I asked for cleaning supplies to wash the toilet and bathroom of this cell as well, as they were also very dirty. The old man brought me all the necessary materials and handed them to me through the hatch at the bottom of the door.

At this point, I began to think that the cell in the detention centre wasn't so bad. The walls were rather grimy, but they matched the dirty beige carpet. A number of blankets were folded on top of each other in a corner of the room, like a high bed, which looked very tempting. I spread one of them out on the floor and put my clothes on it to dry, after scrubbing them under the shower. I hoped I would not be called back before I could wear them. Then I propped myself up against the pile of blankets and breathed deeply.

Now that the cell and its new occupant were relatively clean, it was possible to concentrate on the interrogator. What would he do next? Was he done for the day? Would there be more smooth talk or would he be aggressive again this afternoon? How come he had been so calm and collected after our dreadful quarrel yesterday? He had asked me no serious questions that morning; was he merely entertaining himself at my cost or just killing time? It no longer mattered. Thanks to the food, the shower, and this relatively clean, peaceful and private space, I was feeling so much better that my concerns over the interrogator gradually faded, and the hope of going back home rose in my heart instead. I missed my children terribly. I missed my dearly beloved Siyávash. I wanted to talk to them, listen to them, know what they were up to, and share life with them again.

I was also thinking about the Yárán-i-Iran. I was sure that the gentlemen of the Intelligence Bureau had taken me hostage in Mashhad to put pressure on them. I prayed my colleagues would never accept any compromise for my sake, never surrender to unjust, unfair and unreasonable demands, just to free me. It also struck me that the Bahá'ís all over the world may have heard of my arrest by now and might be praying for me. Perhaps the Universal House of Justice was praying for me, too. A tiny voice whispered in my heart.

Maybe you've stayed calm through all these interrogations because of their prayers.

A long time passed. My clothes were nearly dry, and I was still waiting. No one knocked on the door, no one called me back to the interrogation room. Nothing happened. Before long, dusk fell, the room darkened even more, and the call to prayer echoed from afar.

It was the first time I was spending the night in the detention centre and everything was new. The iron wheels of the food trolley creaked and winced, then stopped outside my door. The old man knocked with unnecessary force, lifted the hatch, and slid the food dish onto the cell floor. I looked at the battered tin bowl, feeling crestfallen. After all these hours alone, it was depressing to think of staying in that gloomy room all night too, without any human interaction. I had not realised that privacy could be a punishment. Going back to the prison seemed more appealing at that moment than being left in this place.

I had decided to fast again the following day, so I set the food aside for my dawn breakfast. But a minute later, the cell door opened, and the old woman – the one whom the interrogator had called Háj Khánum – stood on the threshold.

'Why aren't you eating?' she scolded, in her sing-song voice. 'Don't tell me you're on a hunger strike! That's a crime, you know.'

It was the first time I was seeing her face. She was a peasant woman in her seventies, I would guess, with plump cheeks and missing teeth. I stood up to greet her and assured her that even though I didn't know it was a crime, I had no intention of going on a hunger strike. I just wanted to keep the bread to eat in the morning because I would be fasting tomorrow. Then I asked if she had a freezer bag so that the food might stay fresh overnight.

'Fasting?' she retorted. 'Come on, it's hardly the time to fast now, is it?'

I smiled at her, knowing she understood my meaning perfectly well.

'Háj Khánum, our fasting period is different from yours.'

She looked a little disconcerted but was clearly inclined to talk, even to an infidel.

'Some time ago when I was a guard, I met some of your people here,' she said, drawing herself up stiffly and folding her arms. 'They were good women. But they wore nail polish when they said their prayers.' And she pursed her lips, waiting for my response.

I smiled again. What could I say?

'Well?' she repeated indignantly. 'Isn't that what you people do?'

'Yes, Háj Khánum,' I replied. 'We don't think nail polish invalidates prayer.'

I would have dearly liked to learn more about those Bahá'í prisoners, to know who they were, when she had met them, her impressions of them. But she could not remember their names or the dates of their incarceration, and other things she said did not conform to the facts either. So I could not tell whether she was simply misinformed about the Faith, wilfully distorting what she knew, or just making up stories. Laws of purity and chastity exercised her the most; these symbolised the truth of Islam for her. Her co-religionists, she told me primly, followed the rules properly. Mine, she repeated, didn't. But they were virtuous women, she added, inconsequentially. The contradiction did not seem to bother her.

'I came over here,' she said, wagging her finger at me, 'so you wouldn't have to go back to prison. But I've a thousand things to do for New Year's Eve, so you'd better behave! Don't you go on a hunger strike!'

I assured her that I would not and asked if she might be here if I stayed another night.

She said she would. To earn some money 'for the sake of God,' she qualified. But only until Naw-Rúz. 'After that I have guests,' she continued more cheerfully. 'My children and grandchildren are coming for the New Year. They live in Tehran, but they're coming to see me for Naw-Rúz.' And having mentioned this happy prospect, she mercifully forgot all about purity and chastity and plunged into a description of her grandchildren. She wanted to earn extra 'for the sake of God,' to buy Naw-Rúz presents for the little ones, she said.

That night, the old woman opened the cell door several times to check on me, and each time, we exchanged a few words. I was comforted by her simple, kind voice. She was very devout. At midnight, I heard her chanting prayers softly and melodiously in her sweet accent. But she made a great deal of noise when she rose for the dawn call to prayer. Her bed must have been right behind the wall of my cell. Whenever she breathed deeply or sighed heavily, whenever she turned over or groaned 'Yá Alláh' as she struggled out of bed, I heard it all. Nevertheless, her presence behind the partition gave me a sense of security.

* * *

I did stay another night. And then another. And another after that. Soon, the old woman and I established a daily routine that was a comfort, of sorts. I woke up with her grunts at dawn, drank a glass of water from the tap in the sink, then took as long as I could to say my prayers. Afterwards, I walked around the cell, exercising back and forth, back and forth, and kept myself moving until I was summoned. At that point, the old woman would blindfold me and guide me through the corridors to the interrogation room. I think she even sat behind the door there. She stayed close by me all the time, and this too was a comfort.

On one of those days, while I was waiting for the interrogator, there was an uproar in the room next to mine. All hell seemed to break loose on the other side of the wall. I could not imagine what was going on, but apart from the thundering tone I was beginning to know so well – bellows and roars that could be heard over the roof tops – I thought I heard another man's voice too. It was difficult to distinguish the actual words because this person was speaking quietly, but the interrogator was clearly incensed. He yelled and shouted and cursed and swore. His profanities were monumental.

Finally, I heard footsteps and the interrogator swept like a hurricane back into my room. The air moved with him; I even felt it stir beneath my chador. What now?

'Just come and listen to this fellow!' he shouted. 'The way he speaks, you'd think he was visiting the home of his maiden aunt!'

I kept my mouth shut. I had no idea what he was talking about or who, until he mentioned the man's name. He was interrogating one of the local Bahá'ís of Mashhad.

'You know him, right?'

I nodded, although I had never met this particular friend myself.

'The lazy oaf is just sitting there with his legs stretched out, leaning back in his chair, as if nothing was happening. He's making a fool of himself!'

Rage can sometimes exceed the capacity to express it. The gentleman of the Intelligence Bureau slammed the palm of his hand so hard on the table, he must have hurt himself. He then let loose another angry volley, either from pain or fury.

'When I ask him what his duties are in the Bahá'í community, he replies, "Serving the creation of God". When I ask him, who appointed him to do that, he says, "God has!" When I ask him to whom he is responsible, he says, "To God"!'

The word 'God' had become a curse in the interrogator's mouth. He spat it out in disgust and began to grind his teeth as he paced to and fro behind me. I froze, making as little noise as possible, but now I understood. The prisoner in the other room was doubtless concerned that if he named members of the Bahá'í community, they would be arrested, too. He was also very likely aware that I was in prison and was anxious to avoid causing me further problems. He did not want anyone to suffer. Of course, the authorities knew the names of all the Bahá'ís in Mashhad anyway, and there was nothing about me that they did not already know. His attempts at discretion were only giving the impression that he was withholding information and had something more to hide. My heart ached for him.

After a moment, the interrogator continued, talking half to himself and half to me.

'The idiot should take a lesson from this woman. She's been under interrogation day after day, from morning till night, sitting in that chair for seventeen hours at times. He couldn't cope with it, but if he doesn't cooperate, it will be far worse for the stupid fool!'

Such sarcasm, such contempt. Was he professing to flatter me with these comparisons so as to undermine my confidence in this dear friend? Did he imagine that by praising one of us and criticising the other, exploiting one and manipulating the other, he could weaken our unity? How far he was from understanding trust, or us.

He snorted heavily after delivering this homily, then whirled round and approached me from behind, with a furious expletive.

'Get up! Go over there! Say something to that lazy bum, so he won't push me too far. He shouldn't press on my nerves like this. He'll end up paying for it!'

After a brief hesitation, I stood up and groped my way blindly after him. Moments later, I was standing at the entrance of the interrogation room next to mine. He had evidently left the door wide open so I could hear everything.

'There he is,' he announced. 'Just take a look at the buffoon.'

Of course, given the blindfold, I could see no buffoons, but I figured the other prisoner was probably sitting as I had been, with his back to me, on a chair some paces away.

I greeted him gently. 'Alláh'u'Abhá,[13] dear friend. Mahvash at your service.'

He replied instantly and with great respect. 'Alláh'u'Abhá, Khánum-i-Sabet.'

'Are you well?' I asked.

'Yes, Khánum-i-Sabet. Thank you, Khánum-i-Sabet.'

I took a deep breath and then did my best to reassure him. 'Don't be troubled,' I said. 'You can answer the gentlemen's questions without any worries. It is not important.'

He responded in a rapid, ringing tone: 'I will obey, Khánum-i-Sabet! I will comply, dear Khánum-i-Sabet!'

I held my tongue, wishing he had not been quite so ardent, but at least I had done what I could. The interrogator would hopefully get what he wanted out of this Bahá'í now, without resorting to physical and verbal aggression. But I had not reckoned with that gentleman's foul temper. Suddenly, and without any warning, he kicked the chair violently, slamming the prisoner's knees against the wall. Then he ordered me back to my room.

No sooner had my vertical vision taken me back, and seated me in my chair, than he was pacing behind me again. But he was no longer huffing and puffing; he was no longer half-talking to me either but growling furiously to himself. He had forgotten I even existed and was so exercised, so exasperated, so incensed that he even spat on the floor.

'Look at me,' he muttered, under his breath, 'a Ministry deputy, a government official, with years of experience, and no matter what I ask, this man refuses to reply. Look at him now, look at how he "complies" and "obeys" this creature, how he answers a suspected felon, how he addresses a mere woman with total obedience and respect!'

All the while he was snarling and spitting, I sat like a statue, bolt upright, head held high. After ranting on like this for several minutes, he turned abruptly on his heel and left the room. I remained immobile, waiting for him to return. And all through that long wait, I wished I could have explained something very simple to him. I wished I could have told him that it was not Mahvash this Bahá'í was obeying. The dear man next door did not even know me personally. He had certainly not addressed me with deference because he held *me* in high esteem. Nor had he complied because he believed in the Bahá'í principle that women are equal to men. The respect he had shown was merely for the role and responsibilities I was holding at the time. His courtesy was towards the Yárán.

6

PSYCHOLOGICAL TERRORISM

Night came, and another day arrived and ended in yet another
night. And all this time I was still holed up at the detention
centre, in solitary confinement, with no company except the
old woman. I was still trapped miles away from home, light
years from everyone I knew, and an eternity from those I
loved, who knew nothing whatever of my whereabouts.

I spent days on end sitting in that interrogation chair; I spent
hour after hour under an avalanche of questions quite unrelated to my charge. And even though the interrogator should
have known by now that as long as I was accused of the wrong-
ful burial of a corpse, he was not going to extract anything out
of me apart from dust, it looked as though he was planning to
dig forever. I was thoroughly sick of it, homesick, heartsick,
lovesick, life sick, missing the flowers, the stars, and the vast,
untrammelled sky. Freedom. How I missed my freedom!

Oh, if freedom would sing the tiniest song,
as small as the throat of a bird,
even ruined walls would no longer remain
still standing in this world…[14]

'What are you doing? What are you up to?'

The old woman interrupted my reverie. She could see I was preoccupied. I told her that I had been reciting poetry and saying prayers.

'Without a veil?' she said, scandalised. 'There's a chador hanging there for prayers, you know.'

'We do not have to wear a veil when we say prayers and meditate.'

'But why weren't you properly facing the Qiblih at least?' she quizzed.

'Our Qiblih is different.'

'Oh.' She was rather nonplussed. 'So what do you say when you pray then?'

'We praise the Lord and submit ourselves to His will, just as you do.'

'Well, thank God for that,' she sighed with relief. 'Then we do have something in common. But why did you have to go and change everything else?'

I smiled. 'We didn't change anything.'

'Then who did?' She was clearly scandalised.

'Only God can make such changes. Only His Word has that power.'

'But how do you know it's His Word?' she retorted.

'The same way you know that the Qur'an is God's Word.'

She was silent for a second or two, digesting this quandary, and then flapped her hand at me crossly. 'But why change the rules? Why start something new?'

I replied very carefully. 'Well, when we are children, we need certain food, certain clothes, certain kinds of protection, but when we grow up, we need different things. New ideas. More freedom. Perhaps God wants us to grow up?'

The old woman hung fire for a minute longer. I could almost hear her mind churning. She was probably wondering why on earth I'd brought children into the discussion.

'Honest to God,' she grumbled, 'I don't get any of it.' Then she flapped her hand at me again, still muttering, and turned away, leaving me to my solitary meditations.

My conversations with Háj Khánum helped me steer clear of my own anxieties, which had a way of proliferating in solitude. Most of the time I was a bundle of nerves, my stomach tied in knots. But a new feeling of alarm was also growing within me. I was beginning to worry something might happen to weaken my resolve, shatter my strength and reduce me to a state of psychological and spiritual hopelessness. I might become tired, sick and give up. I knew this was the goal of solitary confinement. Relentless interrogations can bring you to your knees. I decided it was time to give myself a counselling session. Instead of agonising, I had to find a way to avoid yielding to the stress and collapsing.

Just list all your fears, to keep them under control.

I started counting. First, I was concerned about my family. Second, I was afraid I wouldn't act in a manner befitting a representative of the Bahá'í community of Iran. Third, I was scared that if this detention was prolonged much longer, I'd be ground down, worn out. But that third fear brought me back to square one. Self-awareness offered no solutions.

In that case, list the facts instead. Remember the facts, one by one.

And so I began to list them. I had been detained here against my will for over two weeks – that was a fact. I had been indicted and imprisoned on trumped up charges – that was a fact too. And now I was being interrogated by someone who clearly hated everything I stood for, and I couldn't do anything about it. That fact brought me back to square one again.

What else? Facts don't begin and end just with you.

No, the fact was that when Mr Aslání, our former government liaison, became inaccessible from one day to the next, the consequences were devastating for all the Bahá'ís. They had no recourse when their homes were burned down and their properties seized, when their businesses were closed and their jobs taken away, when clerical hostility incited their murder in broad daylight. I remembered Abadih, where such things had happened. I remembered the suffering of friends in Vilashahr, and Najafabad, and Khurramábád, and Dasht-i-Mughan. How many children hounded from schools? How many students deprived of their futures? These were the facts, the most important facts of all.

And now it is your turn. You're facing this same pressure. You know, for a fact, these gentlemen have no other aim than to suppress and crush you. What will you do?

Persevere. Be as steadfast as a mountain and as immoveable. Faith is also a fact.

And with that thought, my heart was finally at rest, my mind at peace. And I slept.

* * *

But not for long. Rest and restlessness, sleep and wakefulness were interchangeable states of being during those days and nights at the Mashhad detention centre. Worries roused me, fear forced me to my feet and panic led me to cry in the dark. I felt hot and cold all over and was never sure whether the cause was internal or external, mental or physical. The room was unheated. First I would lay a few blankets under me, a few on top, and use one as a pillow. Then I would pull most of the blankets over me in an attempt to get warm, but still shivered from head to foot. In the end I'd sit up in the darkness and discover the blanket beneath me was soaked in sweat, as if I had a fever. It was impossible to sleep.

The closer the days drew to Naw-Rúz, the more I longed for release, but also the more apprehensive I became about this ongoing, never-ending detention. It was clear that the interrogator was trying to destabilise me, and wanted me to doubt everything. I did not know what to believe, how much to trust or whether he meant anything he said.

One day, after mentioning my husband's name several times, he once again asked me about Siyávash in ways he knew would unsettle me.

'He used to be a Muslim, right?'

I did not reply. By then it had become clear to him that I would not respond to anything irrelevant to my case. My husband's faith bore no relationship to the dead man's grave and had nothing to do with the brand of dust in which he had been laid. The interrogator was just throwing such statements at me to provoke my unease. He knew how to stir me up, how to torture me emotionally. After a while, he raised the subject again.

'Your husband is an apostate, of course. Where is he now, do you know?' Then he murmured under his breath, 'Come on, she doesn't know. How would she know?'

He wanted to reduce me to such a state that I would beg for a phone call or plead for a visit. An old trick of the trade. First, they drain you of energy by flogging you with questions. Then, when you're at the limits of your strength, they increase pressure on your areas of special vulnerability. And when this pressure renders you stiff with panic or flaccid with fear, they finally suck all the information they want out of you. In my case, the interrogator's tactic was to enquire about the well-being of my family at moments when he sensed I was feeling particularly weak. He knew he could render me helpless that way.

On this occasion, he asked, out of the blue, 'By the way, how old *was* your husband?' He laid particular emphasis on the tense of the verb.

When I replied by saying, 'Around sixty,' he sighed and added, in a pitying tone, 'Poor thing, he was quite young, really.'

No matter how hard I tried to ignore his bluffing, my heart burned at his words and later, in the fretful atmosphere of solitary confinement, I brooded over them. I prayed, of course, or tried to. I imagined my house, projected myself inside it, attempted to conjure up, by some sixth sense, communion with my dear Síyávash, to assure myself of his well-being.

If you can talk to a corpse, you can surely talk to your husband!

But dread darkened my turmoil. I was without news, without contacts, uncertain of everything, so to console myself in the small hours of the night, I decided I would ask the interrogator for confirmation tomorrow. I would request a phone call, tomorrow. I would hear their voices, however briefly, tomorrow. I would beg, I would grovel…

But in the morning, I always felt more resolute, my peace of mind relatively restored by prayer, and pride would not allow me to ask for a reprieve. I rejected my night terrors and determined not to demean myself by begging for bounty. And I would sit in that chair once again, lean on that armrest that brought no rest, with the hairs on the back of my neck rising at each foul breath. And once again in the middle of his cross examination, the interrogator would throw out an old bone to arouse my gnawing hunger for news about my family.

'Your husband's warehouse was on Doosti Lane, wasn't it?'

The sudden statement, again in the infernal past tense, was so much like an epitaph that I almost gasped aloud. Then, without warning, he called abruptly to the old woman.

'Háj Khánum, please come in!'

And she was unexpectedly by my side, as if she'd been there all along, listening.

'Shall we go now?' she asked me, with disarming gentleness.

After she returned me to my cell, relieved me of the blindfold and closed the door on me, I threw my chador onto the blankets and ran to the toilet, feeling ill. I hoped that the old woman could not hear me, but a few minutes later, she was at the door again with the dog bowl of food. My voice could barely crawl out of my throat.

'I am not eating today, Háj Khánum,' I whispered. 'Honestly, nothing will go down.'

The fractured sleep of solitary confinement made me queasy; the sight and smell of food left me nauseous. And the biliousness only abated when a narrow stream of light filtered through the window at last, just below the ceiling. No air came through that window, of course, and I could not see through it to catch even a glimpse of sky or the natural world. But every dawn, a bird sang beautifully right outside, before the call to prayer, evidence that another difficult night had passed, forewarning that another hard day was about to begin. As soon as I heard the bright melody of its repetitive little song, I rose to my feet.

The next morning, the interrogator was in fine fettle. Perhaps he had slept well. Or perhaps he was delighted at hearing from the old woman that I had been unwell. He was still playing his games, still speaking of Siyávash in even more insidious ways than usual.

'By the way,' he rounded on me, 'did your husband become a Bahá'í by himself?'

Once again, uneasiness clutched at my vitals. I felt slightly disembodied, as though someone else was inhabiting the space behind my face, and I was perched precariously on her shoulders. We were two people: one in the interrogation room, the other drowning in a whirlpool of trepidation; one sitting serenely on the chair, the other struggling to keep her head above swirling emotions. But I kept my shoulders rigid, and my chin squared.

The interrogator waited a while before speaking again.

'Why don't you answer?' he probed at last. 'You made him a Bahá'í, right? You are aware of what this means in an Islamic country?'

There was no point in objecting to the 'made him' nonsense. I wasn't going to respond to this kind of goading because I knew that *he* knew that the opposite was true. No one can 'make' a person a Bahá'í, least of all my dear, independent-minded Siyávash. Faith is a personal matter for Bahá'ís. But in Islam, it is supposedly inherited, like the size of your nose. Ironically enough, it is easier to get a nose job in Iran than to change your religion.

'Conversion from Shia Islam is penalised by the death sentence, of course,' added the interrogator unnecessarily. 'You are aware of the laws of the land to which I am referring?'

Once more I said nothing. He knew that *I* knew all about apostasy, and he also knew that my principles were entirely against such notions of coercion. Bahá'ís believe in the independent investigation of truth, and the freedom to choose whether or what to believe. It's a question of conscience. He must have sensed my hackles rising because he stopped nee-dling in that direction and started on another tack.

'What's wrong with your husband anyway?' he pursued. 'Why isn't he coming to see you? All the others have come, your son, your daughter, your brother. I'm serious, they are all here now. They've come to Mashhad. But I've not been able to get permission for them to visit you yet, unfortunately. You'd like to see them, wouldn't you?'

I controlled myself and still did not respond. He was not going to exploit my unspoken desperation in this underhand manner. His combination of promise and threat was repellent. But my silence did not stop him from inundating me with derisive innuendos. By the end of the interrogation that day, he was a fountain of sparkling sarcasm.

'You can surely spit *something* out of that dry throat,' he sneered. 'You don't have to suffocate *entirely*. Just cough up enough to make a phone call, won't you, and let them know you're still alive. They're in torment out there, thinking we've gotten rid of you.'

Then he took me, still blindfolded, into another room. There must have been phones installed there because I heard him dialling and then saw my brother's mobile number high-lighted on the receiver he held towards me. So! He had been preparing for this all along. While the phone was ringing at the other end, he hissed a warning.

'Just a *salaam*, mind, and only say how you are. Nothing else.'

Someone picked up at the other end and my brother's sol-emn voice boomed around the room. They had evidently installed loudspeakers in this place, so they could hear every-thing being said.

I was dry-mouthed. 'It's me.' It was hard to speak. 'Yes I'm fine.'

After a brief exchange of banalities, I asked my brother where he was. He said they had arrived in Mashhad from Tehran two days ago and had been trying to see me ever since. 'Fúrúd and Negár are also here,' he added. 'But they refuse us permission for a family visit.'

At that, the line was abruptly cut.

So much for the inability 'to get permission'! My dear ones were right here, in Mashhad, waiting to see me, and the interrogator had doubtless ensured that they were turned away. His lie cut me to the quick. But just to know of my family's proximity was a comfort.

* * *

The next day, Háj Khánum brought me a dish filled with nuts and dates. They were evidence of that comfort and proof of the interrogator's perfidy, for they had probably been withheld from me for days.

'Your son brought this stuff in for you,' the old woman told me. 'He also brought you some clothes. If necessary, we will give them to you.'

Pistachios, almonds, cashew nuts, hazelnuts, dates and raisins. They aroused such conflicting emotions, such a mingling of sugar and salt: the joy of connection with Fúrúd and my family, the sting of separation, of nostalgia. And revulsion towards the interrogator. For a long time, I just left that dish of paradoxes on the floor, unable to touch it.

One day, not long afterwards, I had been seated for so many hours, and the interrogations had been so difficult that neither body nor spirit could bear it any longer. I did not know what time it was, but I guessed we were long past the moment for breaking the fast. Just then the door creaked open, and I heard Háj Khánum muttering to the interrogator.

'Yes, go ahead,' he replied.

A few moments later, I glimpsed a plastic cup on the armrest from under the blindfold, together with some sugar. The handle was slack from the heat. The cup wobbled and some tea spilt over. The interrogator threw two tissues over my head.

I thanked him, when they drifted down as far as my vertical vision.

And then I noticed the sugar. I had assumed the old woman had given me regular sugar cubes, which I disliked, but these were fragments broken off a real sugarloaf! As I lifted a small piece to my lips, the interrogator must have sensed my appreciation.

'Háj Khánum felt sorry for you,' he jeered.

His words cut like a knife. I guessed he wanted to spoil the tea for me. He wanted to embitter its sweetness and transform the old woman's kindness into a demeaning kind of pity. But I didn't care. It proved that a little bond of friendship was growing between me and Háj Khánum, one I doubt that good gentleman could have ever conceived was possible.

Over the days, the old woman had gradually been telling me more about herself. She never set foot inside the cell, of course; that was her red line. But at night, when no one else was around, she'd open the door without knocking and then start chatting from the threshold. Perhaps she did not like being alone any more than I did. She told me all about her grandchildren, about her life. She had worked at the detention centre since the early years of the Revolution, and although she had retired, they still called her in for emergencies from time to time. It was hard to leave her husband alone; he was old and needed care. But she had agreed to work the night shift, once in a while, 'for the sake of God,' so that they would not take me back to prison. Plus, it helped her earn a little. 'For the sake of God,' of course.

After one of those endless days of sitting and answering questions from morning till night, Háj Khánum brought some food into the interrogation room. It had been served for me an hour earlier, on schedule, in the same battered dog bowl. But as darkness fell and the interrogation dragged on, she had decided to heat it up so I could break my fast. I sensed that the interrogator accepted this initiative on her part very reluctantly. He permitted the intrusion in a begrudging tone and left the room briefly so I could eat. Still, I would have preferred not to antagonise him. I was not particularly hungry and wished the old woman had not done this, but did my best to swallow a few spoonfuls, to satisfy her.

But oh dear, she kept doing it. For three days in a row, she kept bringing me food after the evening call to prayer, so I would have some energy, and – as she put it – so I would not die. On the third day, the interrogator refused permission. I was afraid he would speak harshly to her, but she was the one who raised her voice and began to argue with him boldly.

'The poor creature is dying,' she protested. 'You've worn her out!'

The interrogator said something inaudible, but Háj Khánum would not let it go.

'I'm here for the sake of God, not for you,' she stoutly retorted. 'I'm not a prison guard, you know!' And then I heard her going on and on about God being the judge of hearts.

The interrogator was noticeably more irritable after that. He not only refused to let her bring me any food but stopped treating her with the old fake deference. They were no longer on good terms, which made Háj Khánum more cautious with me, and made me more wary with her from that time on. I feared I may have compromised her situation.

7

THE FIRST NAW-RÚZ

One evening, towards sunset, I heard a loud report, like a pistol shot followed by a sudden bang. I wondered what on earth it could be. Gunfire? A bomb? The noise was repeated, louder and louder with multiple eruptions and explosions like rockets, and then I suddenly remembered: *Chaharshambeh Suri*, the Iranian festival of the fire dance, the 'Scarlet Wednesday' before Naw-Rúz.[15] People were igniting fireworks, and so close too! I could hear the honking of horns and loud music beating through the walls.

Dear heaven, you're not on another planet, after all!

Was I really in the same world as these people setting off fireworks? Had the tyranny and oppression and darkness surrounding me not brought the rest of the world to an end?

I am generally fond of our cultural traditions. I used to maintain them at home as often as possible, but I did not observe the antics of Chaharshambeh Suri as much as Siyávash was wont to do. He had many fond memories from his childhood of the celebrations his family held on the last Wednesday before Naw-Rúz. He wanted our children to have the same souvenirs and experience all the merry pyrotechnics associated with this festival: *koozeh jinni* (a clay jar filled with firecrackers), *haft taraqqih* (a seven-fold firecracker), sparklers, Roman candles and all the rest. On Chaharshambeh Suri, he would take them to some suitable spot, having bought the usual stock of explosives, and then set them off, with much mutual excitement. Chaharshambeh Suri had always been a symbol of vitality for our family.

And now it was happening in the streets of Mashhad. Incredible! A thrill ran through my whole being at the thought of normal life out there. But what about my children? Were they participating in Chaharshambeh Suri this year? How were they feeling tonight? Were they too worried about me to celebrate with their friends, too sad to enjoy themselves? It was hard to resist the flood of maternal angst. But after a moment, my hopes revived to think that the pulse of life was still beating, that our traditions were still snapping and crackling in the streets. If, despite all the oppression, our cultural identity lived on, then life and love and hope must continue in my family too. I decided not to be overly concerned about my children. Siyávash was surely with them. They would celebrate Naw-Rúz together.

* * *

On the last day of the year, as on every other day, I was interrogated in the morning and in the afternoon. When we left the room together, the interrogator stopped briefly in the corridor outside. As he did so, I sensed someone passing by, from a movement in the air.

'We did everything we could to send you home for the new year, you know,' said the interrogator, addressing whoever it was. I recognised, from the response, the Bahá'í friend at whom he had been hurling insults the other day, in the adjacent room.

'Yes indeed, thank you so much,' the dear man said, 'but please send the lady to her home and family too!'

'No,' replied the interrogator, 'we're not quite done with her yet.' And lowering his voice, as the others walked away, he growled spitefully, 'She's not been cooperating.'

He then informed me that since Háj Khánum would not be working during the holiday, I would have to go back to prison for a few nights. I knew this. The old woman had already told me. She also said that she was originally supposed to help out just until the new year, but the Intelligence Bureau had recently asked her to extend her services beyond the holiday. It was a good sign that I had not jeopardised her job, but rather ominous for me. They clearly expected me to be here for some time yet.

So I was driven back, blindfolded, to Vakilabad Prison on New Year's Eve. Once again, I had to go through all the same procedures as before; once again I had to register in the same inspection office and provide all the same information about the dead man. It appeared that the unfortunate fellow was also going to spend Naw-Rúz in prison with me. I was standing at the bottom of the steps thinking about the poor corpse when Parváneh arrived in the lobby from the qarantineh. Her pretty features were strained with anxiety, and she grabbed my arm the minute she saw me. I had never seen her so agitated.

'Quick, upstairs as fast as you can,' she gasped. 'I need your help. They're in really bad shape up there tonight.'

I could hear the hue and cry even from below. Something was seriously awry in qarantineh. And it was not hard to guess the reason: the women were probably feeling miserable on New Year's Eve. I steeled my dispirited self, gathered up my strength, and ran after Parváneh, two steps at a time. The wailing and cursing had reached fever pitch when we entered the long hall, and before I knew it, Parváneh pushed me ahead of her.

'What's going on?' I shouted above the chaos. 'What's happening in here?'

Everyone suddenly quietened down. I looked round the hushed circle of strange faces, all stamped with familiar miseries, and quickly realised I knew none of these women. Everyone who had been here before I went to the detention centre must have been transferred to the public ward, and none of these women recognised me. Since Parváneh had ushered me in and I had caught their attention by raising my voice, I suppose they thought I was a prison guard, although I was not dressed like one. One by one, they began to surround me, protesting their arrests, as if I could do something for them.

'My children are stuck outside our house and can't get in!' cried one. 'I just went to buy them gifts for the New Year and ended up here!'

'They've detained me for no reason whatsoever,' wailed another. 'I've done nothing wrong! They arrested me by mistake!'

'I'm only a pilgrim,' sobbed a third. 'I came to the shrine of Imam Rezá. But they hauled everyone in on New Year's Eve for security reasons, just to quiet the streets around the sanctuary. It's not fair!'

It went on and on. The qarantineh ward was swarming with distraught women, hysterical women, weeping and wailing, keening and crying women in great distress. I had no option but to speak with the authority they assumed I had. I raised my voice again.

'Ladies, as you know it is a holiday. And from tonight onwards, we are here for the duration. We have no choice.

Crying and carrying on like this will make no difference. I'm in the same situation as you. I am a prisoner like you. I am stuck here like you. So let's find a way to celebrate the New Year in better spirits, and in harmony together!'

Some of the women just gaped at me in disbelief. Others drew back, scowling resentfully when they realised I was not a guard and began to cry and curse all over again. But a few, who were grouped around a woman with burgundy red hair, seemed prepared to celebrate, even in these circumstances. They took up the challenge, started singing a popular song together, and began to snap their fingers, wiggle their hips and dance to the beat.

It was not long before the wailing had more or less ceased. Some of the women even embarked on a programme of cosmetic improvement, designing hairstyles, threading each other's cheeks and brows to remove facial fuzz. Parváneh was prevailed upon to loan and supervise the use of trimming scissors. And then I suggested we all take showers.

'Bathing on New Year's Eve is an obligation!' I announced portentously and immediately felt disgusted with myself. Good grief! Why had I used the word 'obligation' instead of 'a necessity?' Or 'a relief'? Ecclesiastic control even infects language in this place.

But a couple of women seized upon the declaration and quickly elevated showering to doctrinal heights. 'Oh yes,' they cried. 'It's a sacred obligation!' Within minutes they had organised a rota so everyone could aspire to sainthood by taking turns to shower.

Parváneh approached me, beaming from ear-to-ear, and offered to 'do' my face, too. While she performed this kindness, she told me to instruct the women to tidy up all their belongings that were lying around. 'And make sure they clean the bathroom afterwards too,' she added. I might have guessed my authority would extend no further than servitude.

An hour later, someone announced that we'd be eating a traditional Naw-Rúz meal that evening – *sabzi polo mahi*! Herbed rice and fish? In prison? But when the food pot arrived, it amounted to a fragment of fish between two or three persons, and a plate of tasteless grey rice. Parváneh dished out the unappetising food with the help of another prisoner, but I could barely swallow my share. The smell of the rice made me sick.

One of the women who'd been eyeing my plate nudged closer. 'Aren't you going to have any more?' she whispered. Before I could even reply, she had eaten all my leftovers.

'Their appetite really improves when they're coming off crack,' said Parváneh.

Finally, it was time for lights out, the hour of mandatory darkness and compulsory silence that was never absolute in the qarantineh ward. It was also the hour when the old year turned towards the new (*tahvil-i-sál*), when the past gave way to the future. I lay awake through my first Naw-Rúz night in prison, feeling lamentably homesick, wallowing in self-pity and full of self-disgust. My lofty exhortations and forced jollity struck me as utterly fraudulent. I felt like a cheat, like one of those people who do not practise what they preach.

The next morning, I rose early, showered and dried myself with my chador. Since Háj Khánum had never been authorised to give me the clothes my son had brought to the detention centre, I had no option but to dress in the old ones I'd worn the day before, in spite of it being the day when, traditionally, everything should be fresh and new. After that I asked Parváneh to let us know the exact moment Naw-Rúz began, because it would help to focus our attention on something besides ourselves. She went downstairs and came back a short while later to announce – so that everyone could hear – that the vernal equinox had taken place, at precisely 9:20 a.m. on Panjshanbeh, 1 Farvardín 1387 (Thursday, 20 March 2008).

So, to mark my first New Year in prison, I went up to one of the women, kissed her on both cheeks and wished her well. Afterwards, some of the others also wished me well, and we tried to console each other as best we could. It was a real test for us all, a challenge to behave like normal human beings in this abnormal place. And we triumphed, in a manner of speaking. We managed to revive some of the arts of civility towards each other.

* * *

On the second morning of Farvardín, even as I was preparing myself for the possibility of staying one more week in the qarantineh ward, someone yelled out my name from the bottom of the steps, 'Get ready! Criminal investigation!'

That was when Parváneh confirmed that it was the Intelligence Bureau [*'Ittilá'át*] summoning me, and that 'criminal investigation' was, as I had suspected, a euphemism.

'The detention centre is actually quite close to us, next door to the prison, in fact, just round the corner. They drive you in circles to disorient you,' she told me, with a wink.

A short while later I was seated in the Intelligence Bureau car again, blindfolded as usual, with my head leaning against the back of the driver's seat. One day, I thought, when I am free, I would love to walk through these streets and see, with my own eyes, the prison, the qarantineh ward, the detention centre. It was a classic case of craving for what is denied. Previously, I'd given scant thought to the existence of such places and certainly had no interest in seeing them, even if free to do so. Now they had become elusive objects of desire.

I could not help feeling rather depressed as I stepped into my grey and beige cell in the detention centre. It seemed so insecure with its unlockable door, placing me at the mercy of whoever opened it, with or without knocking. It felt lonely too, after the hurly burly of the qarantineh ward, and I felt adrift like an atom in the Milky Way, a tiny speck with no will of my own. I had to remind myself several times a day that I was still in Iran, in the city of Mashhad, just 620 miles away from my own home. But the sense of alienation never left me, despite all my efforts to analyse the cause and identify its component parts. I was a stranger in a strange land, a migrant in another universe.

As I stepped into the cell and untied my blindfold, the old man held something out to me. A tiny bar of soap. 'Want some shampoo too?' he whispered hurriedly.

How grateful I was to him! That's all it takes to feel less alienated in this world: a bar of soap and kindness. Besides, despite the solitary confinement and the lack of a lock on the door, it was still better to take a shower in this cell than in the qarantineh ward. I was getting dressed again when the old man called out once more.

'Get ready for your interrogation!'

Slipping the chador quickly over my head and the blindfold over my eyes, I stumbled after him down the same, unseen corridors, around the familiar, unknown corners to the room where the cold, disembodied but all too recognisable voice of the interrogator offered me New Year's greetings. He asked me placidly, as if I had gone on some exotic holiday, how I had enjoyed my Naw-Rúz, what I had done, and whether I'd eaten well while away?

My replies were, as usual, brief, my tone equally cool and impassive. There was something particularly grating about being forced to answer such banal questions on so special an occasion. Then out of the blue, he abruptly changed the subject.

'You will now call your family,' he said. 'Just a short call, mind. You will not give them any information. I repeat: you will not say a word about where you are or what you are doing. Understood? Just let them know that you're still alive on New Year's day.'

My heart galloped. Joy! But I told myself not to overreact. *Hold on. It hasn't happened yet.*

The news might not be so good. Perhaps the interrogator had a reason for using the past tense about Siyávash. Perhaps he wanted me to phone now, just to discover the worst on New Year's day. My anticipation shrivelled into dread.

He took me to the same room where I had previously phoned my brother and told me to enter ahead of him. As I stepped inside, I rapidly raised my chin; it was risky but I wanted to see what I could beneath the blindfold. For a fleeting second I glimpsed two young men bent over some equipment, connecting a line, preparing the phone. Probably to monitor the call. Seconds later, the interrogator entered behind me. I recognised his quick step, sensed his presence from the sound of his breathing and the imperceptible shift of the air around me.

'What number should we dial?' he asked.

I froze. Number? Where should I call? Home? I had no idea. *What's your home phone number?*

I'd forgotten! I think my brain literally seized up for a moment. After giving them the wrong number twice, I eventually heard the phone ringing through the loudspeakers.

Everything would be heard in that room. Every word. My heart almost burst.

After a few rings, someone picked up.

'Speak!' ordered the interrogator.

I took a deep breath, but nothing came.

'Yes?' It was Siyávash! 'Hello?' he echoed.

His words reverberated against the four walls. It was very difficult to contain my happiness at the sound of his sweet voice, but I could hardly get my own out of my throat, after hearing his. He seemed to be uncertain, sad, depressed.

'Alláh'u'Abhá. Happy New Year!' I breathed.

He did not reply. He did not recognise me! I had to repeat myself.

'It is me,' I croaked. 'Happy New Year.'

Siyávash had not been expecting this. His voice changed, his relief was palpable, his tender delight flooded over me and washed around the room in lapping, laughing waves.

'My dear, is it really you? How are you?' he cried joyfully. 'Tell me how you are, won't you? Happy happy New Year!'

I could barely contain myself. Words were so trite. 'And the same to you, Happy New Year. I am well, thank you. How are you? How are the children?'

Was that all I could say? He assured me they were well, they were all well. Was I well? How was I? Really well? 'But where are you?' he asked urgently.

'Hang up!' ordered the interrogator.

'I have to say goodbye,' I mumbled, leaving his question unanswered. 'Please take care of yourself.' And we were cut off. The phone was disconnected.

I was furious. This interrogator was too cruel. To offer me a conversation and then cut it so short like that? To promise so much only to deny it so fast? The man was a sadist. And yet, by the time I was back in the interrogation room, all my anger had vanished, my fury evaporated. I wanted to fly, to soar into the sky. Siyávash was alive, he was well and at home! Nothing had happened to him. A moment later, I had plunged into despair again and was filled with doubt. But why had he been so down? Why did he not recognise my voice? Was he all alone? Where were the children? Couldn't the interrogator have at least given me the chance to ask him about them? Too, too cruel! I was back on the rack, torn between joy and sorrow, hope and despair, swamped by anger, petrified by uncertainty.

Over that first Naw-Rúz, I identified several important techniques employed by these gentlemen of the Intelligence Bureau. They not only wielded the usual weapons that distorted facts and fomented doubts, but they had also refined even more heartless deceptions. They knew how to arouse a person's most intense longings, only to dash them brutally away. They were able to control the very pulse of one's hope in order to slash it open and bleed it dry. By denying us access to our loves, they brought us to the very verge of hopelessness.

That day, the interrogator chose to inform me, in a sanctimonious tone, that he had been compelled to leave *his* wife and children at home on this holiday, just because of me. He was stuck in here, while everyone else was out there celebrating the New Year, just to follow up on *my* case. Presumably, I was supposed to feel indebted to him for this great condescension, to thank him for his remarkable sacrifice on my behalf. I did no such thing.

I knew he was trying to save face. He wished to prove that despite kidnapping me illegally and holding me hostage for almost three weeks, without providing any information to my family or contact with the outside world, he had gone out of his way to permit me less than a minute's phone call to them on the New Year holiday. I suppose he was hoping to exonerate himself, as far as the letter of the law was concerned, to maintain the appearance of having complied with the regulations of incarceration.

After this pantomime, the rest of the interrogation that day was uneventful. He mainly asked me questions about my activities in prison. At the end, he called the old man to take me back to the car but, most unusually, he accompanied me part of the way himself, as I trailed, still blindfolded, in the wake of my guide.

Was I meant to feel honoured by this special attention? Or was his sham display of courtesy a form of increased surveillance to mark the festive occasion? I was unimpressed by both alternatives and would have preferred to celebrate Naw-Rúz any way but this.

8

NEW WORDS, NEW WARDS

I was driven back to Vakilabad Prison in the same car and along the same circuitous route as before, but as soon as we were in motion, my heart stopped beating erratically and I grew more serene. It was a relief to leave the dour isolation of the detention centre after this New Year interrogation period, and head back to the bedlam of the qarantineh ward. I was almost looking forward to my return, because I knew Parváneh would be waiting for me. To feel expected is as sweet as to anticipate arrival. It was pleasant to know that someone would be happy to see me, even if it was only in jail.

When I stepped through the door of the qarantineh hall, the woman with burgundy hair, who had been among the first to respond to the challenge of cheering everyone up for Naw-Rúz, headed straight for me. She was middle-aged, wore relatively decent clothes compared to the rags worn by many others, and had clearly had a radical nose job. A stylish, happy-go-lucky sort of person, she also seemed friendly and affectionate, for I had noticed that she liked to sit in a corner of the hall much of the time, in the company of young women, talking and laughing in a relaxed manner. She seemed so very unperturbed by this appalling atmosphere that my curiosity was piqued. After greeting me warmly on my return that day, she drew close and began to speak to me confidentially.

'How long do you think I'll get this time?' she whispered, as if I were somehow in the know and could give her privileged information about her sentence.

'I have no idea what you're even convicted of,' I answered.

'I'm a *qavád*,' she murmured, with a knowing wink.

'I'm sorry?' The word rang a bell, but I was not sure what it meant.

She drew back for a moment and gave me the full benefit of her neatly upturned nose. 'Well,' she sighed, with a dismissive shrug at my ignorance, 'they say I keep young women in my home.' And since I must have still looked puzzled, she added, with impatience at my obtuseness, 'To exploit them. Sexually, I mean.'

I sat down in a heap on the edge of her bed, and we began to talk. I told her that I was unfortunately quite ignorant of her case, knew nothing of the law on these matters, and therefore had no advice to offer. But I was keen to ask a few questions. This introduction, which levelled the playing field between us, led to a candid exchange and the burgundy-haired lady gradually explained several of the anomalies and mysteries I had noticed in the past few weeks. I remembered, for instance, that soon after I arrived in the qarantineh ward, a young girl of seventeen or eighteen had approached me one day, looking quite dishevelled, and had asked to know my crime. I had been reluctant to mention the Bahá'í Faith.

'What do you think it is?' was my quizzical rejoinder.

She gazed at me for a moment, with shrewd appraisal, as if trying to calculate my worth. And then in a tone of awe, as though referring to an extremely high rank and role in society, she had asked: 'Are you an international *qavád*?'

I had never come across the word before, but now, thanks to the burgundy-haired lady, I started to think seriously about what it took to be the Madam of a brothel. At first, I could not understand the young girl's admiration for this profession or the reason why it attracted such respect in this place, but as I pieced the puzzle together, the proprietorial air of this Madam, with her vibrant hair, gradually become apparent. I discovered that a brothel keeper or procuress is rarely kept in custody for long but uses her time in prison to fish for prostitutes and 'catch young girls in her net,' as they called it. These Madams contact the girls once they are freed and start to exploit them, as sexual bait. Some even make bargains with the authorities to release the girls early in exchange for their immediate services. As a result, an arrest not only provides the Madam with the means to bribe her way out of prison quickly, but it can prove very profitable to her in the long run.

If it was so permissive, prostitution must be more pervasive in Iran than I had thought. Was the industry a political ploy? Was it maintained to divert people from thinking about social justice? And who were these brothel keepers that were treated with such leniency? How had their values been so eroded? Had they experienced similar sexual abuse in youth, and if so, how could they lure others into the same plight with such impunity? I was heartsick to think of these girls being exposed to physical and psychological diseases, abandoned on the margins of society after being exploited, while their Madams raked in the next harvest.

Parváneh told me that the burgundy-haired woman was eager to make the acquaintance of all the women in the qarantineh ward, and to learn the nature of their charges. But why me? She could hardly believe I could be useful for her purposes, let alone in the same profession. She probably thought I wielded some kind of 'power' due to my friendship with Parváneh, which was rather funny in the circumstances.

* * *

On the morning of the fourth of Farvardín (24 March), four days after Naw-Rúz, my brief holiday in the public prison was over and I was conducted back to the detention centre. Háj Khánum had been summoned back too, though she now told me that she would not stay for long. She gave me no reasons, but promised that as long as she was around, I would be safe and should not worry about the door. She was effectively keeping others locked out by keeping me locked in. It was a dubious sort of reassurance.

The interrogator was at my service too and gave me his undivided attention; he did not miss a single opportunity to cross-examine me with inquisitorial exactitude. The daily sessions were shorter than before, and slower; it was becoming obvious that the gentlemen of the Intelligence Bureau were only dragging out my confinement to increase pressure on my dear colleagues, and maybe even on the Bahá'í World Centre.

This thought filled me with apprehension.

Then, one week into the New Year, the old man told me that my time at the detention centre was coming to an end; I was to return to the public prison at the end of that day. I showered off the grime of the last interrogation session with relief, and washed all my clothes, but he knocked on the door all too soon. Nothing was quite dry by the time I had to put on the blindfold and leave the grey cell, and it was only after my arrival at the prison that I discovered, with surprise, that he must have slipped several more bars of soap and a dozen sachets of shampoo surreptitiously into my bag. One of the female guards quickly appropriated them during the inspection process, with the air of having apprehended a thief. She probably needed them herself, but I was sad when she took everything. Those shampoos would have been much appreciated by the women in Parváneh's ward.

I completed the usual paperwork like an automaton, with silent apologies to the long-suffering corpse who still had to be named, branded and dragged along with each iteration of my indictment. And then I started heading towards the steps that led up to the qarantineh ward, a direction I knew robotically well. But I was stopped by a shout.

'Not that way!' another female guard called out. 'Come with me.'

Turning back in surprise, I saw her moving off in the opposite direction and hurried to catch up with her. Since I wasn't wearing a blindfold, we walked fast. I could not ask where she was taking me, but was glad to see the interior of the prison for the first time. It was an old building, solidly constructed, with sturdy walls that had withstood the test of time. The corridors were wide, the ceilings high and the floors covered with fine old glazed tiles. Then a heavy iron door yawned open, and we stepped into the heart of the labyrinth.

The first passageway we entered, which branched off to the left, was teeming with women. They were milling around on all sides as we passed, adrift and aimless, vacant and apathetic. Their skin was chalk white, their eyes lustreless and dull, and although they were not dressed in prison garb, they seemed half-dead in their loose pyjamas and bunched up skirts. Their demeanour, too, was oddly similar, as if they were clones. It was most disquieting.

Many were seated on the floor and some of them were leaning listlessly against the walls. But as soon as they saw us, they all rose to their feet, more from fear than respect, I suspect, and lined up as we walked by, as if for inspection. Several greeted the guard who was conducting me, with timid and tremulous anticipation. Everyone, without exception, gaped at me.

As we walked through this passageway, a group of the younger girls detached themselves from the milling crowd and began to run after us. The guard went down a flight of stairs and I followed, with the girls at my heels. She turned right into another corridor, and the girls and I scurried after her. Then a strong stench hit me. I guessed we must have been passing near the prison baths, for the damp air reeked of sulphuric acid and ammonia. From that point on, the young girls began to announce my passage loudly, as if in warning.

'Solitary! Solitary!'

A glimmer of the setting sun cast shafts of sallow light along the walls, and grey shadows were laddering the floor from barred windows high above as we reached the end of this long corridor. Our way was blocked by a small door. The entrance was narrow as well as low, hardly wide enough for one person to pass through, and the door itself was heavy and made of corroded iron, with a small slot at eye level covered with mesh. The female guard turned the key in the lock and undid the chains with a jangle and a clatter, but was having a hard time pushing the door open. The rusty hinges resisted obstinately, so when she tried to force it open with both hands, several of the young girls pressed forward, eager to help.

'Damn thing!' muttered the guard, as the girls leaned hard against the door and pushed with all their strength. It gradually scraped open, and the guard immediately covered her mouth with her scarf. The smell on the other side was beyond foul. It was noxious. I almost gagged. One of the girls turned back briefly towards me, with frank pity in her eyes.

'What have you done?' she asked.

I tried to smile. What could I say? That I was a Bahá'í? That a Bahá'í did not need to have 'done' anything to be treated to this stench? Would she even understand? She was very beautiful, this girl, and looked no more than fifteen or sixteen years old. I guessed from her accent that she was from Afghanistan. What could *she* have done to be in such a place?

There was a narrow, white-washed corridor beyond the entrance, with three more metal doors on the left, each barred shut with huge padlocks and chains. Three small solitary confinement cells with low ceilings. Three narrow doors with slots that opened and closed from the outside. The drains of the first cell were apparently blocked, which accounted for the stench. The middle cell was ominously vacant, and there was already an occupant in the third. This person began to shout as soon as we entered. Her voice was piercing.

'Let me out,' she screamed. 'Or give me a pill. Or a cigarette at least. Please!'

My conductor told her, roughly, to shut her mouth and then drew back, keeping her own covered with her scarf. All the female guards in the public prison wore the same dreary floor-length coats, trousers and navy-blue scarves. But as the door of the middle cell was being unlocked, an older woman arrived, dressed in a crisp, well-ironed uniform. I gathered from the deference shown towards her by the others that she must be the warden in charge of the women's section in this prison. Instead of making a fuss over the choking smell, she immediately began to give orders to the young girls to prepare the cell for me.

At her instructions, a tatty piece of torn carpeting was dragged in and thrown onto the floor. An outdated magazine was laid carefully on it, and a one-litre plastic Coke bottle, filled with hot water, together with some loose tea leaves and a few sugar cubes wrapped in newspaper, were placed in the middle of the carpet. I noticed a few filthy blankets lying in a far corner of the cell. The girls were anxious to offer what comforts they could.

'What else do you need, Solitary one?' asked the Afghani girl.

'Books,' I instantly replied. 'It doesn't matter what, just books.'

'Do you like novels?'

'Yes, absolutely,' I told her gladly.

'Then I will bring some tomorrow with your breakfast,' she promised.

The well-dressed warden was observing me closely in the course of this exchange.

'Why on earth are you here?' she asked.

My smile must have been equivocal. I had been instructed by the interrogator never to mention the Bahá'í Faith. Frankly, I did not want to utter the words in a place where one couldn't even breathe. And if I had, it would have probably been taken as 'preaching' and only added to my problems. I indicated with a shrug that there was nothing to say.

As they were about to leave, securing the doors behind them with double chains and locks, the warden herself made the final pronouncement.

'The judge says you must stay in solitary for fifteen days,' she said. 'But I honestly don't know why. You're not an addict. This is hardly the place for the likes of you.'

9

VISIONS IN THE DARK

I stood behind the closed door trying not to vomit. The sickening odours from the nearby drains of the baths and the stench of the toilets all around filled my mouth, my throat and my lungs with their toxic vapours. There was no ventilation. The girls had called this room 'the kennel.' It was just about large enough for a dog. Poor dog.

The blanket lying on the floor in the corner of the cell was covered with a shower of white flakes, I now noticed, from the plaster that had fallen from a large damp patch on the ceiling. On the other side of the cell, a few centimetres off the ground, was a squat, oriental toilet, no more than a hole in the cement. It was excessively filthy. Beside it was a rubber hose attached to a tap, with water oozing out of the end. There was no jug, no basin, no container in which to wash. The water trickling out of the hose was lying in putrid puddles between heaps of dried faeces. I noticed a few dead cockroaches lying around, and a couple of large, live ones, too, lurking in the corners. Here was yet another world.

Who had condemned me to this place? The warden had mentioned 'the judge.' Which 'judge'?' Did she mean Judge Hedáyatí, who had offered to free me with a bail bond of ten million *tumans* that first night? The stocky young man, who had said my arguments were convincing? The well-tailored gentleman, whose paperwork was so engrossing that it did not allow him to authorise a phone call? Had it all been for show? Had he been playing with me? Had they all been playing with me – the judge, the interrogator, even Parváneh?

Dismay overwhelmed me, a sense of having been duped, dishonoured, deceived. The flaking ceiling might just as well have fallen on my head at that moment. I stood there, in the doghouse, unable to move for a long time, with my trembling hands covering my face to block out the stink. My clothes were still damp, still smelling of camomile shampoo, but I was not sure whether I was shivering because of the chill or from sheer shock. I only knew that I was tired, so deeply tired of all these tricks and this endless mendacity.

I was tempted to hold the plastic Coke bottle close to my body. It was filled with hot water; perhaps that would control the shivers. The black scrap of carpeting seemed relatively clean and the girl said it had been washed recently. I dragged it to the side of the cell, just behind the door, to distance myself as far as possible from the toilet and its filth. Then I kneeled down on it, using my chador with its wet seams as a sheet under one of the smelly blankets, and hugging the hot water bottle for warmth.

And what if the plastic cracks? What if the bottle springs a leak?
The thought made me laugh.
Well, you'll get scalded, that's all, and soaking wet in the bar-gain, and then you'll have to shout and scream for the guards like the poor woman next door.
I was just beginning to feel a little warmer when I noticed that my neighbour in the third cell had finally given up on the guards, and was now calling to me, screaming non-stop.

'Solitary one, I beg you by the saint Abul'Fadl, do something for me. Solitary one, I beg you by the chastity of Zahrá, help me! I swear by Imam Husayn, I am dying!'[16]

I stood up and brought my mouth close to the slot in the door.

'What are you saying, my dear? What do you want?'

'Solitary one, I beg you by the eighth Imam, give me anything you have, anything – a cigarette, a pain killer, any kind of shit you have.'

The poor woman gave an ear-piercing shriek, which I tried to answer.

'I have nothing, dear. Even if I did, how could I give it to you? I'm locked up too.'

Her screams became even louder. She started making a sort of rattling noise, a snoring sound in her throat, like one possessed. In the midst of the din, I heard the voice of the Afghani girl calling from behind the rusty door at the end of the passage.

'Don't worry, Solitary one,' she said. 'They all say that, but I've been in there and I can promise you, there's nothing. You don't have to be afraid!'

I was bewildered. What was nothing? Why should I not be afraid? And of what and where? I told her that I did not understand what she was talking about.

'That cell is not full of *jinn*s,' she explained. 'If you hear noises at night, they're from the drug addict, not *jinn*s. She faints, you see, and hallucinates; she's also on crack.'

I found myself reassuring her even as she was reassuring me. 'I'm not afraid, my dear. Don't worry about me. But why are you in here?'

'It's my lousy coward of a husband,' she answered. 'He's in the drug business.'

And then she explained that the public prison of Vakilabad in Mashhad was filled with young girls from Afghanistan, some as young as fourteen and fifteen. They were brought over on the pretext of marriage, given in multiples of four to men in the business, and used to traffic drugs. They were the ones who were invariably caught in the firing line and punished. She too had spent time in the dreadful kennel, which explained her empathy.

'Are you an addict too?' I asked, for she struck me as such a lucid, sane person.

'Not at all,' she replied. 'I'll be back in the morning and bring you a book.'

I thanked her and bid her goodnight, but long after she left, I continued to be regaled by the howls of the poor woman next to me. Her voice boomed in that closed-in space, her screams were deafening. She would not, *could not* calm down.

* * *

It helped to concentrate on simple things and not look too far ahead. Since I still felt cold, even with the blanket and the chador over my shoulders, I sprinkled the tea leaves in the water bottle and shook it slowly. The cockroaches were scuttling around the edge of the wall near the reeking toilet, with a repulsive rustling sound; I gave them a leery eye.

You lot had better not come any closer. Don't even think about it, or you'll find yourselves hit on the head with the heel of my shoe.

After a while, I began to feel a little warmer, although it was still hard to breathe. But as the cold subsided, my thoughts chilled me. The behaviour of Judge Hedáyatí had broken my heart. How could he lie to my face like that? How could a representative of the justice system treat another human being so unjustly? Such deceptions were to be expected from interrogators, but I still wanted to believe that a judge would abide by rather than break the laws of the land. Even so, I had to remind myself that in certain places – such as Iran today – judge and jury, arbitrator and interrogator could be hand in glove. They had not even the courage to tell me, to my face, that they had abducted me because I was a Bahá'í.

Such people have existed everywhere, since time immemorial. They crush our freedoms to maintain their own powers. They kill our hopes and cause the suffering of the innocent with impunity. They have committed crimes against humanity in every era, and in every land. People like this judge have corrupted religion throughout history and persecuted the followers of every faith, including mine. Tens of thousands of Bahá'ís were brutally killed in Persia because of them. The herald of our Faith was shot and its founder was banished by such as them. They made him run, barefoot and bare-headed beneath the blazing sun, from Zargandeh to the Siyah Chal.[17] They beat him and bastinadoed him before flinging him into that putrid dungeon. Down, down, down three flights of stone steps, down four long months…

My thoughts drifted as I pulled my legs close under me. The light was so dim that my attempts to read the magazine were useless. So I leaned back against the door and closed my eyes, thinking of those steep and stony steps leading down, down, down into that foul, underground dungeon so long ago. Thinking of the stench of it. Imagining what it would be like to be imprisoned in such a place for four whole months. The Black Pit.

The metal between my shoulder blades felt cold at first, but the heat of my body gradually penetrated it. I was grateful to the door for warming me. And as it grew darker and warmer, I found myself sinking into it, stepping through it, and following those stone stairs down. The air was heavy, the atmosphere impenetrable. Down I went, step by step down the first flight, centuries down, into a sewer and a cistern, into a reservoir and a dungeon, deep underground beneath an ancient Qajar palace. There was a heavy murmur rising towards me from the depths of that far off time, a melody lifting from that pitch black prison, the chanting of men held captive in the chains and fetters of the past – I could hear them.

In Him let the trusting trust!

I heard the words and yet, I could see where I was, sitting against the door of the doghouse, in the prison of Mashhad. I was fully aware of my actual surroundings even as I continued climbing down, step by step, into another place, another time. They were pitted and cracked, those steps, and covered with slime; the light above me was dim, the air foul and unbearably fetid, but the darkness below rang with joyous voices, with shouts of praise.

God is sufficient unto me. He verily is the All sufficing. In Him let the trusting trust.[18]

Each flight of steps brought me closer to the chanting, and my wonder grew as I climbed down first one, then two, then three flights of those steps. For as I approached, I sensed a blaze of light in the heart of that darkness, a blessing in the core of it, a bright Presence that affirmed all that was good and glad and filled with gratitude and hope. And all through that strange descent, while I remained fully conscious of my circumstances, I was also aware of other prisoners down there, men bound by chains and shackled together in the gloom. Chanting. Even as I sat in the kennel, leaning against the iron door, with my arms wrapped around my knees, I was sur-rounded by thieves and murderers and human anguish in the presence of an unimaginable compassion. I had stepped into a timeless world of dazzling darkness where all was resolved, all was forgiven, all was wordless grace.

It is hard to describe what happened to me that night. I had never had such an experience in my life. Not being inclined to dreams and visions, I considered miracles, if such things do exist, to be for those who experience them. Period. They can-not be shared; they cannot and should not be put into words. In fact, I had no idea how to fit this curious experience into time and place, let alone language.

Did it last a moment or several hours? Was I sitting in that cell, as reason would attest, or had I gone elsewhere, according to laws other than physics? In literal terms it may have been for no more than a few seconds. But it felt like an eternity. And as I rose to the surface again, like a swimmer reprieved by drowning, I felt weightless, overflowing with love, with joy, and utter abandon. I felt light and buoyant and free, totally free.

The air of the doghouse, in Vakilabad Prison, was no longer unbearable. The darkness was no longer oppressive, and I dis-covered, to my amazement, that I was not in the least bit hurt by what Judge Hedáyatí had done to me either. Nor was I angry with the interrogator, or anyone else. My broken heart seemed to be strangely healed. How this had happened, I could not tell. By what means, I had no idea. I only knew that as I sat there, curled up on the floor, I felt very well, utterly content, and in perfect health.

I wanted to hold onto this feeling forever. I wanted to stay here for the rest of my life, if only for the chance of another meeting with that compassionate Presence, if only to capture a glimmer once again, from the beams of that blessed brightness.

* * *

The poor woman next door was still calling, still begging for help.

'I swear by Abu'l-Fadl, I cannot stand this any longer, I am dying…'

I counselled myself not to ignore her, to get up and talk to her. I had to force myself to do it, not for any physical reason, but because I did not want to leave the state of mind I was in, the proximity to happiness I was feeling. But once back on my feet, I found, to my surprise, that a hundred suns were throbbing in my heart. I was full of warm energy. I called out to her, eagerly, through the slot in the door.

'My dear one, dear daughter, what is your name? Come! Let's talk together!'

There was a pause in her howls and when she spoke again, her voice was perfectly normal. 'What about?' she asked, reasonably enough.

'Do you want to tell me your story, or shall I tell you mine?' I asked.

And then, on the basis of her silence, which I wrongly assumed was an assent to listen, I started talking about myself: a young woman in love with education and with children; a revolution in her country which led to her being disqualified as a teacher; and how this woman, despite being dismissed from her job, tried to find solutions to help young people further their studies… I paused.

'Do you see them too?' she asked.

'See what?'

'The *jinn*s!' said the poor woman, her voice rising to a pitch of panic again. 'There are *jinn*s in here, I have seen at least ten of them. They come after me, they attack me!'

I let her talk. She told me how frightened she was, how very frightened. I realised, after a few moments, that I could not hope to distract her from her fears; my stories were of no use to her. So instead, I told her that I wasn't afraid, that the *jinn*s did not bother me at all.

'How come?' she asked, in surprise.

'Because I don't believe in such things.'

And the minute I uttered those words, I knew there was no reason why she or anyone else would believe in the marvels of compassion that I had just witnessed in the dark heart of my despair. We need only turn our sight into ourselves to see either our demons rising to meet us, or our bright angels standing within us, mighty, powerful and self-subsisting.

The lock turned, the chains jangled at that moment, and through the slot in the door, I glimpsed two female guards entering the corridor, so I sat quickly on the ground, out of sight. Their steps passed my door, and their keys jangled again, at the entrance to the next cell, in which the shrieks were on the rise once more. From what I heard them saying, I gathered they were planning to take the suffering addict to the prison infirmary.

My heart was at ease. I drew the blanket carefully over myself and tucked in the sides all around me. Then I pulled the chador I was using as a sheet over my head. As I drifted off, I realised I would never be able to tell anyone about this either. No one would believe me when I told them that it was the most peaceful sleep I'd ever had in my life.

10

MAXIMUM SECURITY

Early the next morning, the rattle of the lock and chains heralded a connection with the human race once more, and as that beautiful Afghani girl had promised, a story book. I learned from her that all the other girls had done time in this place too, like her; they all knew what it was like to be locked up in this hell hole with screaming addicts. They had somehow found a means of calming the woman in the cell next door and may in fact have given her more drugs before returning her to the isolation cell, because she was quiet now. Apart from occasional rasping snores, no other sound came from her all that morning. She had spent the whole night screaming but was dead to the world by day. And so, I was, to all intents and purposes, alone in the kennel.

I was also blessed with total silence. Since the light was too murky to read, I set aside the novel the young girl had brought and read my heart instead, meditating on the marvel of the strange night that had passed, pondering over what I had experienced in the penumbra of the cell. The voices of those chanting prisoners still echoed in my ears.

In Him let the trusting trust!

Towards noon, the chains and the lock rattled in the corridor again and one of the female guards spoke through the slot in the door.

'Get ready, you're going out.'

And, once again, I was taken to the detention centre of the Intelligence Bureau. Once again, I found myself in that solitary grey room. I was only there for a few minutes before the old man knocked on the door, and I was blindfolded and taken out again. No time to adjust from one world to the next. No time even for a shower. As he guided me back through the corridors, I smelled the stink of the kennel on me, like a miasma of muck, like the leak from a drain. The reek of it was still strong in my nostrils, in my clothes, in my chador and in all the pores of my skin when I reached the interrogation room.

You can always tell who has been to the doghouse.

I had barely seated myself before the interrogator took a deep breath and began talking at me, all in a rush. I was going to be allowed a visit with my son, he said hurriedly. Well, not actually a visit, just a quick meeting with him. Well, not exactly a meeting, more of a brief encounter, just so my family would know I was still alive, he concluded. Nothing more. Nothing of where I was. Nothing of what I was doing here.

'You understand?' he said.

I was beginning to understand more about this place every day. But there was a great deal I would rather not understand about the irascible and cold-blooded interrogator. Instead, I preferred to take his offer of a visit that was not really a visit, a reunion that was not actually a reunion, as confirmation of the strange vision I had experienced the night before, if indeed it had been a vision, of an encounter unlike any other I'd had in my life.

An engine was already throbbing and exhaust was in the air when we reached the car park and the old man told me to watch my head as I bent down to slip into the back seat. He should have enquired after my heart, hammering in my chest. But it was only after we set off that I had a second shock. Once the blindfold was off, I found myself in the middle seat of the car, as far removed from both windows as possible. Two bulky men were sitting on each side of me and someone I had never met was next to the driver. The man on my right told me to lean my head forward and keep my eyes to the floor, and after we had driven round for a while, the one on the left said I could now relax. All four were strangers to me.

The driver and the men beside me were the kind I had come to associate with the Intelligence Bureau – dressed in a slovenly manner, bearded, thuggish types. But the person in the front seat was another species altogether; he was elegant and sleek. He did not speak to me, never looked in my direction, but I glimpsed his profile when he turned to the driver with instructions to park the car in front of the prison doors. He had a neatly trimmed black beard.

The place was teeming with people. I looked to the right, to the left, in all directions and then suddenly, in the middle of the crowd, there was my son! His eyes met mine. He looked straight at me sitting there in the middle of the back seat. The window was down barely ten centimetres, but I could not call out to him across the bulk of the man next to me. Besides, this Samand car had been adapted for prison transport: the handles on the back doors had been removed so the window could not have been opened any further even if I were right beside it. I nodded to Fúrúd, wondering for a moment whether he would even recognise me wearing a chador and a head scarf. My appearance was probably very different from what it had been when he saw me last. But the moment of contact between us was like my experience in the kennel the night before: a flash of brightness in the dark, seeing and being seen, recognising and being recognised, a single glance of love exchanged.

It was enough!

My son drew near the parked car immediately. I was in such turmoil, longing to reach out to him but terribly afraid these men might do him harm, yearning to express my love but responding like a stone after having habituated myself to restraint these past weeks. I could see that Fúrúd was trying to control his feelings too, trying to hold back, to show as little emotion as possible. He seemed cold, indifferent, as he approached. He did not even look at the man beside me but fixed his eyes on mine. And then he began speaking rapidly, talking urgently, only to me. As if to soak me up, suck me out through the car window.

'How are you, *maman*?' he said. 'How are you feeling? Are you alright?'

I told him I was well and asked after him in turn, thanking him for coming. 'You have gone through so much trouble to come here,' I heard myself stupidly say.

Then, as if this were a perfectly normal social situation, just an ordinary exchange, or as if he were still a little boy needing a lesson in courtesy, I indicated, with a slight nod, that he should perhaps greet the men in the car with me. He did so automatically. It was surreal to hear his polite '*salaam*' and to have the thug sitting between us, who was effectively my jailer, my hijacker, my abductor, respond with a cold hello. Then Fúrúd turned back to me.

'No trouble,' he said, picking up on my last comment. 'It's been no trouble at all. And I'm perfectly well.'

Then he asked me again how I was. I repeated in turn that I was well, that there was no problem. And then, since I was very concerned about Siyávash, I asked how his father was doing. My son replied that he was fine too. We were trapped in banalities, separated by a stranger, confined on opposite sides of a barely open window, and I was getting desperate. I do not know if it was because I was so nervous or because I wanted some news about everyone, some information about anything, but I repeated the question twice.

'How is your dear *baba*, does he take his medications regularly?'

'*Baba* is well,' my son replied. 'We are all well.'

At that point the driver turned on the car engine. 'Time to go!' he barked.

Fúrúd intervened, his voice rising urgently. 'We've brought you some clothes,' he said, 'and other things. To eat.'

'Thank you, my dear,' I began. 'You shouldn't have troubled yourselves.'

I wanted to soothe his growing agitation lest it provoke the ire of the agents, especially the man between us, and I was about to repeat that I didn't need anything, when the driver swung the steering wheel violently round and slammed his foot on the accelerator to back out of the parking space. Before I could utter another word, the car roared away with a screeching of wheels and a groaning of gears, and from the corner of my eye, I saw my son leap out of the way. The driver careened through the streets in random frenzy, turning here and there, twisting this way and that, before reaching the prison, twenty minutes later.

There were still many visitors massed up before the doors. I looked round frantically. Was Fúrúd still in the crowd? No, he had vanished. Had he left of his own accord, or been instructed to go? There was no way of knowing.

My bulky companions in the back of the car hurriedly ushered me out, delivered me to the prison officer on duty, and drove away in a blast of exhaust fumes. And the smooth-faced, well-trimmed, elegantly dressed gentleman sitting next to the driver went with them. The fact that such a man had been present to oversee a two-minute exchange of banalities between a mother and a son seemed bizarre to me. I must either be very dangerous or very important to these people for some reason. Or maybe I was simply very stupid, because I had not remembered, in that fleeting moment, to even mention the bail money to Fúrúd.

* * *

For the rest of that day, the prison girls called greetings to me through the slot of the doghouse door. Some tried to console me in my solitary confinement, commiserating with me for being in such a place. The Afghani girl, whose name was Zaynab, brought her friend to sing an exquisite song for me in her beautiful language, so gentle, so soft! I was deeply touched by these young women, by their kindness and compassion despite their own miseries and deprivations. They all knew what it was like to be in the kennel.

Many of the prisoners I met at that time were women who had endured appalling hardships. Many were obliged to assist with prison work and basically served as slaves to the prison authorities. The female guards kept one or two of these girls at their sides at all times, giving them the worst tasks, the most demeaning chores, and they would always lord it over them from on high, belittling them in the harshest terms.

One of the worst jobs they were given was related to drug prevention. When they told me about it, I finally understood what

Parváneh had meant by waiting *for as long as it took* to see whether the women had brought heroin into prison. Those who were suspected of being addicts had to stay in the doghouse after returning from a furlough, until they had had a bowel movement. At such times, the guards would order these poor girls to search through the excrement of the suspected addict to make sure the prisoner had not ingested drugs in small plastic bags, to use in jail. The guards never undertook such filthy tasks themselves.

The young girls who had arranged the cell for me that first night, with hot water, a scrap of carpeting, and the luxury of a magazine, were under the authority of such a female guard, the one who had marched me over there. But for all their efforts to bring me comfort, they could not increase the oxygen levels in the place. I was suffocating, gasping for air, and often brought my mouth close to the slot in the door, trying in vain to catch a fresher breath. There was none. Although I had not wanted to leave before, I confess it was harder to make my way back down those stone stairs on the second night. I was choking.

Half of that terrible second night had crawled past, when the jangle of locks and chains broke through my haze of suffocation and stirred me back into dazed consciousness. I was still trying to fathom what was happening when the cell door rasped open.

'Get up,' said the guard, covering her mouth with her scarf in disgust, 'you are going somewhere else.'

Where? I asked. Outside? Was I being let out of the prison? I asked hopefully. No, she said. Not quite out. It was just that Mrs Jenáhí – the warden of the women's ward whom I had met the previous night – had decided to put me elsewhere. She had called the guard station at eleven o'clock, from her own house, giving orders on her own responsibility, that I should not spend a second night in the kennel.

I marvelled. Once again, it seemed that a breeze of compassion had wafted towards me from the depths, just like the ocean of light that had washed over me the night before. What an unexpected reprieve! I did not know why it had happened or how I deserved it, but I gulped down mouthfuls of grateful air as we walked away from the doghouse.

From what the guard said, I assumed that I was being taken to the public part of the prison, but this proved not to be the case. They took me first to the Main Corridor, where I had passed by those dozens of pallid, dull-eyed women milling around the previous day, and then came to a stop before another barred and bolted door that led off from it. On the other side was a third iron door set into a massive wall, beyond which lay our ultimate destination. The guards removed the chains and the padlock and ushered me through.

I was losing all sense of direction in this labyrinth. Besides, I was exhausted from lack of sleep and it was past midnight by then. As we stepped through one door with a shriek of grinding metal, only to find ourselves facing another, requiring a jangle of chains and clatter of yet more keys, our destination seemed to narrow down further and further.

A few women were standing behind bars at the far end of the last passageway. Despite the lateness of the hour, a couple of them greeted the guards in a familiar and friendly fashion, offering joking comments and random remarks as we came in. Most of their faces were chalk pale from lack of exposure to the sun; their skin was a sickly yellow and covered with bruises and stains. But unlike the women in the qarantineh ward, whom they otherwise resembled, these prisoners were curious and eager to meet their new guest.

The guard unlocked the door of the second cell in the passage and ordered me in. There I found myself surrounded by five women who welcomed me into this remote and far-flung corner of the prison with smiles and greetings. It seemed miraculous in such a place and at such a time to receive such a warm welcome. Their kindness filled me with wonder.

Since communication with them was easy, I asked who they were, where we were, and why we were kept behind so many extra doors and bars, separated from others? A woman who looked about forty-five, though she was in fact ten years younger, was the first to respond. She introduced herself as Fatimih, the mother of three and the wife of a thief.

'This is a prison inside the prison,' she said. 'When someone does something really bad in the ordinary place, they send her to this dump. See how awful we must be?'

So this was the dreaded maximum security ward of Vakilabad, the ward for dangerous criminals I had been threatened with before! And these smiling women, who had welcomed me so kindly in the middle of the night, were all hardened felons who had committed heinous offences at some point in their lives – robbery, arson, murder.

I tried to make light of it, for I knew they were well aware of where I had come from. The corridor from which this unit branched off, and through which I had walked, only led in one direction – to the doghouse, the kennel, the ultimate pit of hell.

'But I didn't come here from the ordinary place!' I jokingly responded, and they all laughed with me.

'Aha!' said one of them, 'that probably means you're even more dangerous than we are. You must be such a troublemaker that they didn't want you to be near anyone else.'

She was called Maryam and was in her mid-thirties, tall, well-built and dynamic. At first encounter she came across as rather loud but proved over time to have an attractive personality and sweet temperament. She liked to stand by the bars of the cell, chatting and laughing with the others in the corridor, calling out whenever possible to this or that passing prisoner. I didn't know what she had done to be in maximum security but was delighted that she'd accepted me there, and considered me, as she charitably put it, 'one of us'.

In addition to Maryam and Fatimih, three other women shared this cell and greeted me cordially that first night. One of them, a skinny young addict with a face covered in unsightly spots and blemishes, was called Naneh; she was highly strung and irascible, with a nervous temperament and a tendency to fuss over everything. She had grown up in the suburbs of Mashhad, burdened by many family problems, and had become a notorious thief as a result. The night I arrived she told me that she had stopped stealing for a while, but when her brother decided to get married, she had so desperately wanted to give him a special gift that she had robbed someone in the shrine of the eighth Imam for his sake.

'He's my little brother, you see, and I love him,' she confessed. 'I went all out for him and stole a gold necklace lying there. They arrested me on the spot.'

The two other occupants of the cell were middle-aged women, each serving ten-year sentences for the last misdemeanour they had committed. One was fat and the other was thin and they were both called Zahrá. The well-endowed Zahrá was very patient and did not say much; I discovered in time that she was the wise elder of the group. The smaller, wiry Zahrá was frank and talkative, rarely indulging in sentimentality. She once confessed to me, with a sardonic smile, that they were all fed up with her forthrightness. Both women had spent many years in captivity; I came to think of them as my Big and Little Zahrás.

This communal cell in maximum security was about fifteen square metres, with a single aperture high up on the wall, close to the ceiling – a non-window. It faced a busy yard but was locked fast so that no fresh air could circulate. There was also a toilet inside this common room, as well as a shower without a vent, which did not help clear the odours either. The toilet area was dark and damp with very little light filtering through, but it was relatively clean. The women had tied two pieces of string in there, to dry their washing.

My ladies in maximum security were quite hygienic, overall, despite the lack of fresh air. They showered regularly and loved standing under the water for a long time, just to 'let it come,' as they happily told me. They scrubbed their clothes frequently and did what they could to maintain their looks. And they were in the habit of carefully examining any newcomer who joined them to make sure she was clean too; they would search each other's hair for lice, and at times even shaved it all off to avoid infestation.

Despite their alleged crimes, these five women were also innately generous souls. They not only welcomed me that first night but immediately accepted me among them. As I learned more about their circumstances and became familiar with their trials in life, I marvelled at the strength of their characters and grew increasingly fond of them. Although other women came and went in maximum security, during the course of my imprisonment in Mashhad, these five friendly troublemakers were my true and trusted companions. I was deeply grateful to be out of the kennel and in their company that night and slept with a light heart in the top bunk bed which they told me could be mine.

11

SPRING

I remained in the public prison of Vakilabad for several nights after that, returning to the detention centre for interrogations in the mornings. Sometimes, I would be kept all night in the grim grey cell and only brought back to the prison the following day. And on the journey between these two places, I was always blindfolded and told to keep my head bent against the back of the car seat as they swung round corners to confuse me.

But on the 13th day after Naw-Rúz, the holiday called *Sizdah Bedar*, the agents drove me back to the prison from the detention centre very early, and without a blindfold. As a result, I was able to look around me for the first time in almost a month, the only other occasion having been during the fleeting 'visit' with my son, Fúrúd. I stared through the windows like a starved person, hungry to catch a glimpse of normal life again, hoping to see people coming and going. But Mashhad was empty that morning. I had expected more traffic, but the streets were bare, the buildings hushed. Nobody was around.

Even so, spring was stirring and, since the whole city was still asleep, the air seemed alive to its imminence, just for me. The breeze was cool and fresh among the lilting leaves and the plane trees were decked in delicate green, just for me. Sunlight beamed through the window and the clouds were puffs of white and the sky a perfect blue. Music was in the air, an exquisite symphony was playing, and all the branches in their shimmering silks were dancing for this prisoner wrapped in her smelly old chador in the back of the car.

Even though I did not know why I was being taken back to Vakilabad so early that morning, I was inexplicably optimistic. I talked to the branches in my heart, to the fresh leaves and the joyous birds, and begged them to stay beautiful, to sing beautifully always, to dance in beauty forever. I even dared to presume it was God's will that I had been allowed to look at the blessed beauty of the world that day. The tiny atom of my existence felt coupled and cradled within the mighty orbit of the living, limitless and infinitely lovely universe.

But once back at Vakilabad Prison, I discovered that I was totally alone. The corridors echoed vacantly. The maximum security unit was empty. The plastic bag containing the novel and the magazine given to me by the kind Afghani girl in the kennel hung limp in its loneliness on the bar of the third level bunk bed where I had slept the previous nights. And all my friendly murderers and thieves and arsonists were gone. There wasn't a single human being around.

The guard told me it was because of the holiday. All the prisoners had gone out on a daytrip, for a new year's excursion, and the doors had also been opened, exceptionally, to the five friendly troublemakers in the maximum security unit. It was the first time in many months that they had been allowed out of doors. I realised then that I, alone, had the unique privilege of being left behind in the women's section of Vakilabad, on Sizdah Bedar, the one day of the year when it was considered unlucky to stay inside according to Persian tradition.

Being in solitary confinement is bad enough. Being placed in the maximum security unit is no picnic either. But to find yourself the sole detainee in prison, on such a day as this, is a challenge even to the most cheerful. The sense of isolation and the resounding silence in a place usually crammed with bodies and roiling voices was depressing, to say the least.

For lunch, they gave me a tin bowl of lentil rice and a small fifty-gram carton of yogurt. The smell of prison food made me nauseous; it was saturated with camphor or whatever it was they used to preserve the rice unrefrigerated.[19] No matter how hard I tried, I could not eat it. I removed the rice from the rest of the food and ate a spoonful of lentils with the yogurt for my lunch. That was quite enough. And afterwards I lay down on the bunk, walked about the cell, thought a great deal, and finally started to read the novel.

Dear God, what a blessing books are. What freedom they offer!

Towards the evening, the clang of doors, the rattle of chains and a bustle of approaching footsteps announced the return of my cell mates. A hubbub of happy voices filled the corridors as the women arrived. They crowed with delight at the sight of me, for I had not been there when they left. Although they knew I was being interrogated in the detention centre, they did not know why. When they asked about my 'crime', I had told them I was a prisoner of conscience and briefly mentioned our so-called 'underground' university, which did not interest them. Of course, I said nothing about the Bahá'í Faith.

That evening, they were not much interested in what I had to say anyway. They hardly even noticed the shampoo sachets and soaps the guard let me bring back for them. Oxygen had done them a world of good, and they chattered nonstop, full of their own stories. At times, they included me in their conversation but mostly not, because they were full of events of the present and memories of the past; they recalled with particular relish the holiday riots that had taken place in the Mashhad prison during the early years of the Revolution. A mob of male prisoners had burst into the women's wards, stark naked, on the 13th day after Naw-Rúz. What disasters ensued! What a jolly mutiny it had been!

Both Zahrás recounted these tales of horror in glowing terms, accompanied by peals of laughter. They described how the prison guards rushed in after the men broke through the security barriers and began shooting indiscriminatingly, how many innocent people had been randomly killed that day, with absolute impunity. And they laughed some more.

'They'd kill us all if they could, with or without a warrant,' Little Zahrá said breezily. And I thought, how true it was then, and how true it is now.

* * *

The next morning, I was conducted back to the detention centre, as usual, and subjected to several more days of intense interrogation and an equal number of nights of solitary confinement, so I missed the rest of their stories. I missed them, too, as my isolation seemed to go on forever. Only in mid-Farvardín (early April) was I transferred back to the prison and restored to their company. Shortly after my return, however, the doors were unlocked once more, and a new prisoner was thrust into our midst.

From the minute she entered, the quarrels began. There was an uproar of protest. Voices were raised. Curses ensued. Everyone was strongly opposed to this person being in our cell. They knew her to be an inveterate troublemaker. She had been in jail with them before, and there was evidently a history of bad blood between them; their conflict went back a long time. The new arrival sat herself down on the floor and hurled accusations back at the other women; she argued and cursed roundly at each of my cellmates. Then she rose to her feet and went to the toilet. A few minutes later, she came out, having slashed the vein in one of her wrists. Blood was spurting everywhere and Naneh started yelling for the guards.

'Yoohoo! She's cut her wrist, she's going to die! Yoohoo!'

It was to no avail. No guard came. And no one had any interest in trying to assist the would-be suicide either. Naneh's laconic *yoohoo*s summed up the attitude of all the women.

I was sitting on the top bunk when this drama unfolded and became terribly upset. My instinct was to come down immediately and help the poor woman, but the others, noticing my concern, gathered around the bunk bed and urged me not to budge. Stay out of it, they advised. Have nothing to do with her. She's a pest, a mischief-maker, and she has done this before, so don't worry. It's only a superficial cut, just to get attention.

In fact, they had all done the same thing. Many times. To prove it, they began showing me scars on their bodies, telling me how and when they had mutilated themselves.

When I asked them why, they answered, almost in unison – 'Blood calms us down!'

Given their reactions, I thought it best not to interfere. But neutrality has humane limits; I could not bear doing nothing at all. The wrist-slasher was just sitting there, haranguing everybody one minute and playing the victim the next. She was rocking back and forth and wailing, cupping her bleeding wrist in a cloth and swearing at the universe. So I urged her to at least press down on the perforated vein and tie the cloth more tightly, to control the blood flow. And she managed, with the help of her teeth and histrionics, to do as suggested. An hour or so later, a guard finally came in response to the *yoohoo*s. She tied the dirty cloth properly around the woman's wrist and chained her leg to the bed. When I woke up the following morning, the wrist-slasher was still fast asleep and snoring. She had lain there, spread-eagled on the floor beside her bed, all night.

It was just part of the routine.

* * *

Another routine in the maximum security ward was that every evening an announcement boomed out over the loudspeaker, identifying all those who would be released or taken to court the following day. One night, soon after my return from the detention centre, the list of names seemed particularly long. I wasn't paying any attention to it and had just settled down to read in my bed, when one of the women called up to me, urgently.

'Hey, did you hear? They just gave your name for a court hearing tomorrow!'

I was in shock. What court? What hearing? I had already been given a hearing and a judge had agreed to a ten million *tuman* bail. What were they planning to do to me now?

'It's better this way,' another reassured me. 'At least you'll have your situation sorted and be given your sentence.'

Sentenced for burying a dead man in the wrong soil? Sentenced without trial, after they had already kept me imprisoned illegally all this time? Or had these endless interrogations, which I thought were designed to blackmail the Yárán, provided the gentlemen with new reasons to condemn me? Were they going to sentence me for having proven the charges of the Ministry of Intelligence null and void?

I could find no answers to my questions, and after a sleepless night, I rose at six, full of trepidation for the day. The chains and locks clattered and clanked. The doors opened, and a guard conducted me out. She took me to an area in front of the guards' station of the women's ward, with metal lockers ranged along the walls and plastic baskets scattered about the floor. They were heaped with clothes; I could smell the sweat on them even from a distance. Many women were already rummaging around, tossing trousers and head scarves about; I gathered that all female prisoners had to wear court uniform before the judge.

The guard told me to strip, leave my own clothes in one of the lockers and put these sweaty clothes on instead. I could not believe it. Strip naked? Here? Now? Take my clothes off in front of everyone, and dress in a smelly outfit required by the court? I stood some distance away from the swarming women, in a quandary. What a prude and a snob I was. How awkward and embarrassing this was. Yet I could not bring myself to strip; it was too humiliating. As I hung on the edge of the group, another guard noticed me.

'You don't have to wear those,' she whispered. 'They are filthy. Come with me, I will give you a uniform that has just been washed.'

She hustled me inside the guards' room and opened a large old-fashioned wardrobe in the corner, with wide mirrored doors and shelves on one side. The shelves were stacked with a jumble of the same grey uniforms, some still damp.

'These have just been brought over from the laundry area,' she told me. 'The weather is fine, and they will dry on you in a few minutes, once you're outside.'

I was deeply touched by her kindness. Torn between shame and relief, I meekly accepted the offer. There were long coats, baggy trousers, headscarves and chadors, all made of the same synthetic grey material. All ugly, all slightly wet, all bearing an ironic logo of the scales of justice. But at least they were clean. The guard let me keep one of the wardrobe doors open and change behind it more privately, before leaving my own clothes in a locker outside. I did not know how to express my gratitude to her. Thank heavens there were still some with a trace of empathy in this prison, people who had kept their humanity.

After the usual registration procedures, we were conducted in our hideous court outfits from the guards' station out into the large prison yard. There we were ordered to walk along the whole length of the wall in single file. No one said a word. Each was deep in her own thoughts. I had not walked in single file like this since primary school.

A row of buses and minivans were parked in front of the prison offices, and as we drew near these buildings, a commotion suddenly broke out among the vans, with soldiers and police officers running all over the yard. We women were rushed back inside the building and hustled into a glass-fronted room, several floors up, as though a terrorist attack were taking place. A few, like me, immediately went to the windows to see the cause of the uproar. But others were impervious as if they had witnessed all this dozens of times before. They just sat here and there or stood around talking, ignoring the din outside.

A group of men all wearing the same grey uniforms as ours, with their hands and feet bound in chains, were shuffling in from the two ends of the yard. They were handcuffed and ordered to sit side by side at the foot of the wall, with their legs shackled to each other. I leaned forward staring down at them and noticed that a few were looking up towards us, seeming to search among our faces for someone they knew, sometimes even calling out a person's name. I guessed they might have been trying to find the women who were facing indictment, separated from but condemned along with them. We are segregated in this country even in crime.

Most of the men were young, under thirty. Many seemed despondent, with faces bent and heads drooping between their knees. Some tried to hide the shackles around their feet. No chanting here, no joyous voices rising from the black pit in which these men had been flung. I had never seen such a sad scene in my life and was transfixed at the window, full of grief at the sight of these young men who had supposedly posed a threat to the court proceedings.

What kind of a society was this? Were there really this many pitiful men and women facing trial in Iran, every single day? Was it conceivable that there could be so many crooks and felons in the holy city of Mashhad alone, criminals so young, and presumably so dangerous, that they had to be chained together in this inhuman fashion? And was it possible that these youths – born after the Islamic Revolution, raised in families, educated in schools and living in a culture dominated by Islam – were all criminals?

Rows of chained men continued to file sluggishly into the yard. Young soldiers ran about, urging them to hurry, hurry. Police officers, some in civilian clothes, paced here and there, ordering them to move it, move it. I guessed they must have been afraid of an uprising, a revolt with so many prisoners in one place. They were trying to disperse everyone as quickly as possible, to fill the buses and send them off as soon as they could.

One particularly bad-tempered officer was yelling invectives at everyone. He marched up and down the yard, pushing his way roughly through the crowd, bellowing orders at soldiers and prisoners alike. As the buses drew near, the male prisoners approached the doors in single file, flanked by soldiers. At that point, the fetters linking them to each other were unlocked, and their own feet were chained together instead. They struggled up the steps, shuffling into the bus like cripples. Some could barely walk, and the soldiers were obliged to physically lift them. Once all were inside, the buses set off with their sorry load.

Only then were the women directed downstairs and led to our buses, in groups of thirty; only when we were seated did I learn that we were heading to the same Revolutionary Court I had gone to on my first day in Mashhad. Two soldiers stood guard on our bus, along with the bad-tempered officer. He was in his element, waving his gun about and swaggering up and down the aisle, as the buses ground their way, one after the other, out of the prison compound.

* * *

Spring! I gazed greedily out of the window. It was wonderful to see the changing world, even from inside a prison bus, even on the way to a court hearing. And how much it had all changed since my first arrival that cold day a month ago; it had even changed since my drive without a blindfold after Naw-Rúz. The glimpse of a young sapling, covered in white blossoms, filled me with awe. The flowers on the Mashhad ring road made my heart soar. And the sight of a large fruit tray on a pedestal near a roundabout almost moved me to tears. Of course! Mulberry season. People were gathering in the suburbs to buy the first crop of those delicious fruits, so characteristic of an Iranian spring. And I was reminded of the many times my mother and father would drive to the outskirts of Kan at this time of year and bring back bucket-loads of sweet ripe mulberries to Tehran for us children to eat. How much had happened since then, how many berries not eaten.

I was lost in these poignant memories when the voice of the bad-tempered officer brought me back to reality. He was threatening us with dire punishments if we looked outside or tried to interact with any passers-by. It was as if even spring was out of bounds for us.

'Keep your heads down,' he barked, 'or you'll be sorry!'

The courthouse was quite far away from the prison, but I had hardly noticed the distance; I had been lost in my dreams of the past. But when we disembarked, under the intensified surveillance of the police, it was difficult not to come back to the present. The street was crowded, and the pavements were lined with people, waiting for the hearings. We were kept well away from everyone, however, and the police and soldiers flanked us on both sides as we crossed the short distance from the bus to the courthouse entrance.

Names were being called out by family members and messages were being shouted at some of the prisoners as we walked in. How wonderful to have friends and relatives waiting for you! For a fleeting moment I wondered if someone might be there for me too. But how was that possible, when I myself had only learnt of this hearing at the last minute? These onlookers must have contacts with officials to be here, and no officials were accessible to my dear ones. No one I knew had any idea that I would be facing trial that day.

Once inside the main lobby, we noticed that an area on the west side of the building – presumably the one reserved for entry of the general public – was blocked off. We also discovered that the male prisoners had arrived before us and were already seated in rows on the lobby floor. We women stood in a line behind them. The officer in charge took up his position in front of everyone and began to read our names out loud. At each name, a soldier would unshackle the prisoner's feet and march him off to his assigned section of the court.

The names were all called, for the women as well as the men; everyone was taken away, one by one, and I was the last left standing. The officer walked towards the steps leading down to the basement and then nodded for me to follow him.

12

A SECOND HEARING

The basement was dirty, dark and depressing. It consisted of a long corridor leading to waiting rooms for the accused and a few barred cells. I waited outside the door of one of the rooms as several officers conferred about my case. The reason for the delay was apparently the absence of the judge. He had not arrived at the courthouse yet.

After a long wait, a soldier was ordered to take me back upstairs to the relevant section of the court. And who should I find in one of the rooms but Judge Hedáyatí himself, the same stocky young judge in his well-tailored suit who had condemned me to fifteen days in the doghouse after granting me bail which he never let me have. He was seated behind a large table and when he saw me walk in, he put on a grand show of fake surprise.

'Are you still here?' he said, as if he had no idea that he would be judging my case.

'I was never allowed to make a phone call for the bail money.'

'That's strange,' he said. 'And why was that?'

'I was told you had banned me from making phone calls.'

He shrugged this off and acted as if he knew nothing of what had been happening to me. 'That's certainly not true,' he objected. 'Who said you were not allowed phone calls?' He then called out, ostentatiously, to his assistant, in the next room. 'Háj Áqá,' he shouted, 'have I ever banned Mrs Sabet from making phone calls?'

'Absolutely not, Háj Áqá,' came the obsequious reply.

I held my tongue. The judge busied himself with his paperwork again, shuffling files back and forth. I knew from experience that this was his way of dismissing me as discourteously as possible. Since it was futile to pursue any further discussion, I left the room to wait in the crowded corridor. But I was boiling inside, fuming as I sat by his door. When the judge came out, I stopped him, peremptorily, before he could get away.

'Háj Áqá, please provide written authorisation for me to have access to a telephone.'

'I already have,' he countered. 'It's strange that they didn't give you one. That's the fault of the prison authorities. They are responsible for allowing you a phone call.'

'That's not true,' I replied. 'If you had written your permission, no one would have dared to disobey. But I am certain that no such authorisation from you has reached either the Intelligence Bureau, or the prison administration!'

It was a real showdown. Not only was I challenging a judge but was doing so in public. It was only too obvious that they had deliberately condemned me to isolation, with no access to a phone, and no possibility of being in contact with anyone, so that no message could be sent to my family. He began to object, to dispute the facts, to justify and contradict himself:

'Your son comes to Vakilabad Prison very often,' he protested, 'and I have told him everything. He is the one who should have brought the bail money!'

Incredible! Was he really trying to distort reality to such an extent? Did he dare blame my son for my continued detention and taunt me like this after permitting no more than that heartbreakingly brief meeting through a car window? Besides, how could I believe he had told Fúrúd 'everything' when I had been given strict instructions, doubtless under his orders, to say nothing to my own husband, to keep him in the dark? Had such an accusation not been so outrageous, it might have been comic. But I was certainly in no mood to joke.

The judge then told me to step aside and wait until he could instruct his assistant regarding my case. After a few moments, he left his office without giving me a second glance. Now what? Was that the extent of my 'hearing'? I waited. After a long delay I was summoned in again by his assistant, who turned out to be an unshaven young man adorned in the mandatory uniform of an extremist – collarless shirt, khaki pants, military overcoat and a three-day stubble. He called me gruffly over to his desk and placed a form in front of me.

'Fingerprint, here!' he said, covering a section of the page with one hand and preparing to stamp it with the other.

'I have to read it first,' I protested.

He removed his hand, turning his face away from me. But no matter how hard I tried, I could not read what was written on the form. It was a poor photocopy of an illegible, barely decipherable, handwritten text, the prose convoluted, the vocabulary arcane. I struggled to make it out for several minutes but finally gave up; I couldn't understand a word of it.

'Haj Áqá,' I turned to him in bewilderment, 'what's this all about?'

'Can't you read?' he replied.

'I can, but I cannot figure out what it says. The print is too pale and the language too prolix. Can't you state it more simply to me, please?'

'It's a prolongation of your detention, that's all.'

'What? After I've already been released on bail?'

I was outraged. My hearing, an accusation against my son for not bringing bail money? This scribble, my sentence? I remonstrated. I asked him how my detention could be prolonged, when I'd never been issued with a proper sentence in the first place.

'Well, it's been issued now!' he said bluntly.

'For how many more days?'

'A month.'

'I object!' I answered firmly. 'I've been charged on one specific issue. I already presented my defence on that issue and was granted bail, which I've been effectively denied. I've been charged for no other crime and have already been held hostage illegally all this time. So, on what grounds is my detention being extended?'

'If you're not happy about it, you'd better write down all your objections then, hadn't you?' he smirked, as though inviting me to condemn myself still further.

As soon as I had done so, he dismissed me.

* * *

I slumped down angrily on a bench some way down the circular corridor outside the judges' rooms. The place was crowded. Many people were squatting on the ground leaning against the walls, some wearing handcuffs, some without. Soldiers were scurrying back and forth and there was much toing and froing in the congestion. I sat in a corner, fuming in the middle of this milling crowd, agitated and distressed. The judge owed me an explanation; he should have specified my situation more clearly. Although I was supposed to wait for a soldier to escort me away, I decided to return to the judge's office again without permission and confront him. He was alone this time, without any assistant, and I took him by surprise.

'Haj Áqá,' I said, 'you accepted my defence on the first night of my arrival here, and talked about bail money, and now you have extended my detention. Why?'

'It is just for a brief period.'

'You call a month brief?'

'It might be shorter than that,' he prevaricated. 'It might be just a week.'

Our conversation ended abruptly when a soldier entered the office to take me back to the basement. I had no choice but to follow him to that same dark, dirty, depressing place. On the way, I heard a few men in another corridor, chanting salutations to a prisoner who was being released. I was so indignant that I could not even be glad for the man.

The transport officer was still in one of the basement rooms when I sat down to wait in the hallway. I could hear him through the wall, joking and laughing with some soldiers. They had apparently brought him some fresh bread and eggs for breakfast.

No one else was in the corridor apart from myself and a soldier. I was the only woman there. Everyone else was either in cells or in hearings. One of the soldiers kept going in and out of the officer's room, dashing back and forth to prepare his breakfast, I assumed. I smelled hot butter and heard the breaking of eggs. Then there was a sudden yelp, followed by a splatter. One of the eggs had apparently slipped out of someone's hand onto the floor.

The bad-tempered officer came to the door and cast an imperious glance at me.

'Come in here and clean this up,' he said brusquely.

I did not reply but stayed rigid in my seat, frowning, without budging an inch. When he called me again, with the same order, I turned my face slowly away from him and lowered my eyes. It was the severest sign of protest I could give. He raised his voice then, and shouted a third time with even greater impertinence.

'Hey you, woman, I'm talking to you. Come over here and clean up this mess!'

Up till then, I had maintained almost total silence, but at this, I rose to my feet. 'With due respect, sir.' I gave him a level stare. 'I am not your housemaid.'

I had fixed my eyes on the offensive man, but I was poised to run up the stairs; if he said one word more or lifted a finger to do anything inappropriate, I intended to run straight back to the judge's room. I knew I had already caused offense by my insubordination towards the judge, who would do little to defend me, but as the only woman in that basement, facing an aggressive man, I had few options. This officer was no doubt aware that I was a political prisoner; he probably considered me 'a threat to the security of the state', so I suspected he was trying to rouse me just to report me as a troublemaker and add to my problems.

But just as he was about to become even more belligerent, a soldier showed up. He retrieved a broom and a dustpan leaning against the wall and went into the room to clean up the eggs himself. I do not know why, but the officer suddenly decided to leave me alone after that and turned back into the room too, slamming the door hard behind him.

I sat there, in the basement, for two or three more hours, waiting for everyone else's hearings to be over for the day. The prisoners came down, one by one, and sat on the floor with their backs against the wall. All of us were in the same state: tired, hungry, sleep-deprived and heartbroken. I did not see a single person who seemed relieved or happy, except the one man for whom they had been chanting the salutations of release.

The women also gradually arrived in the same low spirits, and sat beside me on the only bench, or settled down on the floor and leaned against the wall. The beautiful young girl who had been next to me on the bus was charged with prostitution. On the way to court, she had been very worried about her fate and asked me to pray for her. But now, after the hearing, she was quiet and resigned and sank into a hopeless lassitude.

Finally, when everyone was assembled, the soldiers began a head count and the officer, whose prolonged breakfast was over at last, emerged with orders that we should get a move on. We all filed up the stairs and walked through the yard, where everybody sat on the ground once more. The men were handcuffed but wore no foot shackles. As the names were called out, we rose, one by one, walked to the car park and climbed into the buses like robots: men first and women afterwards. The beautiful young girl and I sat together again, in the second or third row behind the driver. And all the way, from the court to the prison, that incorrigible officer bandied vulgar jokes with this girl, ogling at her and sniggering over his own salacious insinuations. He even gave her his phone number.

Once back in prison, we put on our own clothes again, placed the court uniforms into the baskets, then waited to be delivered back to our various cells. You have the impression, as a prisoner, that you are less a person than a parcel. Even your own legs have no authority to carry you from one place to the next, unless some paper is stamped, some order given. Every movement involves an escort, and you end up with a sensation of paralysis.

But the mind keeps moving.

* * *

It was while I was sitting in the courthouse, waiting for someone to take me back to the public prison, that I saw a terrible sight in the room next to the guard station. The door was open, and they were whipping a young woman, lashing her back. She was seated with her face turned from me, hugging a wooden chair to her breasts. Her red blouse was raised to her neck and a female guard was standing next to her, lashing her with a whip. The guard was holding the edge of her black chador between her teeth, biting hard on the cloth as she brought the whip down again, and again, and again, on the girl's raw back.

I was overwhelmed with painful memories, for I had felt the bite of that lash too, on my own body: the body of a little girl starting school in the provincial town of Zavareh. I was just eight years old, eager to learn, with sharpened pencils in my pencil case and new notebooks in my satchel. But on that first day I had been told to sit apart from the rest of my classmates, and had no idea why. That had been the start of my troubles. When the teacher announced it was because I was *najes*, I did not understand the word, even after my classmates kindly explained that it meant I was 'unclean'. I assured them I wasn't, and showed them my washed hands, but they only laughed. When I came home and asked my mother about the word, she was not much help either. She merely said it arose from ignorance, and that I should not worry. One day all this nonsense will pass, she assured me; you just make friends, learn your lessons, and be the best in class.

Well, I made friends, and became the best in class, but the word did not pass away. One day it was in the mouths of a group of juvenile zealots who suddenly decided to attack me at school. Perhaps they had heard the taunts of 'Najes! Najes!'[20] on the recent broadcasts on the radio, inciting hatred against the Bahá'ís; perhaps they were just bored and needed entertainment. The boys were twice my size and I was completely at their mercy. When they started battering me with their fists and kicking me, shouting this word in my face, all I could hope for was that the school director would come and save me.

It took a long time for her to arrive, but when she did, she did not save me. She asked no questions, did nothing to ascertain the truth, and made no attempt at even a show of fairness. Her aim was to appease the fanatical pupils and doubtless their parents too. She pulled me away from the battering fists and kicking feet and took me to the middle of the school yard where the pomegranate switches for 'discipline' were soaking in the pool. Then she proceeded to whip me, again and again, to lash me with these thin, thorny branches so relentlessly that the skin of my hands and my body was flayed raw, and I fainted.

* * *

The flesh of the young girl's back in the courthouse room was covered with swollen red welts. No sound came from her, except a faint whimper when one of the lashes was particularly hard. I don't know how many strokes she received, but it was more than I could bear to watch. At the end, the poor thing stood up, pulled her blouse down carefully over her flaming back, and then, with defiant indifference, started chatting and laughing with other prisoners sitting outside in the sun.

It had been an exercise in futility and bravado, a punishment that was palpably ineffective and openly mocked. My own experience as a child, being lashed by the director, expelled from the school, and then stoned as I ran home, was supposedly an appeasement rather than a deterrent and less easy for me to mock, for it led to serious infections, a burning fever and months of convalescence. It also made me wonder, even at that young age, how one word could make people behave with so little humanity towards each other.

Just then a female guard finally arrived to conduct me back to the women's maximum security ward, where I found my sweet cell mates waiting for me. They could see immediately that I was hurt and bitterly disappointed; far from being granted a reprieve, my hopes had been crushed at court. They clucked over me like mother hens, poured me tea from their worn-out thermos flasks, and sat around, asking me to tell them everything, *everything* that had happened. And when I did, they sympathised and tried to do everything, *everything* they could to console me. They told me jokes, performed droll acts to make me laugh, dredged their memories for amusing tales to cheer me up. And all the while their eyes were fixed on me, anxiously, to see if I would smile at last.

Most of the relatives of these women were thieves and robbers, addicts and prostitutes; when they were not in prison, they lived on or under cardboard shelters in the wilds of the city streets. Several had lost touch with their families altogether and had no one left in this world. I could sense sadness between the lines of the comic tales they told me; I guessed they had rarely experienced a happy, secure or calm moment in their lives. And yet here they were, cheering me up, trying to make me happy, wanting to see me smile again.

How I loved them. How I grieved for their lost opportunities, their wasted talents, and the good lives they had a right to, and might have lived. My private descent all those days before, down the stone steps of despair into the dazzling darkness of the doghouse, had brought me face to face with a spirit of compassion, love and forgiveness that I associated with all that was most sacred in my faith. But after the callous treatment I received in court that day, I found myself overwhelmed by the compassion, love and forgiveness of my cell mates, who had no belief in the sacred and who rejected all they had seen of faith. It was among these victims of a sick society that I rediscovered the beauty of mortality.

It was extraordinary how attached we became to each other. Whenever I was taken to the detention centre, they would tell me, as they said goodbye, how much they looked forward to my return. Although I returned to Vakilabad Prison less and less frequently in the weeks that followed, they welcomed me gladly and with open arms whenever I did. I grew to love them like family and longed to restore the dignity that had been stolen from them, the self-esteem that had been stripped from them, the love that had been denied.

Since I had little to give them apart from sachets of shampoo, I praised them, extolled their qualities, celebrated their innate generosity and acclaimed them for the purity of their hearts, the nobility of their characters. I assured them that their destiny lay in their own hands, even though they might not think it, because even though they could not control the world, they were the only ones in command of themselves. We often discussed the meaning of free will together, and the need to exert it for change to occur in our lives. They questioned me about the necessity of prayer, when they saw that I believed in it, and asked what confirmation meant to me. They were a living example of true honesty, genuine humility.

It amazed me how thoughtfully they listened. At times they would laugh, other times they would weep at what I said or quoted for them. But they always listened. They had abandoned all expectation of mercy, favour and forgiveness from the world they lived in, and blamed all their deprivations on a god they had stopped believing in years ago. But they would sit and listen to the Bahá'í prayers with extraordinary attention. And I noticed that the words had a visible impact on their behaviour, a positive influence on their conversations. They would restrain themselves from using vulgar language within earshot of me, and even reminded each other, at times, not to swear in my presence. It was deeply touching, even when funny. I knew I would be indebted to those women for the rest of my life.

Especially my two Zahrás.

13

A WORLD OF WOMEN

As a result of passing twenty years behind bars, Big Zahrá had gained considerable experience as well as maturity. She was a born leader, in her way, and all the others in the cell looked up to her. The prison years had also transformed Little Zahrá into a modest, patient person; she was down-to-earth and uncomplaining and always called a spade a spade.

One day, Big Zahrá decided to tell me how she and Little Zahrá had become friends.

'Would you like to know where we met?' she asked. 'It's quite a funny story!'

I expressed my eagerness to hear it, and they both collapsed into fits of laughter. Big Zahrá explained that she had first met Little Zahrá in prison, long before befriending her. Then one day, when she was 'out at work' as she called it, picking the lock of a house she planned to rob, she suddenly found herself face to face with the other Zahrá again.

'Hang on a minute!' she said, 'I know you! What are you doing here?'

Little Zahrá was afraid of being caught red handed in the act of larceny, so she had gesticulated, rather desperately, to show that she was only looking for a toilet. Big Zahrá told her coldly that there was no need to wander around peoples' private houses for such a purpose and pointed to the corner of the yard. Some months later, they found themselves back in the same prison cell for committing another petty crime and real-ised they had been trying to rob the same house at the same time. That's how they became the best of friends.

'Well, how did I know that place was your territory?' said Little Zahrá as they both began giggling again at the recollection of having invaded each other's turf.

None of the women in maximum security liked to be called a 'thief'. They preferred the word 'burglar' as if it conferred greater dignity on their 'work'. It had a literary aura to it and carried a certain weight. Since it was less commonly used, my two Zahrás may have felt that it implied a more respectable profession. They needed to preserve their dignity.

Both Zahrás continued to commit misdemeanours behind bars, whenever necessary, so as to extend their sentences and avoid release. They were very cool and calculating about it, maintaining their identity as 'troublemakers' with persistent determination, even professional pride. In prison, at least, they had a roof over their heads, some food to eat, and people who would not shun them. Above all, they were not at the mercy of men. When I told Little Zahrá that I hoped she would be free one day, she pulled a face.

'Don't wish it on me,' she said. 'Where'd I go? I haven't even a tent to live in.'

Nor was she the only one in this situation. Many of the women in the public prison were behind walls by choice. They literally had nowhere else to stay, no place to flee to, no refuge to turn to: it was either in jail or on the streets.

* * *

The relationships between the women in the prison ranged from close friendship to bitter enmity, from jealousy to love. And the configuration of these relationships was subject to a seismic shift whenever a newcomer joined the group, or one of them left.

One day, a young girl of seventeen was brought into our cell, whom Fatimih introduced as her 'relative'. She was so extremely pale, this girl, with lips so very white and dry that I thought she must be severely anaemic. When I enquired what kind of relative she was, the girl replied rather primly that she was Fatimih's 'stepmother.' I could not believe it. She was so young that she might have been Fatimih's daughter. And then with surprising detachment, she started to tell her story.

'I am a prison child,' she said simply. 'I was born in prison. I grew up in prison. After my mother died, I was raised in prison by the women here.'

She paused for a moment, as if searching for the words, and Big Zahrá came to her aid. The child had lived inside these walls all her life, she said, and had never seen the sun; she had been under the care of the women prisoners here –

'But mainly at the mercy of Masumih,' added Big Zahrá, raising a laconic eyebrow.

I did not know who this Masumih was, but they evidently all did. Knowing looks were exchanged as the girl gave a shrug of studied indifference and picked up the story herself. She spoke with a naïve turn of phrase, which lent a kind of dignity to what she said, and used curiously archaic terms, like someone older than her years.

'One day that Masumih used her finger to break my virginity,' she said softly.

The women sighed and clucked. I stared at them, stunned. They knew the story well.

'She was very young at the time,' Fatimih qualified, as if that made it any better.

But her 'stepmother' just laughed at my dismay. I had thought her naïve but was even more so myself. I looked into her beautiful eyes as she described how she left the prison for a whole seventeen days, how she knew no one and had nowhere to go, how Fatimih had kindly introduced her to her father and how he had agreed to 'look after' her.

'He said he would marry me for the sake of God,' she continued. 'He said he would take me under his wing on one condition: I had to earn my own living.'

He taught her how to steal, in order to earn her daily bread. And then he dumped her.

'She was frightened of everything,' interrupted Fatimih, 'absolutely everything – the streets, the cars, the people – my father had enough of it. She couldn't do her job.'

'I was petrified,' the girl concurred. 'I stopped at the first crossroads in front of the prison and didn't know what to do next. I'd never seen so many cars in my life or so many crowds. I'd never seen so many men. I hated being outside, taking my husband's role like that; it was hell. So I quickly did what I could to come back into prison.'

She had learned to commit petty crimes inside the prison since then, to stay permanently incarcerated. She could not survive, she repeated, in the male world outside.

'I dislike men, you see,' she lisped in her sweet Mashhadi accent. 'I prefer women.'

That night Fatimih's 'stepmother' crept into Maryam's bed. I could hear Fatimih objecting strongly and Maryam retorting back. Big Zahrá warned them a few times to keep their voices down and to have regard for 'the lady'. I presume she meant me. But they took no notice. The argument swelled and grew heated, despite Big Zahrá's loud and prolonged hushes. I did not understand what was going on, so I peered over the bunk bed to see what all the palaver was about. And immediately lay back down. Everything was clear.

Until that night, Fatimih had been what they called Maryam's 'partner', but now Maryam had decided that she preferred the 'stepmother.' Since no one should limit male desires in a patriarchal culture, Maryam was doing what she wanted as a 'man', and since women had to submit to men in this culture, Fatimih's 'stepmother' could not repel such advances. She was obedient to command and followed the norms.

The irony was that although these women had been consistently mistreated by men and abused by them, they mirrored their behaviour down to the last detail. Although they had suffered systematically under patriarchy ever since they were born, they chose to replicate it within the prison walls. Their 'male' and 'female' roles imitated all the oppressive patterns of 'free' society. This was a quintessentially Iranian situation.

Maryam liked wearing men's-style loose trousers. She cut her hair short and left her eyebrows un-plucked. With her tall stature and strong build, she was quite mannish in appearance and probably modelled her behaviour on the men she had known. Fatimih, by contrast, was very feminine; she instinctively followed stereotypical female behaviour, almost to the point of travesty. She would flirt and act the coquette with Maryam; she would spread out the tablecloth like a traditional wife and fuss over her 'man's' mealtimes. And Maryam would sit there, with one knee drawn up under her arm, the other leg bent on the floor, acting just like a conventional male, waiting for Fatimih to cater to all her needs.

It was almost comic, when it was not troubling, because Maryam could be quite authoritarian sometimes, quite oppressive and overbearing. Once, to my great surprise, she objected to Fatimih wearing a pair of trousers, frowned at her severely and said, in disgust, 'Those are too tight for you. Don't wear them again, or I'll tear them to pieces!'

Fatimih turned pink and pouted. But I noted there was a gleam in her eye and a certain note of smug complacency in her voice; she was acting the hard-done-by wife measuring her sexual worth by the flack she received from her husband. 'Honest to God,' she wailed, appealing to the rest of us, with a seductive quiver, 'd'you call these tight?'

Now with the arrival of the newcomer in our cell, there was a crisis between 'husband' and 'wife'. In the opinion of the other women, Maryam was behaving like this just to make Fatimih jealous. And in the opinion of Fatimih, who wept quietly into her pillow that night, the only option was revenge. This 'family' squabble went on for days.

I had never witnessed such relationships before, and it was the first time in my life that I had encountered homosexuality at such proximity. It was as if a veil had been lifted from my eyes. Far from perceiving these women as unnatural and perverse, I realised they were simply fulfilling their natural biological needs the only way they were allowed; their affairs, sometimes gentle, sometimes cruel, conformed to the unspoken laws of prison life. And, more often than not, their relationships were temporary and the result of loneliness, the need for kindness. That was sufficient to explain the level of their intensity and why they were so commonplace. Moreover, many of the women were bisexual, adjusting easily one way or the other to the conditions inside and outside prison, according to circumstances.

Still, it made me feel sad for my friends. Although I understood their reasons and would never judge them, I feared that patriarchy was keeping them doubly jailed. They were trapped in a prison of gender roles within the confinement of the prison walls.

* * *

There were only a few times during my period in the public jail of Vakilabad when we were allowed to leave the suffocating atmosphere of that enclosed cell and breathe fresh air. We would hear the familiar clang of chains and clatter of keys and find ourselves, to our delight, stepping through the doors of the maximum security ward and walking into the miraculous outdoors. The others knew their way to the open-air quad, so I just followed. This brief relief was only granted to me twice during my stay in Mashhad. The rest of the time I could only breathe fresh air when I was being driven back and forth to the detention centre, usually with the windows closed and my blindfolded head bent low.

But whenever we went on these fresh air 'outings', we of maximum security were not allowed to be in contact with anyone else in the women's sector of the public prison. It was as though we were contaminated. We were only given permission to step out after lunch, during the noon break, when all the other women were taking a siesta. And yet, even though there was supposed to be no communication between us, some of the women in the public prison were aware of our schedule. They would call out softly to us through the air vents as we walked around.

'Political one, political one,' they would whisper as I passed.

They sometimes used my first name, and other times my surname. I think I heard Parváneh calling me once or twice.

Sometimes the women did not want to walk in the quad. They just needed to breathe. They would spread a carpet on the ground and sit contentedly, recounting stories. Talk and talk and talk. The combination of words and the open air was enough for them. The small space where we had our fresh air outings was an enclosed courtyard, no bigger than thirty square metres, surrounded by four brick walls about five or six metres high, with rows of iron bars and barbed wire overhead. It was effectively an outdoor cage inside the public prison.

Naneh, the nervous addict with the irascible temper, had no patience with talk. She was jumping out of her skin with frustration most of the time and needed to express herself physically rather than verbally. She also preferred to address the greater powers of the universe rather than the other women. She would hurl herself at the walls whenever we were allowed outdoors, and somehow managed, by dint of clinging to the protruding bricks, to climb them at an almost vertical angle, in an attempt to reach the bars and barbed wires overhead. There she would hang like a scrawny bat and bellow at the top of her voice.

'O God!' she would yell, 'God, let me out, let me out!' She had even managed to find a place where she could push her head out through the barbed wire. 'God,' she would shout into the air, at the risk of garrotting herself, 'I don't want to be here! Let me out!'

I prayed He might hear her. Unlike the two Zahrás and even Maryam and Fatimih, as well as the young 'stepmother', Naneh could not bear being in Vakilabad Prison and was desperate to leave. But she did not want to live on the streets again; she simply wanted to be transferred to a different jail on the outskirts of Mashhad. She had previously been held in custody at this other place and preferred it; perhaps it was closer to her beloved brother.

Communication may have been forbidden between my cellmates and the other women in the public prison, but there was a curious complicity between them. I sometimes wondered whether Naneh's calls to God were not also directed at our fellow prisoners, for whenever we were allowed outside, these women managed to throw cigarettes up vertically to us, through the air vents of the cells below. They knew that most of the ladies in our unit were addicted to nicotine and desperate for a smoke. It seemed to me, sometimes, that they were tossing up hope and resilience to us, rather than mere cigarettes. It was unbelievable how much solidarity, and even unity, there was between all these women.

Of course, one of the reasons my ladies were not allowed cigarettes was because of the fire hazard involved. The potential for pyrotechnics combined with Naneh's temper could have been fatal. One day I smelled something burning inside our cell. The women kept rushing back and forth saying, 'Open the window, open the window,' even though there was no window to open. Then I saw them running out of the toilet carrying a blackened metal bowl.

'Look what we've made,' they told me proudly. 'Just look!'

And I stared in disbelief. They had pulled the cotton padding out of some sanitary towels, soaked it in melted butter which they had hoarded from breakfast, and burnt this unappealing combination in the toilet area over a small fire which they had somehow managed to kindle with stolen matches. What remained in the cinders at the bottom of the bowl they called 'kohl' – and they ecstatically deployed it as eye makeup. They weren't in the least concerned with hygiene or the possibility of eye infections; their only worry was that the smell of burnt butter and cotton should not reach the Main Corridor.

* * *

The principle preoccupation of the women, apart from cleaning and preening themselves, gossiping and quarrelling, was food. They were always hungry, and since they were habituated to the poor quality of the meals in the public prison of Vakilabad, they ate with relish. I was the difficult one – fussy, finicky and fastidious – because the smell of camphor made me nauseous. So they often ate my share as well.

The staple for each meal was rice, a dry, tasteless brand from India bartered at the lowest price and preserved in D.D.T. for a longer shelf-life. Since it was contaminated with arsenic, it was toxic in sustained doses. But what better consumer for it than a prisoner?

This rice was served in a variety of ways. For example, *eslamboli polo* was a traditional rice made with tomatoes, potatoes and at times meat and string beans. The pot would be placed on the ground, and we would all sit around the cloth with one person in charge of serving. The rice in this so-called *eslamboli polo* was white, with a hint of pink, mixed with a few random potato cubes. Another classic was *adas polo* or lentil rice in which you could count the lentils on the fingers of one hand. One day, they said we would have *morgh polo* – rice with chicken. Great excitement! Well, the rice was the same, and the chicken was a bowl of red-coloured liquid, with a few bones and bits of skin floating about. The quality of the food was truly atrocious. Another meal was *ghormeh sabzi*, a sauce normally made of chopped greens and beans with lamb. But the prison version bore no resemblance to the usual recipe. The sauce consisted of long herb stems, sometimes with the string still attached, fried in a black oil with a few kidney beans, and if you were lucky – or unlucky – some skin and fat from time to time.

The person appointed to serve would set aside the 'best part' in a separate plate and divide it into six equal portions before everyone's eyes. No one could touch anything until this was done. The task of serving hungry prisoners on crack was especially difficult, and sometimes risky. One mistake in the distribution of portions could lead to bloodshed.

Breakfast consisted of bread and a very small amount of cheese. On rare occasions they would serve us tiny portions of jam too, a great treat. Dinner was boiled potatoes and boiled eggs and this, to my taste, was the least unbearable of the meals and my favourite. Or they would sometimes serve a thick, pulse-based soup called *aash*.

Fresh fruit was never available to the prisoners in Vakilabad. They sometimes asked me to describe the food I was given at the detention centre, just to relish the words, and they were especially eager to know if fruits were served. Some among them had not eaten a piece of fresh fruit for decades. Once, when I was being transferred back to the prison, I asked permission to take an orange for my friends in maximum security, which I had been keeping in the grey cell just to enjoy its colour. Old Háj Khánum had unfortunately been replaced by a young recruit by then, who only consented to a box of dates and dried fruit, not the orange.

I shared these nutritional treats with the young girls too, who did the dirty work for the female guards. They would cluster about me like little birds, as they followed me back down the corridor, crying, 'What about me, Mahvash Khánum? Have you anything for me?'

The meagre gifts I offered them were nothing compared to the relief they gave me, and the reprieve I felt, each time I left the deadly inhumanity of the isolation cell and returned to my raucous, crazy cellmates in the public prison. There at least, I felt alive, despite the squalor, and the violence, and the pain. There it was possible to be honest, living together as human beings, suffering together, even learning from each other. And since truth telling was my crime, I felt at home in that world of women, because they were so truthful with me.

14

AN OFFER

About a week after the second farcical hearing at the Revolutionary Court, I was back in the detention centre again. Sitting in the interrogation room. Waiting for the interrogator to arrive. He was taking his time. When he did show up at last, he had news.

'Some gentlemen are here to talk to you today,' he announced rather pompously.

Some gentlemen? I could hear the self-congratulation in his voice as well as the threat. So, was it actually going to happen? Was I going to be honoured by a visit from the superior cohorts of the Bureau of Intelligence in Mashhad? All through the first month of my detention, I had been half-expecting to meet these gentlemen. I assumed they might come to check on me while I was trapped here. I had also imagined that when they did, their methods might be a little different, with a veneer of respect perhaps, a show of deference in contrast to the interrogator. Now it was happening, and I found myself in the same chair, with the same armrest, wearing the same blindfold, facing the same wall. And they were behind me, these gentlemen, breathing down my neck like any garden variety inquisitor.

The first was soft-spoken and did initially deploy a semblance of courtesy as he drew near my chair. 'Miss Shahríyárí? Or should I call you Mrs Sabet?'

'Yes.' I was unwilling to accommodate his binary options.

'How many days have you been here?'

'I was arrested some five weeks ago, on 15 Esfand (5 March).'

'How have you been doing all this time? How do you feel?'

I took a deep breath, and decided to be frank. 'How would you feel after five weeks of solitary confinement? Some gentlemen,' I said, emphasising the word, 'whose identities are still unknown to me, dragged me here against the laws of the land, took me to court against the laws of the land, and refused, in spite of the laws of the land, to grant me permission to telephone my family, or request the bail which the judge himself had allowed for my release. So that's how I'm feeling,' I concluded defensively. 'Rather upset!'

His response was very smooth, very composed, without a hint of apology. 'Well,' he said, 'we needed to talk first, didn't we? We had to discuss the matter fully between us.'

Then after hedging and evading the 'matter' for several more minutes, he started to justify and rationalise the treatment I had been receiving, hinting that I was in the wrong, that I owed them an apology, that they deserved some kind of compensation from me.

'You see, Mrs Sabet,' he concluded, his voice still low, still poised, 'we are the representatives of the government of this country, and you Bahá'ís have, until now, lived reasonably well in this country, and until now, we have provided for your security. But if we are to carry out our duties efficiently, we expect some collaboration, some cooperation.'

I swallowed the bile in my throat. 'What kind of collaboration are you referring to?' I asked icily.

'We are the Ministry of Intelligence, Mrs Sabet, so we obviously need intelligence of all kinds and in all fields. We are asking you to provide us with it.'

I lifted my chin dangerously high. 'In other words, you want me to be a spy?'

'That is hardly the label we would apply,' he retorted stiffly.

'Yes, indeed,' I interrupted, 'I understand the word could offend you. But whatever label you use, I assure you there's no need for such underhand methods. The Bahá'ís hide nothing from you. We provide you with all the intelligence you require, openly and honestly. And I'm not that sort of a person anyway.'

My response annoyed him. I could hear an increased testiness in his voice. 'You are not *what* kind of a person, Mrs Sabet? After everything you just heard me say to you, I hardly expected such an answer. You are not even thinking clearly. Don't you people still have a right to live in this country? Why shouldn't your children live too and benefit from the best opportunities we can offer? What kind of person are you then, Mrs Sabet? Don't you want to help your children or your co-religionists?'

'Not like this!' I retorted. 'Not by being an informer!'

At this he lost his temper and raised his voice. 'Khánum,' he snapped, 'you are as stubborn as a lump of wood and just as dumb; no wonder women are called the weaker sex!'

He was trying to upset me, to arouse my 'feminist' indignation, I suppose; he wanted us to argue, to get into a stupid quarrel about misogyny. I sat utterly still and quiet in my chair and refused to give him what he expected.

But a page had turned.

Their tactics changed from that moment. Since I had clearly rejected their 'offer', they moved from bribes to threats. The first gentleman, who had been speaking until then, pretending to be calm and logical in his arguments, now withdrew and a second took his place. The voice of this second man was hoarse and harsh, his comments aggressive, his assertions unreasonable. He began by reeling off several names, bombarding me with random references to people. Do you know so and so? he yelled at me. Or such and such? And how about this one? Or that one?

He was bragging about how many informers they had, boasting about how many moles were already working for them. He was trying to suggest that spying for the Ministry of Intelligence was a perfectly reasonable activity, and there was nothing wrong with it. He wanted to imply that everyone did it. Even Bahá'ís did it. It was normal! His aim was to prove that this kind of infiltration was in fact necessary for the protection of our community. And above all, he was trying to imply how greatly my family would profit from it, how much they would benefit if I became an informer.

When he allowed me to speak, I took another deep breath before answering him.

'Everyone is responsible for his or her own actions, sir,' I replied 'I cannot judge peoples' motives, and I don't wish to know what others may or may not have done. We all have our reasons and our consciences. I have mine and I choose not to do such things.'

He erupted in anger, his tone coarser than ever, his voice rising to a high pitch. He was working himself into a towering rage. 'In that case, you will all be the losers,' he hollered. 'You will all have to pay. We wanted to give you another chance, offer you another way. But you're too stupid. You don't understand that a little collaboration by one person can relieve thousands of others!'

He did not stop hurling abuse at me, deriding my lack of intelligence. I had the feeling that while he may have tried to control himself in the beginning, he was mightily pleased to open his mouth and spew out all his dislike and disgust at last. There was no rhyme or reason to his hatred. His words gushed out like bilge water – all fabrication, ruses and lies. The first gentleman soon joined the swelling tirade, both of them attacking me verbally, flinging insults at me, calling me degrading names. It was as though a sewer had backed up.

But my mind leapt over their words. As they went on haranguing me, thousands of images unrolled before my blindfolded eyes: scenes of suffering incited by gentlemen such as these, miseries they had inflicted on so many Iranians, crimes they had committed over the years. Families torn apart and scattered in exile. Children deprived of fathers and mothers. Households broken up, properties confiscated, lives lost, hopes reduced to ashes. And worst of all, the minds of millions of my countrymen and women filled with fear and misunderstanding, with prejudice and suspicion, because of their incitement of hatred, their distortion of truth. And all this while using the pulpit of religion and the podium of politics to ransack the coffers of the nation, the hard-earned money of the people. I listed all their crimes to myself and answered them in silence, as they ranted and raved behind me.

Oh, you brave gentlemen, after all you have said and done, how can you talk of security and pretend that you want to defend peoples' rights? Do you really think you can dupe me? You may blindfold me, but you will never pull the wool over my eyes.

Answering them in my mind was a wonderful way of keeping calm. I marvelled at how low we can sink, in language and as well as in life, when we try to impose our will on others. The interrogator who usually questioned me had not spoken all this time, deferring to the grander histrionics of the Ministry gentlemen. Now he addressed one of them, who I assumed from his oily deference must be his superior.

'Haj Áqá,' he said, in a sycophantic tone, 'according to the religious fatwa of the Glorious Imam, the lives and properties of these people are lawfully ours, are they not?'

Perhaps he was trying to ingratiate himself with this obsequiousness. Perhaps he was also trying to frighten me. Whatever his motives, I knew the statement to be utterly false according to the constitutional laws of the country. I could not let it pass.

'I beg your pardon?' I interrupted. 'What did you just say?'

The interrogator backed off and hurriedly answered his own question by confirming the rights of minorities. 'But of course, under the government *fatwa*, they can stay alive under the protective shade of the Islamic government, can't they?' he added with a sneer.

The smooth-talking gentleman, who had initially seemed so courteous, now resumed control of the interrogation. 'Well, that's why we want to help them. We are trying to protect them, aren't we? They are the ones who refuse to accept our assistance and reject our offers. And then they go out into the world and act like martyrs.'

At that point, I had had enough.

'Gentlemen,' I said quietly, 'please do not tire yourselves unnecessarily. There is no need for you to go to such lengths. No one is here except ourselves, and we each know what we know. You're well aware of what has happened to the Bahá'í community during the past few decades. You know that innocent blood has been shed, and households scattered to the winds. You know what has happened to the jobs and careers of hundreds of thousands since the establishment of your regime. You're aware of the ongoing dismissal of pupils from schools, of students refused entry to university, of corpses denied permission for burial. And you're fully responsible for all the deprivations that constrain our freedoms and make our lives and even our deaths difficult. Since I know all this, too, how can you imagine I would believe your claim that you want to protect the Bahá'ís and offer us security? Apart from anything else, if you were sincere, you'd address me in a more respectful fashion, through proper dialogue and frank discussion, face to face and not hiding behind a blindfold.'

The first man lost his veneer of courtesy and grew more vehement, more overtly hostile. 'It's you people who cannot face up to us,' he snarled. 'If we let our supporters loose on you, if we arouse the Muslim youth against you, you'd be finished! You think you have established a great propaganda machine abroad, don't you, but the loudest of your amplifiers, your Bahá'í International Community offices at the United Nations, in New York, in Geneva, can be quashed in a second if we choose to snuff them out. Mark my words, we have the means for it; when we grease peoples' palms, they do our bidding.'

The distortions of truth were unending. The threats went on without respite. Before long they were launching ultimatums while I sat there, motionless. If they didn't kill me immediately, let them do so later. I did not answer them or even twitch a foot.

At last, there was a pause in the onslaught, a moment of silence. Was it over, or just a lull before another storm? I could hear them moving about restlessly behind me.

Then the second man suddenly erupted in fresh rage, slamming his fist down on the table. 'To hell with you all!' he spluttered. 'Ali Khánjání[21] was here and didn't even mention your name. We arrested you and they did nothing about it, nothing whatsoever. God knows, it's made absolutely no difference.'

They did nothing?

A rush of joy surged through my veins.

It made no difference?

I could barely contain my elation. This was utterly wonderful news! Despite all his previous distortions and lies, I was ready to believe the gentleman now. So Mr Khánjání had been dragged in here and hadn't breathed a word about me? Hadn't 'even mentioned my name'? – Oh heaven! If he wanted me to infer that the Yárán were giving up on me, that the Universal House of Justice did not care about me, and if he imagined that this would make me lose hope and collaborate with the Ministry, he could not have been more wrong. For it was the best intelligence he could have given me! It was the most liberating information I could have heard. Thank God, the Yárán had not mentioned me. Thank goodness, these gentlemen would never be able to bargain over me, or demand concessions for my release, or put the Bahá'í community under pressure for my sake. I was ecstatic, euphoric.

They struggled with me for another hour that day but eventually left the room in disgust. I fear I may have disappointed the good gentlemen from the Bureau of Intelligence in Mashhad. When the old man conducted me back to my cell I was still walking on air…

* * *

The suggestion that I should spy for this Ministry revealed how poorly these brave gentlemen understood the Bahá'í Faith. Pretending to protect the Bahá'ís and then accusing us of playing the victim after blaming us for every crime under the sun further demonstrated the limits of their logic. They wanted to bribe the secretary of the Yárán-i-Iran with this 'offer' because they thought it would demoralise everyone else. But they had merely lifted my spirits and made it easier to be resilient. The idea that the other members of the Yárán might be coerced by these gentlemen had been gnawing at me ever since I was taken hostage. My greatest dread was that my beloved colleagues would be forced to submit to unjust demands just to protect me, to save my life. But no, they had remained firm, and I would too. I would follow the standard the Yárán had set and defend the truth just as they were doing.

I started pacing furiously around the grey cell after this meeting, walking back and forth, from corner to corner. I do not know how long I kept going, but movement was indispensable to understand what I had heard, digest what I had learned. It was tiring, but I had to restore my equilibrium, re-establish my sense of self, re-discover time and space.

Time is not the same in prison as it is in the free world. Without a watch, in artificially lit cells, most of which are windowless, you simply lose track of the temporal dimension, and with it, all sense of reality and yourself. This can lead to even more serious mental and emotional losses. So you create new ways to gauge time: you measure it according to the squeak of the meal trolley wheels approaching down the corridor, the echoes of the call to evening prayer, the temperature of your morning tea. Sometimes you estimate it by the sheer weariness of your body. After the meeting with the two gentlemen from the Bureau of Intelligence of Mashhad, I tried to restore a sense of time by walking around in circles. When I stopped my giddy round, I was ready to sleep: exhausted, but content.

* * *

The following day, the interrogator's impulse for harassment reached new heights. He told me, in a tone of venomous glee, in a language larded with smug sarcasm and spite, that not only had Mr Khánjání been there for questioning, but Mr Tavakkolí, another member of the Yárán, had also obeyed their summons and responded to their demands. He wanted to tell me, 'Ha! You see, we have you all now, you're finished. You are in our power.' Before leaving the room that day, after referring once more to Mr Khánjání, he threw a hideous question over his shoulder, which hung in the air after he slammed the door shut.

'And if we choose one of you two to be executed…?'

A day or so later he raised the subject again and tried to intimidate me a second time.

'Did I tell you that Tavakkolí's also been here, as well as Khánjání? Oh, yes! We're going to shred you all to pieces.'

This time I reacted. 'That you have always tried to do.'

It was a mere murmur, but I intended him to hear me, and he did. I wanted him to know that if I was still sitting there and he was still attacking me, it was precisely because we had *not* been 'shredded,' we were *still* not in 'pieces.' His response was predictable.

'Yes! You'll see! This time it will be different. This time we'll break the necks of you people, once and for all. We'll do something so that none of you can ever rise again!'

Whenever you hear such gentlemen using this kind of language, you must be very cautious in your reactions. You cannot dismiss what they are saying out of hand, but you need to pare away the abuse to decode the real intention. Only after you see that all these words are merely aimed at seeding division and disseminating doubt can you defend yourself; only then can you rise above such provocations and avoid the traps of fear that have been set for you. They want you to argue, to become confrontational and upset. They want to cow you and crush your spirits. But if you allow that to happen, you will be playing their game. You must never allow them to be your oppressors, never let them turn you into their victim.

Whenever the good gentlemen of Mashhad tried to goad me during interrogations, their goal was always the same. And however I responded, mine was too. They wanted to let me know, in no uncertain terms, that their antagonism against the Bahá'ís would not end until they obliterated all trace of us in Iran. And I was determined to show them that we had no intention of being obliterated, that we would never become their victims, that we were committed to working towards unity and justice for the future well-being and prosperity of Iran, and that nothing they might ever do would detract from our efforts to promote those goals.

15

JUSTICE AND THE LAW

Justice had no place in the debate, but the gentlemen of Mashhad were obsessed by the law. Their interpretation of it was highly idiosyncratic. They wanted to extract proof, exert pressure, and force me to admit that I was breaking the law, that the Bahá'ís were breaking the law, that everything we did was in violation of their definitions of the law. It may have begun with the burial of a corpse, but it extended to every single Bahá'í activity.

They insisted, for example, that the Bahá'í Institute of Higher Education (BIHE) was some kind of illegal organisation, established and maintained through the aid of 'foreign powers'. When the interrogator came up with this line of attack, I informed him very firmly that he was mistaken. The Bahá'í Institute of Higher Education was an internally conceived project, unique to Iran and sustained voluntarily by its own people. It had been set up by the Iranian Bahá'ís to compensate, in part, for the educational deprivation suffered by thousands of Iranian youth, and it was open to whoever wished to benefit from its services. I also said that we considered this accomplishment entirely legal, given the highly illegal actions taken by the government against young Bahá'ís, who were either being refused entry into university, despite proven ability, or denied diplomas at the end of their studies. Since the country's Constitution held that every Iranian should be entitled to higher education, we were, in fact, promoting the laws of the land by ensuring this right for the Bahá'í youth, too.

Furthermore, if this 'university' was criticised for being 'underground', where else could seminars and tutorials take place but informally, in our homes, given all the blocks and hindrances the government was putting in our way? Indeed, private homes were the only recourse we had left, and so far, none of these were 'underground' – yet! Nor did we have any regrets regarding this endeavour. Iran should be proud of our achievements; BIHE students had been accepted in some of the most prestigious universities in the world.

The interrogator brushed my defence aside as if I were a fly. He claimed that according to the laws of the land, even Qur'anic classes had to be licensed, and a Muslim child would need permission to attend one. So how dare we have embarked on such a project without authorisation?

My reply was a one liner: Authorise us then. Had we been protected by the laws of the land, we would certainly have received a licence, but whenever we applied for one, it was denied and unlawfully withheld. We were repeatedly 'disqualified'.

Every time I mentioned the laws of the land, it infuriated him. He would erupt and scream at me in rage; he would lean down and holler loudly in my ear.

'Listen to what I am telling you. I am the law here. I am the governor who decides and implements laws. I do as I see fit, and that's the end of it. You can forget about the rest!'

* * *

The interrogator also quizzed me repeatedly about the *Khádimín*. These individuals, living in communities all across the country, had been appointed, like the Yárán, on an *ad hoc* basis after our elected institutions were dissolved; like the Yárán, they too were set up with the tacit approval of the authorities and in addition to internal community duties, served as a liaison between the government and the Bahá'ís at a local level. Since he knew that the Khádimín had held a meeting in a particular town in the provinces some months before, the interrogator was insisting that their deliberations should have been vetted and controlled.

'Why,' he said, 'do you conduct your business in secret? Why do you turn off all your phones when you meet with each other?'

It was further confirmation, as if I needed one, that our phones were being hacked. But more preposterously, it was an allegation that if we turned them off to say prayers, we were being 'subversive,' that if we tried to solve personal problems discreetly, respecting peoples' privacy, we were 'undermining the Islamic Republic.' Despite the Bahá'í principles of non-involvement in politics and obedience to government, he invariably interpreted whatever we did as a threat to the regime and therefore against the law. And yet, could any group of people have behaved with greater restraint given the unlawful measures taken against us? Could any community have exhibited such willingness to abide by the rule of law more openly? Or shown more patience? Or been more upstanding and peaceable?

He could not accept the distinction between elected Bahá'í institutions, which had decision-making authority, and appointed individuals, who had no power at all to do anything but advise and offer guidance. It was a difference he was either unwilling or unable to grasp, because to have done so, perhaps, may have required him to re-assess the power wielded by people like himself or by individual clergy. So he swerved away repeatedly from this line of argument and returned instead to the issue of overseeing our activities.

'If you're really obedient to the government,' he persisted, 'then why not give us copies of all your reports? In fact, why not conduct all your activities directly through us?'

When I tried to tell him that what he called a 'report' was merely an anodyne update, a sharing of general news about the Bahá'í community, nothing more, he snorted that we were withholding secrets from the state. And when I tried to explain the difference between secrecy and confidentiality in Bahá'í consultation, he dismissed the distinction as sophistry.

So at the risk of provoking another dismissive sneer, I tried to explain the principles of this practical problem-solving tool used by Bahá'ís all over the world. Consultation encourages people to share thoughts frankly while letting go of personal opinions, I told him; it is based on collective decision making rather than on one person's will imposed on others, and is like alchemy – more than the sum of its parts – because the result rather than the process is important. When we consult, I concluded, we try to support and to implement the results in action and in unity but we do not share the process, not even with our spouses.

'In that case,' he argued, 'why do you send your minutes to the House of Justice?'

It was useless to reiterate that there was nothing sinister about our communications with the head of our faith or to point out that all major organised religions maintain some system of communication in this regard, however different it might be. Why should the Bahá'ís not do so too? But when it came to our relations with the Universal House of Justice, it took very little perspicacity to know what was exercising these gentlemen of the Ministry of Intelligence. They could only define the head of our Faith in terms of political power and clearly perceived this institution as a threat to their own authority. That was why they insisted that they were equal to and had the equivalent rank to the Universal House of Justice; that they shared the same motives and had the same concern for the well-being of the Bahá'í community as the Universal House of Justice. Since their task was to ensure the security of the country, they wanted to safeguard our security too. Like the Universal House of Justice.

Whenever the discussion reached this stage, my response was swift.

'How can this be true when your aim is to eliminate us? Is it not clearly stated, in your Confidential Memorandum circulated in 1991, that the Supreme Revolutionary Council wants to uproot our community and erase all trace of us in this country?'

I knew very well that he was fully acquainted with this 'secret blueprint' which called for the 'quiet strangulation' of the Iranian Bahá'í community through poverty, ignorance and fear, because the public exposure of this policy of the Islamic Republic in the annual report of the UN Commission of Human Rights in 1993 had provoked international outrage. But when I provided current examples of how such repression had been followed through and was being systematically implemented today, he denied it; he even expressed indignation, blaming 'parallel groups' for instigating such goings-on.

In the beginning I did not know what he meant. But I soon realised that he was not just shrugging off responsibility onto the thugs paid to act independently of the government – a well-oiled tool of authoritarian regimes – but dropping hints that certain Bahá'ís could be acting in 'parallel' with such groups. In other words, he wanted to insinuate that there were factions within our community. He knew he couldn't argue about our beliefs, so he was looking for ways to subvert them instead. His primary objective was to sow disunity among us, disseminate distrust in our system of administration, by undermining, demeaning and debasing our confidence in the legislative body governing the affairs of the Bahá'ís worldwide, namely, the Universal House of Justice.

* * *

Our belief in the efficacy of the Bahá'í Administrative Order, according to him, was frankly absurd. He kept harping on how irrelevant the system was, how incongruous.

'A religion doesn't need administration!' he spat. 'Faith is not about management!'

I knew he did not believe what he was saying, given the heavily bureaucratic system of religious administration that controlled our country. The clergy of Iran run a huge and complex organisation, with special budgets allocated to every activity, large and small, with a system for maintaining every-thing from daily prayers to the running of mosques, from the control of oil to the funding of interrogations. But he scoffed at my response, ridiculed my attempts to reason with him. I tried to tell him that since there was no clergy in the Bahá'í com-munity – no rabbis, no priests, no mullahs – and since no indi-viduals could wield power in this Faith, elected institutions were authorised instead, to serve the community through the process of collective decision making I had described. The government had forced us to dissolve these institutions, but we still had to help people in need. We still had to bury the dead.

That's when he slammed yet another form on my side table.

'But your institutions don't exist in all countries, do they, eh? Why's that?'

I saw from under the blindfold that this new form required me to list all the countries in the world without a functioning Bahá'í administration.

'Write!' he shouted. 'Write!'

He wanted to prove that if some countries had no Bahá'í institutions, then why should we have any in Iran. I said I did not know all the laws of those various countries, but that since it was one of our principles to abide by them, the Bahá'ís were doubtless doing so, just as they were in Iran, even when it came to finding solutions for the burial of the dead.

Which naturally led to the next question.

'In that case,' he pounced, 'why do you still maintain an administration in Iran?'

'Because as you well know,' I responded, 'it was illegal according to the Constitution to have disbanded our administration and someone still needs to oversee the burial of the dead.'

Whenever I mentioned the Constitution, the interrogator became extremely agitated. His huffing and puffing would increase, and I would hear him pacing behind me, seething with rage. And then he would launch into a highly discriminatory interpretation of the Constitution, which professed that although the rights of the Iranian Bahá'ís were technically protected on grounds of citizenship, they were denied on grounds of theology, because the Bahá'í Faith, he kept repeating, was a sect, a pernicious sect, an illegal sect.

'There is a ban on the administration of this sect, so why are you still maintaining such thorough records and conducting such detailed activities?'

Again, I was obliged to repeat that these *ad hoc* programmes were for people in need, that's all. Why should attempts to enhance the educational opportunities for youth, to alleviate the financial burdens of the old, to offer support for the sick and vulnerable members in society, be perceived as an 'illegal' threat? We had only launched these programmes after the government denied us our civil rights. We had been forced to run these institutes to compensate for the depredations suffered by Bahá'ís whose constitutional dues were being systematically eroded. And our efforts were entirely free of *political* motives.

Even though he peppered my back with the same questions again and again, he would often demand that I also provide answers for him in writing on these subjects.

'Write,' he would yell at me, 'write!'

And I did. And I thanked him for insisting on it.

* * *

It was transparently obvious that these gentlemen of Mashhad had been reading the Bahá'í writings and analysing the messages of the Universal House of Justice for years. They had even kept abreast of the current activities of the Faith worldwide as well as studying its history. They provided their interrogation teams with material that could be easily twisted out of context to create misrepresentations of the Bahá'í Faith and lead to confusion in the minds of those they questioned. The interrogators would deploy splinters of these messages and echo fragments of bowdlerised quotes, giving the impression, to people who were either too naïve or ill-informed to know the difference, that they were in full command of the facts. And then they would use the contradictory replies they had extracted from such people to increase their own arsenal of intimidation against others during subsequent interrogations. The mountain of fake information they had accumulated paralleled the twin landfills of Tehran.

I had already witnessed these methods being deployed against prisoners some years before, during my first detention, in 2005. The interrogators would poke and prod until they extracted some small factoid out of one person and then would use a portion of it to probe under the skin of another. They would bluff, lie and devise all kinds of mind games to unearth more from the second person, and then cobble together whatever they had mined from the two previous ones to attack a third. And so on. This technique could be tailored to a wide range of so-called 'political activities,' from AIDS programmes to literacy classes, and the wheel could turn indefinitely, indeed for as long as it took for some poor soul to break down and make false confessions. The easiest targets among the Bahá'ís were those who thought the interrogators already knew everything about the community anyway, and who would then speak to them frankly, trustingly, hopefully, unaware of their subversive methods.

When you engage in subversion, you suspect everyone else of doing the same. When you hide behind lies, you assume others do too. The interrogator once even stated this openly to me, unaware of how he was betraying his own motives and incriminating himself.

'You are all subversives,' he told me, bitterly, 'all of you are insubordinates! We know about such things! We know you are planning to overthrow our government.'

After I denied the charge, he repeated the accusation, with numbing persistence over the course of a long and challenging conversation. He was very pleased with his conclusion.

'The aim of you people is to overthrow all the governments of the world!'

When I objected, yet again, to this absurd allegation, he parried with another charge.

'Don't you believe in a united world government? Isn't that your ultimate aim? Don't you want all governments to be Bahá'í?'

I sighed. This was such a distortion of the truth that it required clarification. 'Before discussing this issue,' I answered, attempting objectivity, 'we need to define our terms. We need to share a common understanding of what such words mean, before we use them.'

'So you're saying we should first work on our A-B-Cs?' he jeered.

I tried again. He must surely agree that language evolves. Words such as 'power', or 'government,' or even 'unity' no longer mean today what they did centuries ago; even philosophers and thinkers from diverse cultural traditions define these terms differently. So before talking about 'world government', perhaps we should distinguish between discredited definitions of totalitarian control implied by these words, and what they could mean in a future world with different values. Who would want to live under an oppressive system…?

He interrupted me hotly. 'But that's just what your Bahá'í administration is!'

I begged to differ. Words like 'power' and 'unity', I told him, were redefined in the Bahá'í Faith, precisely because the old meanings had become so toxic. Election to a Bahá'í institution entailed service, not power and privilege; unity meant diversity, not conformity. In the same way, fresh definitions of 'world' governance would surely emerge in response to global crises and global needs – for clean air and water, for example, for peace rather than war – and that kind of governance would necessarily imply very different sets of priorities.

'But who knows,' I concluded, 'whether nations will choose a "world government" or unite by default through common principles and due to common needs. I certainly have no idea what it means for a government to be "Bahá'í". We have yet to come together on such concepts, because most of us are still in denial of our common humanity.'

Whenever I suggested that words might acquire new meanings and human understanding could evolve, the interrogator would accuse me of evading the subject because he rejected the idea of social evolution. He would yell at me to answer him. Now. To tell him what the Bahá'ís were doing to establish world unity, now. And when I replied that I had just done so, he would sneer and disparage my logic.

'Oh sure!' he would say. 'Of course! Whenever you're stuck for an answer, you start using metaphors and say that everything will be made clear in the future!'

A thought flashed through my mind. 'Tell me,' I asked him, 'was the view that the Muslims had about the Imams during the time of the Prophet Muhammad identical to the understanding that you have today? Is it the same, in your opinion, or has it evolved?'

He went very quiet then, breathing heavily, threateningly, in a way that either meant he thought I was too stupid to speak to or because he was too angry to trust himself to speak. He often derided my replies or rejected them out of hand. But I knew the tenor of his voice by then and could distinguish between provocation and frustration. He thrived on confrontation; he wanted us to be at cross-purposes and resisted every attempt I made to find common ground. Nevertheless, there were times when he appeared to agree with me, when he seemed to accept that yes, well, maybe, perhaps I might be justified. It was a mere show of open-mindedness, of course, a ploy to take something I said and twist it out of context.

Soon afterwards he left the room and, on his return, he slapped another interrogation form on the armrest of my chair. He had typed out the question about world government.

'Write down everything you just told me about different priorities,' he snapped.

He wanted me to think I was condemning myself, sentencing myself indefinitely every time I put pen to paper. His injunction, 'Write!' was an invitation to crime.

* * *

Although I tried to correct his misconceptions about Bahá'í administration, one subject I had no intention of discussing with him was my faith; I was determined to avoid all religious matters and any doctrinal discussion of beliefs. My principle of silence on this question was so adamant that a little while later he said he would be obliged, due to my lack of co-operation, as he put it, to bring in a specialist, a theological expert who could assess my opinions. This apparently demonstrated how far he was willing to go to accommodate me. He believed an expert could evaluate my beliefs and clarify my silences in a manner that would satisfy the Bureau. I did not see how even an expert could evaluate my beliefs if I said nothing about them, or how anyone besides myself could clarify my silences. But I was given a clue when he produced a book and rustled the pages ostentatiously behind my back.

'I want you to read this,' he said, 'before you speak to our specialist.'

From the expanding ripples of his voices, I could sense him gloating behind my back. I could almost see him smiling. He was extremely pleased with himself. This book would be the final straw, he seemed to imply, the *coup de grâce* that would finish me off. He told me, with the patronising patience of a teacher speaking to a recalcitrant pupil, that he wanted me to read and respond to each theme, one by one.

That night, the book was delivered to my cell in the detention centre. It was as thick and heavy as a tombstone; its sheer size confirmed that homework of this nature could indeed lead to the grave. The unwieldy tome was written in the guise of a university text purporting to provide students with an 'objective' analysis of the Bahá'í Faith. But the chief editor, who was a cleric, had whipped up a confection called 'Bahá'ísm' based on unsubstantiated opinions and pseudo-facts which bore no relationship whatsoever to the truth.

After reading a few pages I saw that such misconceptions would be easier to dissolve with humour than reasoned through analysis. But I suspected the interrogator would not be amused.

16

LONELY TIMES

Except for a few nights when I was mercifully permitted to return to the public prison and sleep among my boisterous and warm-hearted murderers, thieves and prostitutes, I was locked away in the detention centre from that time on, and was kept busy producing cannon fodder for the Intelligence Bureau of Mashhad. The days were dull and the young woman who had replaced Háj Khánum even duller, for she seemed to have been recruited for her connections with the Ministry rather than her wits. A couple of times, when I was being driven to the prison, the gentlemen would also give her a lift, and enquire about her parents, in a tone drooling with sycophantic respect; they would send these distinguished personages their cordial greetings and refer to them deferentially as Háj Khánum and Háj Áqá. I could well imagine such worthies would be proud of their daughter's career choice.

The Intelligence Bureau Girl, as I named her, certainly seemed content with who she was and where she was working; in fact, she seemed delighted with her new assignment. Her self-confidence was neon bright. Perhaps I provided an escape from even more stultifying circumstances. Perhaps I constituted a promotion for her. Although it was obvious, from the distant tone she adopted towards me, that she'd been warned I was potentially 'dangerous', I suspected she may have also thought political prisoners or prisoners of conscience were not quite human. Apart from the one time she reluctantly permitted me to take a little dried fruit to my fellow troublemakers in the public prison, her exchanges with me were free from all trace of charity. She exercised the cold science of exclusion so consistently that I felt myself turning into a lab specimen in her presence, a guinea pig on which she was experimenting. And yet the banalities she uttered were more cringeworthy than scientific.

'I am leaving now,' she would state, haughtily, 'and I will return at lunch time.'

She made it sound like a law of the universe.

Or 'I have to go to an appointment now,' she would say, with a self-important toss of the head, 'and I will return to check on you in about two hours.'

I was grateful when she left but equally thankful for her return, because despite her pretensions, she provided me with a kind of reprieve in those bleak circumstances. She was doubtless unaware of it, but I was conducting experiments on her too. The solitary confinement cell of the Intelligence Bureau of Mashhad was an ideal environment to explore the theory of relativity, and she was *my* guinea pig.

I had always known that time was not a fixed quantity, but in solitary confinement I realised it had no fixed quality either. For the quality of time varies with circumstances, and depends on the point of view of each person. It was hard to believe that time was the same for me as it was for the Intelligence Bureau Girl, for her hour's lunch break must certainly have tasted different to my sixty minutes. I calculated that when she returned to 'check' on me after what she called 'teatime' that day, the gulp of a second for her had taken a whole month for me to swallow. I was able to walk across a desert for the length of two long years, while pacing my cell during her two-hour periods of absence.

Those were lonely times in the detention centre. By the end of the month of Farvardín (mid-April), a month and a half – six whole weeks – had passed since my arrest, and I was truly weary of these conditions. I was with the interrogator all day, with the Intelligence Bureau Girl each evening, and with my miserable self each night. There was nothing to sustain my spirits, no news from family, no books, no television, no newspaper, no telephone. And no respite from the physical privations and inhuman treatment I received, from the carping, cantankerous and confrontational tone that characterised every communication I was granted. To all these was added the ongoing uncertainty – which was the greatest worry of all – that because of me, my dear fellow Bahá'ís were suffering more pressure every day.

It was hard to eat in the circumstances, and since I lacked appetite, it was easy to lose weight. In fact, my clothes were hanging off me to such an extent by then that I was obliged to tie a knot in the waistband to keep up my trousers. I also developed a cold and a cough that lingered for days and was suffering from endemic sleep deprivation. But even without rest or medication, I felt the better for being lighter. It was just a pity Siyávash was not around to appreciate my new slim silhouette…

* * *

As time passed, the interrogations were gradually becoming tougher and more hard-hitting, their tone increasingly insolent and sadistic. The subject matter, moreover, was so complex that the effort of remembering, let alone evaluating, what had transpired, was beginning to elude me. The interrogator was now overtly trying to force specific details out of me related to my work as secretary of the Yárán, and this too I was determined to avoid. So I spent every night reviewing what I had said, how I had said it, and trying to gauge whether my answers could be misrepresented by the 'intelligent' gentlemen of the Ministry.

How had I responded to this or that untrue statement? Was my answer expressed in the right or wrong tone? Could the words I used be taken out of context to distort the principles of the Bahá'í Faith? Had I said anything that might be used to torture others? By then, debate over burials had broadened into a discussion of general Bahá'í procedures – but had I inadvertently mentioned subjects totally unrelated to my charges?

Being bombarded with aggressive questions for hours and hours, day after day, leads to battle fatigue. It is easy to make mistakes. It was therefore important to take myself to account each evening. I had to be my own consultant, my own guide and critic. Sometimes I tried to encourage myself with the way an interrogation had gone during the day. Other times I was miserable over how I had reacted and would castigate myself all night. More often than not, I would lose all ability to assess anything. Again and again, through the numb hours, I would get up, walk about, engage in close combat with one uncertainty only to be invaded by another. Finally, after achieving a temporary truce, I would lie down to sleep, but had barely found a reprieve before another onslaught of worries woke me. Defeat was perilously close.

Many days and nights passed in this way. Time stretched out of all recognition. It became shapeless, like my too-large trousers. It became tasteless and pointless, like the food served in the dog bowl through the slot in the door. There was no light at the end of this endless tunnel of time. As a result of disrupted sleep, the difference between day and night ceased to exist, and I would often find myself literally in limbo in the detention centre, not knowing when I was. The only relief was the thought of the next interrogation.

It was a shock when I realised that, when I admitted to myself how much I was looking forward to 'not-seeing' the interrogator again. These daily encounters were the only challenge in my life, the only objective way to verify who I was and whether I was still a thinking, living, feeling, human being. Or not. Despite their intensity, their severity, their ruthless and arbitrary cruelty, in my heart of hearts I knew I was waiting for the next session. I was eager to be summoned back. That room, that chair, that armrest even, that blank wall I faced, blindfolded, as the interrogator prowled behind me with his snarling questions, his exhalations of disgust, that surreal world had become a field of vital combat for me, an arena in which to test my strength, confront my weakness, and evaluate both.

Each day I stepped into the interrogation ring, it was to assess new skills. Each night in the cell, I struggled to find other ways to face another onslaught the following morning. And with time, it dawned on me that only through the dust and heat of the next public round with the gentlemen of Mashhad could I perhaps triumph over the negativity that such a conflict inevitably entailed. That was the real contest I was facing, the true inner fight: I had to stay steadfast without becoming oppositional; I had to remain patient without indulging in false piety; and I had to learn to forgive, to forgive, to forgive.

Forgiveness can never be expected, of course. It is one of those mysterious commodities that should be given but not required. Once these gentlemen were disappointed in my rejection of their 'offer', once my unwillingness to spy for them was irrefutably apparent and their plans to extract confessions from me proved futile, I would surely pay for it. They would undoubtedly resort to greater hostility, impose more hardships and subject me to further abuse. They had already mounted their pressure over the past weeks. They had incarcerated me in maximum security, among those they considered the trash of society. They had humiliated me in court, as an exercise in futility. They had extended my detention indefinitely without justification. My family had come all the way to Mashhad only to be turned away without right of visitation, and the solitary confinement was becoming increasingly onerous. They had no intention of exercising the arts of forgiveness on me.

But with each passing day, these adversities were also a growing source of relief to me. They confirmed that the Yárán-i-Iran were standing firm, that my dear colleagues were refusing to compromise. For had these gentlemen achieved their aims and imposed their will on other Bahá'ís, my freedom might have been bought by now, the conditions under which I was being held might have relaxed. If circumstances were worsening, it was a good sign. It was a small victory! This conclusion helped me cope with the detention centre.

* * *

There was one particular hardship, however, which I could not overcome: the silence. Apart from the chirping of the unknown bird on the roof, I heard no pleasant voice, no hopeful sounds around me. Some days the interrogation was cut short, or I was not summoned back in the afternoon, and I would find myself suffocating in the relentless silence of this solitude. And during these lonely times with no one to talk to and nothing happening, I would reach a dead end, a blank wall. The silence was becoming harmful to my mind.

I had to learn to scale that wall. After praying and chanting for hours, I set myself the task of recalling all that I had memorised of Persian literature and started reciting poems to myself for hours too. I reviewed films I had seen and novels I had read, recounted stories, deconstructed history, but above all declaimed out loud the odes and *ghazals* of Hafez and Sa'adí and any other poet whose work I remembered. Perhaps the Intelligence Bureau Girl would think me a mad as well as 'dangerous' guinea pig, but I did not care. I needed to hear myself uttering clever, interesting and, if possible, beautiful words.

Literature was my escape, and I began to yearn to write my own thoughts from that time. Perhaps I owed this impulse to the interrogator who had set me on this path. *Write!* I told myself, echoing him. *Write!* I began constructing poems in my mind, evoking the people I had met in prison and my experiences there. At times, I would build a narrative account, and tell the story of my arrest to myself, citing everything that had happened in detail, however daunting, however painful. I tried to examine the situation from a psychological point of view, like a critic. And then I would imagine myself teaching my students, helping them to grasp the complexity of the situation. I would walk about the cell and conduct make-believe classes. Or I would discuss the consequences of solitary confinement with them, raising questions about the human psyche. Or I would challenge them, and myself, with questions about the limits of social justice and individual freedom. My intention was to keep my brain alive, to prevent myself from forgetting things. At the same time, I needed to speak out loud, if only to hear a voice in that grey room, to touch the texture of words on my dry tongue.

By repeating words and constructing sentences, I built an architecture of meaning within those dirty walls and on those non-descript beige carpets. I was tired of doing nothing and language saved me from meaninglessness. And yet, ironically, it was this 'nothing' that finally saved my sanity in the end, not the words themselves, not actual language.

In the silence of unrelieved solitude, you go deep into the world of thought. You review your past, as well as your present. You think about your friendships, relationships, services and colleagues in ways you have never done before. You discover that you have assigned certain values to yourself and to your children, to your spouse and to your community, and have certain priorities when it comes to questions of belief and faith, of self-esteem and personality. But once confronted by a crisis, all those priorities change. You see, or rather hear, new concerns resonating in the silence of solitude; you discover new priorities whose significance you could never have imagined until now.

I was pulled out of a very busy life and thrust into this silence. I was cut off overnight from endless responsibilities, non-stop duties, urgent organisational work and flung into this desolate corner, far from everyone I knew. Outside the prison walls, I had always tried to complete the greatest amount of work in the least amount of time. Now, everything was reversed, and I had to stretch the minimum activity across the longest period. In that other world, I had filled my days with obligations, family duties and pedagogical activities, while managing to ignore, to some extent, or at least take for granted, the foundations of my existence. Bound to the wheel of daily tasks, caught up by the demands of haste and hustle, speed and need, I had not listened attentively to the voice of my innermost being. But now, with the unravelling of the life I had woven, this enforced silence caused me to turn inwards and attune my inner ear to stillness. I was living in a new world here, becoming another person, with all the time to contemplate and all the space to think.

It was a novel experience.

Worlds within worlds. Worlds intertwined with other worlds, like human lives woven into a rich tapestry, an unrolling carpet. And yet, all these worlds are one, and the shining, luminous thread running through them constitutes the warp and woof of a shared spirit, one that makes you kinder towards others, draws you closer to them. When you feel the tug of that bright thread in your heart, you learn to forgive, to be more patient – even with yourself. You consider more deeply the meaning of love, the reason for hate. You ask yourself if you are more familiar with the former or the latter. And why?

In fact, as I began to listen to the silence in my soul, I realised that hatred, even towards the interrogator, the agents of the Intelligence Bureau, or the guards had not taken root in me. It was curious. I could not feel the least upset or offended by them for long, whatever they might say or do. In the case of some, like my dear Intelligence Bureau Girl, I actually found that her callousness was amusing, her arrogance comic.

I was cheered by this thought. It was a breakthrough.

Or was this just a kind of laziness on my part? Had I reached a stage of resignation and submission because I did not want to be bothered to hate? Was this simply a form of giving up, of giving in, a sort of fatalism? Or, conversely, was it the first glimmerings of other capacities lying latent that I had never known were in me, the discovery of new and as yet undeveloped qualities that I had totally neglected until now? The capacity to move beyond crises and turn them into opportunities, the willingness to change life habits and rise above anxieties, and the spiritual power to overcome the fears and defeats that surround us – all these marvels I unearthed in the silence of the solitary cell.

And then, to my utter disbelief, I found that I was not only growing accustomed to solitary confinement but beginning to appreciate and value it. In fact, I was learning the meaning of free will in that grey cell. Solitary confinement had been forced on me, yes, but it was up to me how I chose to live with it; it was my decision whether to accept it consciously, or to merely endure it in turmoil and resentment and growing terror.

The choice was entirely mine; I was free to do as I willed.

17

HIGHS & LOWS

It would soon be Urdíbihisht, the Festival of Ridvan, a period sacred for millions of Bahá'ís the world over. These twelve holy days, between 20 April and 1 May, mark the meeting of the material and the mystical in the Bahá'í calendar, and celebrate the occasion when the founder of our Faith, Bahá'u'lláh, announced his mission of unity to the world. There, on the banks of the Tigris, in a garden outside the city of Baghdad, the sorrow of his second banishment was transformed into joyful tidings of a new age. And now, all over the planet, elections of Bahá'í national and local institutions coincide with that historic moment.

The Iranian Bahá'ís had been deprived of participating in the electoral process since 1983, but it was still the most sacred time of the year for us. We could not exercise our right to vote in this country, but we could still commemorate Bahá'u'lláh's message of spiritual regeneration and the oneness of mankind. We could still recall that time and place when the grief of separation was transformed by him into reunion and recognition.

The paradox of joy and sorrow symbolised by the Ridvan Festival was particularly poignant for me this year, and my prayers and meditations were most ardent. Ever since my strange experience in the doghouse, when I had stepped into that bright Presence, bowed beneath chains and shackled to his fellow prisoners in the pit of darkness, I was able to summon the palpable mystery of it, feel the surging waves of it rising within my heart whenever I brought it to mind. Even after all these weeks, the recollection of that strange incident swept over me, replenishing my strength, spreading through me like a shining sea.

A few more days of interrogation, a few more nights in solitary confinement, and at last, on a certain Friday evening, I was taken back to Vakilabad. I had gradually become familiar with the prison authorities there over the past two months and they welcomed me kindly whenever they saw me. Many were surprised to find me still in custody after all this time and found an excuse to speak with me. They wanted to know how my case was progressing, why it was being prolonged. Members of the police force, officers in the guard stations, even the soldiers expressed their regret at my long detention; some were visibly dismayed to see me still there, and several even commiserated with me. A few went so far as to voice criticism. Only the female guards showed no emotion. They treated me with the same callous disregard each time I returned, as though they expected to keep me behind bars.

So when the chief officer at the main desk delayed sending me to the women's section that Friday evening, I was not surprised. He had often kept me waiting till the crowds dispersed, in order to exchange a few words. He was very discreet about it, only glancing in my direction after the place emptied. Then he spoke as if he had only just noticed me.

'Oh, it's you, is it, Mrs Sabet?' he said kindly, 'are you are still here? Why is that? How come your situation has not yet been resolved? Tell me, what has been happening?'

I told him about the two court hearings and the extended detention, and he expressed his heartfelt sympathy, repeating that he thought the case had been closed a long time ago. Then wishing me a speedy release, he summoned a soldier to conduct me to the women's section and sent me off with a respectful goodbye. The soldier took this as authorisation to add his two cents, to air his astonishment, too, that I had been detained all this time without a trial. Even the officer on duty at the women's station – the same person who on previous occasions had complained to me about his life and work – also delayed before calling for a female guard to take me to maximum security that night. He looked carefully around, and once he was certain nobody could hear him, he also expressed his sincere regret at the treatment that I was receiving. Then he decided to vent his personal feelings.

'Mrs Sabet,' he said earnestly, 'all my life I have been a good Muslim. My father was a staunch believer too, and so am I. But ever since this Revolution, I have come to detest religion and anything to do with it. I swear, I'm only working here to earn enough money to feed my wife and children.' Then he leaned towards me confidentially and added, 'Would you believe I've been living on tranquilisers and sleeping pills for years?'

Yes, I believed it. No, I was not surprised. Even when he told me how depressed he was, even when he complained about the grifting and cheating everywhere he looked, the corruption and venality at all levels of government, and how deeply all this was affecting him, I was in no way shocked. Considering his job, who and what he saw, when and where he performed his duties, it was small wonder that he was dejected.

'It's perfectly normal you should feel unhappy,' I reassured him.

'Life here has made me lose hope in humanity,' he told me mournfully.

He had lived for years among the wretched of society. He had witnessed daily brutality and nightly depravity. He had every right to be sick and tired of it. But even so, he could surely sympathise with these people in prison, he could surely try to help them, a little? I reminded him that many of them were suffering even more dreadfully than he was.

'In my opinion the whole lot of them should be annihilated,' he retorted angrily. 'This entire society deserves to be burned to cinders, and its ashes buried too!'

I tried to reason with him, as I had with myself since coming to that dreadful place, to encourage him to be patient, to be understanding, urging him that these troubled people deserved to be loved, to be believed, that their miseries deserved attention. As did his.

'Corruption has poisoned our roots,' he said bitterly. 'This land is cursed!'

Naturally, I could not agree. I told him that the Bahá'ís believed Iran had a wonderful future. It was destined to lead the world in honour and in truth. He did not laugh. He did not contradict me. He just gazed at me wistfully for a few moments, and sighed.

'I have heard that the Bahá'ís are decent people,' he said. 'I've been told that they can distinguish between what's lawful and what's forbidden. Some say they would take the food out of their own mouths to feed it to others. Is that true?'

He had clearly been in a doghouse of his own for a long time, this man, but with no reprieve, without a glimmer of that blessed light. So, since it was one of the radiant nights of the Ridvan Festival, I took the unprecedented risk of talking to him. In a discreet corner, where no one could see or hear us, I told him that throughout history, in the darkest times and the most corrupt places on earth, God revealed Himself to liberate the very people who were the most despised, to revive the hearts of the most hopeless. And then, I whispered to him of the new Revelation that had shone from the blackest pit of Tehran over a hundred years ago; I told him how Bahá'u'lláh had breathed a new spiritual life into the world and that his message marked a divine springtime for humanity. Despite his gloom and cynicism, I think I surprised him. He was dangerously eager to know more.

'What shall I do when you leave?' he cried, full of excitement.

'One day we'll rebuild our country together,' I assured him. 'Be certain of that!'

'I would so like to believe in this hope,' he said plaintively.

'So allow yourself to,' I laughed, 'instead of wasting energy on your doubts!'

Whenever I had these kinds of encounters – with officers and soldiers who accompanied me back and forth, asking questions out of curiosity, with prison wardens, as well as the prisoners themselves, with my dear ladies in the public jail, and even with people like Háj Khánum, and the driver for the Intelligence Ministry in the mustard-coloured jacket – I found myself musing about freedom and captivity. Something curious was going on here, I thought, as the female guard finally arrived to escort me, with considerable ill grace, back to the maximum security ward. Was I really the prisoner in this place, as she and the brave gentlemen would have me believe? Or was I actually free, and everyone else in chains? Why did I not feel like a captive, despite all this jangling of keys and rattling of chains? And why did others not treat me like one?

It was odd.

*　*　*

Shortly afterwards, back in the cramped cell among my friendly criminals, I was lying high on my bunk bed, deep in these thoughts when the locks and keys jangled again and Maryam, our watchperson, cried out, 'They're bringing someone in!'

A newcomer was ushered into our cell. She was frail and thin, with a dark complexion and large, lifeless eyes. The sight of her filled me with sorrow because she was eight months pregnant, with a belly the size of a small melon. As soon as she arrived, she placed her bundle under her head and lay down to chat with the women she knew. She told them that all she had ever eaten during her pregnancy was fruit leather (*laváshak*) and crack. I could not believe it, but the others did. It was the first time I had heard a mother talk so casually about contributing to her newborn's addiction. It was also the first time I had encountered a case, notorious on the streets of the capital, of child trafficking by the desperately poor.

'This baby I am carrying belongs to other people,' she said. 'They bought his little brother for a hundred thousand *tumans*, but when he was born, I gave him too much smoke, and he died. So I have to pay them back with this one.'

The woman hardly ate a thing, even though she was an addict. Most of them received methadone every afternoon when a nurse came round and poured a quota into each one's mouth. Apart from this prescribed opioid, they managed to buy pills from whomever slipped a few into their hands, now and then. Then they would sit in a circle ceremoniously and grind the pills with the bottom of a glass, before sniffing it up together, in pairs.

I had no idea what these pills were, just that they seemed expensive. They were not painkillers, and probably did little for the women, who were already receiving maintenance therapy to assuage their addiction. But I think it was helpful for some of them to recreate the social atmosphere of taking drugs together. This ceremonial act filled an emotional need and possibly averted the impulse of violence towards themselves and others.

The pregnant woman seemed calm without methadone, but she was swallowing painkillers with the zeal of the desperate. They must have made her feel better.

'Who's the father of this one?' asked Fatimih. 'Did he agree to the sale?'

'What father?' the woman quietly replied.

'Where will you give birth?' another asked.

'I broke the law on purpose so that I could come inside for it,' the woman said. 'I want to give birth here because there's nowhere else to go.'

She then sat up, opened the bundle and brought out two sets of worn-out baby clothes. She seemed thrilled to have prepared for the birth of her child.

'See!' she said, with a wan smile. 'Here's what it can wear!'

* * *

Towards the end of that same Friday evening, I heard my name called out again. I was apparently on the list to go to court for a third hearing the next day. I felt the same flutters of anxiety, the same worries as before. What was going on? What new plots and plans were they up to now? Would my charges be changed at this new hearing?

The night was, as usual, sleepless. The morning was characterised by the same ceremonials of dress code and rituals of transportation. And we all trooped out, male and female, bus after bus to the court. Once inside, I was conducted to the same branch, to the same judge, and in the same room. The secretary placed a form in front of me as soon as I arrived. I noted an official stamp on the side of the page as he pointed to a spot in the middle.

'Fingerprint!' he repeated curtly.

I pulled the form close and read it as steadily as I could. Fortunately, the text was not as prolix nor as arcane as the previous one. It was also more legible. It stated that I was apparently appointing two lawyers and giving them power of attorney to represent me, one in Tehran and another in Mashhad. The first, Mr Abdu'l-Fattah Soltaní, was known to me by name for he was a co-founder, with Shirín Ebadí, of the Defenders of Human Rights Centre. He had already been imprisoned for his activism three years before. Was he now offering to defend me, to speak on my behalf and protect my rights? Such courage! Such kindness! A surge of gratitude ran through my veins. I suddenly felt safe. A lawyer, at last! I also had a parallel surge of anxiety, both for his sake and my own, because this must mean my case was becoming more complicated. But I signed the form. Frankly there was not much choice. I balked, however, at having black fingers again.

'If you have my signature,' I asked, 'why should I also provide a fingerprint?'

He shoved the stamp pad towards me with his own thick index finger. 'It is necessary,' he said, without raising his head.

I placed my print on the page and quickly rose to my feet, because Judge Hedáyatí was about to walk out of the room. I was determined to talk to him. I rushed forward and stood in front of him, blocking his way with a raised black finger.

'Háj Áqá,' I said, trying to catch his eye, 'how long will my case go on for? You do know I'm being held here illegally?'

Judge Hedáyatí barely gave me a glance. 'Not much longer,' he replied casually.

Then he immediately changed the subject, as if to deflect any further demands on my part. His smile was smooth and his voice oozed with insincerity.

'By the way,' he said, 'your son's been here, did you know? He comes here very often. I have told him that the road from Tehran is dangerous; he shouldn't risk driving so many times a week. I've even invited him to come and live in the flat above our home; it's vacant, you know, and he can stay there until your case is sorted. In fact, he was in front of the entrance of the courthouse today. Didn't you see him when you arrived? He's probably still there now.'

My heart practically leapt out of my rib cage; it thumped so loudly that I was afraid even the secretary, sitting at his desk, would hear it.

'No, Háj Áqá, I didn't see him,' I said, forgetting all about my question and barely able to contain my excitement. 'May I ask you to please send a soldier to find him for me?'

He turned then and addressed someone behind me. 'Hey, you,' he said, with a grand gesture, 'run downstairs, will you, and tell her son to come up here!'

A short, small-boned man in a too large uniform hurried forward from the door with a sharp, military salute. 'Yes, Háj Áqá, of course, Háj Áqá,' he said, and then he turned and disappeared into the corridor.

Then I remembered the crowds amassed before the doors of the courthouse. Running a few paces after the soldier, I called out to him, urgently, giving him my son's name.

'Do you know who he is? Will you recognise him?' I cried.

The soldier vanished between the people in the crowded corridor, and I sat down, full of hope, thrilled with anticipation, longing to see dear Fúrúd's face and hear his sweet voice. But time passed and nothing happened. More time passed and, finally, after an age, when I understood that nothing would happen, I rose to my feet and entered the judge's office again. What he had done was very wrong, and I intended to tell him so.

'Háj Áqá,' I said gravely, 'I have fallen into a cycle of trickery that is illegal and unethical, and no one but you can stop it.'

And then I told him everything that was on my mind, and spelled out point by point exactly what had happened since my arrest, how wrong it was, how unjustified, and how inexcusable, how illegal. I was very upset. There was nobody else to tell, no one with more authority than the judge, and I guessed that I might never have this chance again.

He listened to me. Or appeared to. He did not interrupt or turn his back on me. But when I stopped speaking, he leaned forward and, to my great astonishment, turned off his mobile phone, lying face up on his desk. He had been recording everything I said! He would probably turn it over to the Intelligence Bureau now. It would show them that their techniques on me were working, prove that I was distraught, that I was struggling, and having a hard time. He probably did not care a fig for what I had just said, but it would doubtless put him in their good books.

I gave him a long reproachful look, which meant nothing to him and did little for me. My heart was aching. And then I turned away and sat in the corridor outside again, waiting listlessly for a soldier to take me downstairs. The judge left his room without saying another word to me. A few minutes later,

I had an idea. It was a delayed reaction, because my reflexes were slow from disappointment, perhaps, but I went straight back into the room and asked the secretary for a piece of paper. Then I sat down and wrote a statement with the same comments I had made to the judge, asking for my case to be attended to as soon as possible. If he was going to play tricks on me, then I wanted to leave a written record of it.

Another soldier finally came and marched me off. We went downstairs into the basement, just like the last time, and I waited in the depressing corridor just as before, along with a long line of other prisoners. The bad-tempered officer was having his breakfast again but this time he came out of the room with two boiled eggs in the palm of his hand. He glanced at me, then at the other prisoners standing around, and called two of them forward.

'Hey, you and you!' he said, as if summoning a couple of dogs to heel.

The two men came forward, and the officer placed a boiled egg in the hand of each.

'Go and eat!' he said grandly.

How proud he was of this silly show. How it belittled him in the eyes of all present.

* * *

By the time I returned to maximum security, the meal had already been served. The women were resting but had saved some food for me, an unusual gesture, because the ravenous crack addicts among them would have had a hard time letting any food go by. I generally ate little or nothing at all, and on this occasion could hardly swallow a mouthful. No one objected. They assumed I would not be staying for long, and everyone knew that the food in the detention centre was better anyway.

When the plates were cleared away, they were eager for me to tell them what I had seen and heard at the court. Although they really had no notion of my charges, they were all experienced in the ways of judges and full of advice about what I should do next. But I was too heartsick to speak much, after being lied to about my son. The pregnant woman who had come in the previous day was gone and I didn't even have the will to ask about her, to know whether she had gone into labour or not. But there, on her bunk was someone else's baby – a tiny two- or three-month-old infant, who lay fast asleep with a faint smile on his little purple lips and the distinct air of a pre-natal addict. The women told me the little one had been sleeping for some hours, and nothing seemed to wake him. His mother, who had replaced the thin pregnant girl, was at the guards' station, getting some methadone.

A few minutes later, a trim young woman came back into the cell. She sat on the floor, barely giving the baby a second glance, and began talking about herself. She showed us her arms, her sides and her belly, telling us in detail how she had undergone seventeen plastic surgeries to reduce her weight by over forty pounds. Then she described how she and her husband's friend, with whom she was in love, had robbed a store to furnish a flat where they could live together. They had set up quite a nice life, she said, and she had been planning to divorce her husband and marry his friend when they both got arrested. Such a shame.

When asked about the child, the mother spoke very well of him. An awfully good baby he is, she said. No trouble at all. Takes his little smoke three times a day and that's enough for him. She gave him drugs to keep him quiet, and he left her alone in return.

'He sleeps day and night,' she said happily.

'Whose baby is it?' asked Little Zahrá. 'Your husband's or his friend?'

'No idea,' the woman breezily replied.

Some of the women glanced round and saw my shocked reaction, and then everyone began to laugh. The mother laughed too, and the child continued smiling in his sleep. But I was not shocked for the reasons they supposed. It was not the actions of the mother but the fate of the child that exercised me, not the present abuse he was being subjected to, but the grim prospects for his future. Who would be responsible for this little boy or educate him as he grew up? What kind of parenting could he possibly hope for in the years to come?

The relationship of these women with their children was often tenuous and their concern for their upbringing frequently non-existent. I had gathered from listening to their talk that the education given to some children by their mothers had not extended beyond survival skills: their fathers taught them to steal, and their mothers showed them how to live on the streets. Often, with both parents in jail, they were left to the care of their grandmothers. And this pattern was being replicated generation after generation. The mother of one of my Zahrás was a peddler selling her wares near the metro station.

This innocent, blue-lipped baby would doubtless inherit poverty and distress too, once he was out in the world. In his case, the violence had already begun within these walls, and he would doubtless replicate it beyond them. The idea of such wasted lives, multiplied millions of times across the planet, lay heavy on me after the experience of my third court hearing that day. My spirits had sunk so low that I did not even offer to help the women who were spreading a blanket between the bunk beds and pinning a sheet for the baby to sleep on.

In fact, I was desperately tired and longed to lie down myself, but my path was blocked by the women, who had spread themselves all over the floor. Since it was impossible to step over them, I kept them company for about half an hour before inching my way round towards my bed. Arriving at the foot of the three-tiered bunk, I began hauling myself up to the top. But just as I let go of the bars of the second bunk and reached out for the third, some lack of co-ordination, some break between thought and action occurred, and I let go with both hands at once. Holding nothing but air, I suddenly fell backwards and blacked out.

The women said afterwards that I had been very lucky. Two of them were sitting nearby and reached out to grab me as I tumbled down. Although I slipped out of their grasp and hit my head on the ground, the impact was also softened by the baby's blanket. Despite this, I cannot remember falling. All I recall was the moment I let go of the bars with both hands. That brief glimpse of clutching at emptiness was vividly imprinted on my mind.

When I came to my senses, the women were repeating my name, and Maryam was shouting from behind the bars, calling for help, over and over again.

'Come quickly, she fell, she fell, the political one fell!'

I heard the clanging of locks and clattering of keys and then two or three of the female guards were hovering above my head, asking questions, to test the level of my alertness, I suppose. I was all right. I sat up slowly, checked my arms, my legs and back, with careful movements. Everything was fine, except for rapid palpitations. I dismissed these as unimportant, though I had never experienced anything like them before. The blood pumping in and out of my heart was practically visible in my throat.

Back in the detention centre the following day, the interrogator greeted me, as soon as he entered the room, with a broad smile and a query about the fall.

'I hear you were laid low yesterday,' he said. 'What happened? What caused it?'

I told him it was a momentary lack of hand and eye co-ordination, that was all. He then asked about any aftereffects, and the next day, the Intelligence Bureau Girl parroted the remark by saying that if I felt unwell, she would arrange a visit with the doctor. Her callous tone and dismissive manner were in such sharp contrast to the genuine care of the women in the public jail that I found it very easy to decline the offer. I preferred the kindness of my companions in maximum security to any medicine given by a prison doctor.

18

VIOLENCE

Although they were kind-hearted by instinct, the women in maximum security were often at the mercy of irrational whims and subject to incoherent fits of rage. They owned little but were strongly attached to their meagre belongings and kept them close beside their beds, because they did not trust each other. They once quarrelled furiously over the shampoo that I had managed to bring out of the detention centre for them. When one accused another of stealing her sachet, all hell broke loose. They were ready to fight over the slightest thing.

Food frequently led to conflicts and even culminated in violence at times. Whenever they became angry, they lost all control, even in front of me. They simply could not help it. One night there was *aash-e-reshteh* for dinner, a kind of noodle and vegetable soup. Each person was given a plastic cupful of the soup together with a tablespoon of *kashk* or sour yogurt. Fatimih, Maryam's 'wife,' liked being in charge of serving; she made a hole in the corner of the small plastic bag containing the sour yogurt, and squeezed out a tablespoonful for each of us, to pour onto our soup. As was the custom, she was expected to give the almost empty plastic bag, together with the final portion it contained, to the last person.

That night, Naneh, the young addict, wanted to have the plastic bag, but Fatimih had other ideas and refused to serve her last. Naneh was so infuriated that she threw her soup into

Fatimih's face, and so the fight began. I was up on my bunk bed when it happened; I had never seen or heard such a quarrel in all my life. Frankly, I was not even aware of how and when it started, but before I knew it, they were all beating each other up in the most savage manner. Everyone was at it, without exception. It was as if a five-headed giant of fury had reared its ugly head in that cell and was ready to rip the whole world apart.

They were screaming at each other, yelling at the tops of their lungs. It amazed me that Naneh could bellow so loudly and utter such astonishing vulgarities. She was at the mercy of towering rages. This frail little person who weighed no more than ninety-five pounds and moaned endlessly about her aches and pains could overturn a triple bunk bed in the blink of an eye. Trapped above them on the third level, I could have toppled over and been crushed under the weight of the metal had Naneh decided to give the beds a powerful push. There was no way to escape. So I grabbed hold of the bars on the sides and clung on for dear life as the metal structure shook and shuddered beneath me. And I kept my mouth shut tight while my dear cellmates howled and shrieked like harpies.

The quarrel over the plastic bag of sour yogurt was just one of many bitter fights that took place in those confined quarters, but violence was pervasive among my friends, and probably inevitable in such a confined space. They came from violent homes and had grown up in violent families; they lived with violent men and participated in violent crimes. Several were married to members of armed gangs and had participated in violent robberies. They were accustomed to taking terrible risks. A few were even killers.

* * *

One of the women, who joined us in our cell during my last weeks there, came from Shíraván. She had fair skin and light-coloured eyes and was called Ummu'l-Banín. Like me, she was at the interrogation stage of custody. But she had committed murder.

When we met, she was still in shock, perhaps, or in denial of what had happened. Her laughter was piercing and alarming. She blushed to the roots of her hair whenever she addressed anyone and although her prominent pink lips opened in a smile, her eyes had no spark of life in them. She may have thought she was laughing and may have even been trying to laugh, but to my mind it was just a nervous reflex. She wanted to present herself as normal, to accept the conditions in prison as natural, but it was a defensive reaction against horror.

'What have you done?' she asked me, somewhat reluctantly, one day.

'She taught at a university,' Maryam interjected.

Ummu'l-Banín wavered for a moment and then decided to trust me with what was really on her mind. 'What do you think will happen?' she murmured.

'About what?'

'Me?' The rising inflexion of uncertainty in reference to herself was revealing.

'Why, what have you done?' I asked.

It was clear from the way she hesitated that she did not want the others to hear her.

'Are you married?' I asked her quietly.

'Yes,' she said, 'and I have two children.'

And then, after another pause, Ummu'l-Banín began to tell me her story. When she was still a child, her father had arranged for her marriage. She and her husband loved each other and

were blessed with a daughter. Her husband was in the scaffolding business, like her father, and had big dreams, high ambi-
tions, so he took the family to Tehran. They were alone there,
far from family, but happy, until she became pregnant again.

'When I was eight months pregnant with Mustafa,' she
murmured, 'my misfortunes began. God knows how I
suffered.'

Her husband fell off some scaffolding and died on the spot.
She had to pack up her life and come back to her father's home
in Mashhad. When the child was born, her in-laws, who lived
in Shíraván, came and took both children away from her. Even
the newborn.

'See here,' she whispered to me, 'my breasts are still full of
milk!'

They claimed that according to the laws of the land as well as
of religion, they were now the custodians of their son's children.
She had no rights. Despite her pleading, they refused to listen to
her. They said she was no longer related to them; they wanted
nothing more to do with her and sent her back to her father.
And he said there was only one recourse left for a beautiful,
young widow: his daughter had to get married again, and fast.

'I was still in mourning for the death of my husband,' she
said, 'when he gave me to one of his friends. I was still grieving
the separation from my children, still full of breast milk, but
he insisted this would be to his benefit and mine.'

Her father's friend was a much older man and turned out to
be an addict; the new groom's children, from a previous marriage, were even older than the bride herself. She would not
allow him to touch her and tried to run away to Tehran. But
she was caught and brought back; her husband made her
swear, at the Shrine of Imam Rezá, not to leave again.

'I had to give my word,' she said quietly. 'Even my mother forced me.'

Then one day, she could bear it no longer. She went to the pharmacy and bought two hundred sleeping pills, and when her husband came to her father's home to talk business that evening, she made the meal, ground the pills into two jugs of *doogh* yogurt, and left it for the men to drink. She hoped they would fall into such a sound sleep that she could run away after the morning call to prayer and join her mother in Shíraván.

But when she woke up early the next day, she noticed with horror that her little sister was dead, and white foam was spilling out of her brother's mouth. They must have both drunk from the bottom of the jug where the sediment of sleeping pills had accumulated.

'I touched my brother,' she whispered. 'He was ice cold!'

Ummu'l-Banín was petrified. All she could think of was that no one should know how this horror had happened. So she brought a barrel of petrol, emptied it on the carpets, and set the house on fire. The whole building went up in flames.

'All burnt to ashes,' she said, her eyes wide. 'My nineteen-year-old brother, my thirteen-year-old sister, and my father – turned to smoke. But that man stayed alive!'

Her family members had evidently served their guest from the jug first, as hospitality dictated, and since he had not fallen into such a deep stupor, he had escaped the fire. The police thought he had burnt the house down to take revenge on her father over some financial dealings, so they hung him up by his wrists and tortured him. But Ummu'l-Banín was tortured too, by remorse. Eventually, she told one of her uncles what she had done and then went and confessed everything to the police. She was instantly arrested.

'Now, my mother has sent word,' she said, 'that she's going to pay the bail. But seven uncles on my father's side, whom I've never seen in my life, want blood money.'

By now, the other women in the room had gathered round and were listening to her story. They understood her plight; she was at the mercy of her paternal uncles, who wanted her to 'pay' for the deaths of her father and brother. Her mother had even made matters worse by consenting to bail so when she left the prison she could not escape from her husband. Everyone showered her with sympathy. They all felt sorry for the young woman.

Over the course of the next few days, Ummu'l-Banín was taken to the prison health centre so that psychiatric specialists could decide whether she was sane when she committed the crime, or psychologically unstable. The two Zahrás were of the opinion that she was perfectly sane and had acted in ignorance. The others believed that she was out of her mind and obviously 'mental', as they put it. But when the day came for her hearing, Ummu'l-Banín gave them all something else to think about. She put on a bright red robe and make-up and went to the court exuding self-confidence, dressed in her best.

The minute she left, the women started to buzz like bees and gossip about her. Of course, she would be forced into the same smelly grey court uniform, like everyone else, but the fact that she had chosen to step out of the cell wearing red meant something worse than insanity to them. It meant that she had killed in cold blood. According to my cell mates, her crime was not just murder and arson but the colour of her lipstick and her clothes. To my astonishment, they saw her dress as evidence that Ummu'l-Banín did not feel any remorse.

As if to prove them right, Ummu'l-Banín came back from court laughing that day. She laughed as she described what had happened. She laughed as she spoke of her mother's grief. But that same night the poor woman crept up to my bunk and sat there, weeping bitterly. She was haunted by memories of her sister and brother, heart-broken over their deaths in the prime of their youth. And her father, she sobbed, had always been loving towards them; he had only married her off because he was worried about what people would say.

'Better to kill me than give me bail,' she whispered. 'My life is a disgrace.'

* * *

Around noon the next day a social worker came to the public ward to visit us wearing a full hijab. She was tall and angular, around forty years old, with strained features unrelieved by make-up. She summoned the women to sit round her on the floor and began speaking to them on religious and spiritual matters, exhorting them to patience, urging them to tolerance and advising them to improve their conduct. I came down from my bed and joined the listening group. She had a mild manner but a leaden voice; I had the feeling that she was speaking by rote. She must have repeated this sermon many times.

The women sat quietly in a circle, listening with great respect. When she finished, there was an expectant pause. I suppose she hoped for questions.

'Would you please ask them to give us a television?' one said. 'We get bored.'

It was hard not to smile; the remark was not exactly on topic.

'Don't you go to watch the films?' asked the woman, in surprise.

And that was the first time I learned that the prisoners in the public prison were allowed to watch films on certain days, in a certain room. But the choice of what films were available for detainee consumption clearly did not appeal to my cellmates; they preferred television and repeated their request. They also asked for the skylight to be opened to let the air circulate a little more in the room, or to at least have a ventilator, they said, for the toilet. The smell was unbearable, even after they cleaned it. They needed fresh air.

I am not sure how the social worker evaluated her meeting with them. Television and ventilation bore little relation to the exhortations she had mouthed. But I had an idea after she left and suggested that we put their requests in writing. Why not send a letter about these matters to Mrs Jenáhí, the head of the women's ward? Everyone was enthusiastic and Maryam asked the guards for pen and paper.

The response came within a surprisingly short time. The head of the women's ward arrived at maximum security herself the very next day, together with a few female guards. This was unprecedented, everyone said. Absolutely unprecedented!

Mrs Jenáhí was a woman of around forty-five with a sallow complexion. Like the social worker, she was also slim and tall and wore the mandatory black chador and complete hijab over her crisp uniform. She stepped inside our cell with a commanding air, clearly accustomed to wielding authority. I recognised her immediately, but she did not look at me.

As was routine when welcoming any official, we all scrambled to our feet as soon as she entered, and the conversation took place standing. After the customary greetings, I noticed my letter in her hands. I had withdrawn slightly outside the circle of women, but she ignored me and addressed herself exclusively to the others, her eyes fixed on the letter.

'I see that you now have a scribe,' she said. 'Who wrote this?'

The women mentioned my name and pointed towards me and only then did Mrs Jenáhí glance in my direction. She asked me to explain each point I had raised in the letter and responded by summarising the actions she had already taken with regard to these very issues. For example, she said, the women used to have a TV but during one of the fights, they had smashed it to pieces. She was also afraid that a ventilator could be another source of quarrels because some might want it on, others might be annoyed by its noise, and prefer to turn it off. And so on. With each example, she seemed to be waiting for me to guarantee that I would take responsibility for the consequences. I suppose she wanted to see if my words extended to deeds, if I was willing to take the blame if anything went wrong.

I answered each of her concerns as best as I could, apologising in advance for my limited knowledge. I explained that some of these issues were inevitable in such a confined environment, and that tension was bound to occur when people were under this kind of stress and pressure. She nodded, without committing herself to do anything. Then just as she was about to leave the room, she turned round and called me by name.

'Please come with me,' she said.

The other women, and even the guards, were taken by surprise. They did not know that I had met the head of the women's ward before and since she showed no sign of recognition, they were unaware that she might remember me. Once out of the cell, Mrs Jenáhí asked me to walk beside her, with the other guards trailing behind. Even I was surprised by that mark of respect. We walked down the corridors of maximum security to the sewing workshop, a large hall where some forty or fifty women were sewing in rows on machines. Mrs Jenáhí did not speak and I did not say a word either, but when we stepped into the hall, she stood at the threshold of the workshop and looked straight at me.

'I am sorry about this place,' she said quietly. 'Tell me, are you well?'

'Oh yes. Quite well. And thank you for rescuing me from the doghouse that night.'

She acknowledged my recognition, in a matter-of-fact way with another rapid nod of her head, and I had enough wit to respect her discretion and say no more.

'Where you are now is not so good,' she acknowledged, 'but at least it's better than the other place.'

'Definitely better!'

'If anything further is required, or if you need something in particular yourself, let me know. How do you evaluate the condition of that cell?'

'The ladies are patient,' I told her, 'with the exception of Naneh, who I think has really reached her limits. Something needs to be done for her. Also, a television will definitely contribute towards calm among the others.'

She repeated that the women had already broken one television, so she did not wish to give them another. I said no more, and she moved on. But just before entering the public section of the prison, she stopped again in the middle of the corridor.

'Be sure that this phase will not take too much longer,' she added quietly.

She then instructed her guards that whenever the supervising judge came to the prison, they should take me to him so that he could follow up on my case. After that she wished me a gentle goodbye and good health, and left.

When I returned to the cell, the women flocked around me, asking what had happened, what was going on, and what she wanted. They were thunderstruck to see Mrs Jenáhí treating a prisoner in the public jail with such respect. I was astonished too, quite honestly. It was interesting that such a woman with all her experience and authority would choose to talk to a Bahá'í prisoner, accused by the Intelligence Bureau of being a security threat, and to treat her with respect, even before her own staff.

After that incident and on Mrs Jenáhí's recommendation, I met with the supervising judge of the prison on two occasions. He offered me advice, which proved to be useless; he suggested I write letters, which led to nothing. But I suppose it was a way of leaving a paper trail, to show that I had tried to seek redress for my plight through all available legal channels. For that reason, if none other, such efforts might have had some value.

However, the visit of Mrs Jenáhí did lead to the desired transfer for Naneh, who was mercifully sent to another prison. I hoped it was the one she preferred for even the right to choose one's prison is a kind of freedom. It also marked the last time I was in Vakilabad myself, the last days and nights I spent with my dear companions in maximum security.

19

REACHING THE LIMITS

I had arrived in the qarantineh ward at the end of the winter season, when it was still cold, and was moved to maximum security at the start of spring. But as the days lengthened and the solitary confinement cell in the detention centre began to grow unbearably warm in early summer, I was also beginning to reach my limits, like Naneh.

As the days grew hotter, the interrogations became correspondingly intense. It was clear that the gentlemen of the Intelligence Bureau had emerged from an initial period of indecisiveness to be more focused on their goals. Although the charges against me still related to the corpse buried in 'Bahá'í dust' instead of 'Muslim earth', I knew that their real aim was to condemn me as secretary of the Yárán. Since I had resisted questions outside the purview of the burial charge, apart from broad principles of Bahá'í procedure, they now focused on a frontal attack. They wanted to criminalise all my duties and responsibilities, plans and programmes, and above all my communications conducted on behalf of the Yárán.

So the next time I found myself leaning on the armrest of that infernal chair in the detention centre, the good gentleman proceeded to give me what he called 'a serious thrashing.' After flinging the usual invectives at me, he began to hurl abuse at the Universal House of Justice. For perhaps the hundredth time, he asked me to enumerate the methods we used to communicate with the House of Justice 'situated in the city of Haifa of the fake Zionist regime.'

I replied that every Bahá'í, the world over, was free to contact the Universal House of Justice directly, whenever he or she wanted. Since we could not do this from Iran, the only way for individuals to communicate with the institution was through members of their families, through friends abroad, or anyone they knew living outside the country.

'But what about you people?' he shouted behind my ear. 'I'm not asking about individuals! How does your group communicate?'

With that he tore up the page on which I had written my answers and threw the pieces of paper at my head. Then he re-wrote the question and instructed me to answer it again.

'I have already answered this question several times,' I told him. 'Would you like me to re-write the same words for you all over again?'

He burst into more curses. 'Write!' he roared at me, in a voice that reverberated round the room. 'Write!' he repeated, as if the weight of the word could shatter my head.

He wanted me to write what he wanted me to write. In other words, lies, fabrications, distortions, anything to incriminate the Bahá'ís. But I wrote the truth. I gave him exactly the same answer I had submitted to him on previous occasions, stating that our methods of communication with the head of our Faith were precisely what I had already spelled out. Since we were not permitted to contact the institution directly, we did so through families, through friends, through anyone we knew living outside the country. We had no other practical way, no other means.

He usually referred to the Universal House of Justice scathingly as 'the justice house.' This time he let his language sink even lower and demanded, once again, using increasingly disparaging terms, that I provide information on 'All communications with the filthy centre of the sect situated in the city of Haifa of the fake Zionist regime.'

I was very tired. I had no idea what more he wanted of me or what else to tell him that might assuage his mounting fury. Since he had used the belittling and inaccurate term 'filthy centre of the sect', I wrote '*I do not understand what you mean*' and returned the piece of paper, holding it backwards from the side of my chair to where he was standing.

He was behind me all this time, prowling about, breathing heavily. He snatched the paper from my hand, read it and slammed it down hard on my head. Then he began to swear at the Universal House of Justice. A stream of vulgar expletives poured from his mouth.

As his voice rose and his obscenities multiplied, the composure I had been cultivating, rooted in my deepest beliefs, gradually gave way to indignation. This was going too far. Patience and forbearance were no longer appropriate in these circumstances. I remained immobile in the chair with my back to this fulminating man but was preparing myself to stand up at any moment. I had decided to leave the room, should he continue using this kind of offensive language towards the House of Justice.

'I am not going to answer any more questions,' I said coldly. 'Kindly return me to my cell!'

The interrogator swore at me again, using even more foul language, hurling even more filthy curses at me than before. And as his vituperations expanded to include the Universal

House of Justice, I stood up abruptly, slamming my hand down too on the armrest. In a voice that had never come out of my throat before, I roared back at him.

'I will not answer you anymore. You have no right to insult my faith. You have no right to speak to me like this. I will not accept it.'

He snarled something in response, but I could only hear my own voice. It was so loud. I had the feeling that this new voice of mine could be heard throughout the Intelligence Bureau. It was booming through the walls and echoing across the heart of town. I started to remove the knot of the blindfold from the back of my head.

'Let's finish with this game,' I cried, tugging at the cloth.

'Don't turn around!' he screamed. 'Sit down! I am telling you to sit down! Do you hear? I am telling you – do not turn around!'

'No, I will not sit down,' I roared back in my new voice. 'Take me to my cell.'

I sensed him panicking. Was it because of my threat to pull off the blindfold or because of my voice? He must have been wondering how it had ever come out of me. The last thing he wanted was to have such a voice of protest raised in that hushed setting, such loud dissent breaking the silence of the Bureau. But the worst for him, I think, was my insubordination. He was ordering me to turn round and sit back down, and I was refusing to do so. I had finally lost patience with him.

I stood silent and rigid for a few more moments. He stopped screaming. There was a soft tread of steps in the room. Someone else had come in and was standing next to him, steering him gently out of the line of fire. The interrogator uttered one last word.

'Sit!' he spluttered at me, half-choking.

Then he left the warzone, slamming the door behind him. I waited until I was sure no one else was in the room. Then I lowered myself gingerly down on the chair and huddled over for some time. A long period of silence ensued. Long enough for my heart to beat normally again. Long enough for my freezing hands and feet to warm up. After a while I stopped shivering. Whatever he may have wanted to do, he had not broken me.

Then, the old man entered.

'Come on,' he said kindly, 'let's go back.'

* * *

In my cell, I immediately went into the shower. Water. Warm water. I stood under the gushing water with my eyes closed for a long time. My thoughts were shattered. I was in a state of shock, traumatised by this war. It had started a long time ago, and the attacks and assaults had been going on like this, under kings and clergy, shahs and soldiers, secular and religious regimes, for well-nigh two centuries. It was an unfair and unequal war, unethical, unjustified and unpardonable. I was weary of it.

That night, for the first time, I wondered whether I would ever leave this trap alive. My mind and heart were heavy with exhaustion and loneliness. There seemed to be only one way all this would end, and it was clear whose bones would be strewn on the battlefield. And would that be such a terrible ending? For me, perhaps, but for the Bahá'í community?

The first thing you think of at such times is whether you can be steadfast and endure.

Mahvash, are you sure?

Given the possible outcome, I had never been so certain of anything in my life.

Mahvash, can you bear it, though? Can you really undergo these trials?

Such steadfastness would not come from me, I knew that. Perseverance to that degree would be a gift from my God. I could ask for it, and He would either grant it. Or not.

Mahvash, they might go too far. Unbearable tortures. Unbearable pain. Death.

And then I remembered the steps again, leading down to the Black Pit. I remembered the dazzling darkness, the black hair flowing down like a mighty torrent on those shoulders, and my eyes closed as I gazed on Bahá'u'lláh. His compassion. His patience. The strength of a hundred suns rose in my heart.

It will all be for the best.

That night, as I appraised the situation, I realised that no matter from which angle I viewed it, the outcome could only be for good. Whatever happened, this was a win-win situation. As long as I remained firm, as long as I stayed honest and true, one way or another, the principles of the Bahá'í Faith would prevail.

I did not sleep at all that night. I prayed, and thought, and thought, and prayed. And I felt light, very light, as though my blood had been drained out and replaced with some thinner substance. It was as if I were no longer really attached to this dusty world, as if mortal life had lost its meaning for me, and the one thing remaining was my steadfastness in the path that lay ahead, my firmness of faith in the face of the future. Nothing else mattered.

And as I tossed and turned, I tried to prepare myself for that future. Would there be another cross-examination tomorrow morning? If so, how would the interrogator behave towards me now, after the violent confrontation that we had just had? What was appropriate for me to say to him? Or do? Perhaps he would continue in the same vein until he crushed me completely. Perhaps I might just be transferred back to the public prison…

The following day, nothing happened. I had hoped they would not summon for me for a while, and my wish was granted. For a few days no one came and there was no change in the routine. The old man pushed the battered dog bowl silently through the slot at the bottom of the door. The Intelligence Bureau Girl made her chilly appearance each evening, after being away all day. She would announce her arrival and then depart without a word. They were evidently punishing me by cutting off all communication. But I did not care.

Then one day, the old man showed up suddenly, to take me back to the interrogator. 'Get ready, *bábá*,' he said. 'Time to go. Just follow behind as you always do.'

His voice was noticeably gentler, using an endearment as if to his own daughter. Perhaps he pitied me and felt sorry that the interrogations were starting all over again. Maybe he had been listening to all the abuse hurled at me, and had heard my replies.

But today the interrogator took a different approach. There were no further screams and shouts and curses. He was indulging himself, airing creepy insinuations. Like the judge.

'Your son keeps coming all this long distance to see you,' he said. 'It's dangerous, you know. The roads are not safe. Well, what can you expect, with a car?'

Another time he raised the subject of my son in relation to the length of my detention, which he implied could go on indefinitely.

'He has brought you some more clothes,' he told me. 'Some dried fruit, and money, too. He has brought enough food for five years!'

That evening, the young girl confirmed that new clothes had indeed been brought for me and asked whether I needed anything. And I was left alone to contemplate the mixture of truth and lies I had been told, to try to distinguish between them. So it continued, one day after another, the same routine, the same innuendos. But the interrogator never spoke of my insubordination again, never once mentioned our confrontation. And neither did I.

* * *

In the course of that seemingly endless and increasingly airless time, during the second half of Urdíbihisht in early May, the Intelligence Bureau Girl opened the door one morning in a joyful mood. Half-swinging herself into the cell, while holding on to the doorframe, she called out to me to hurry, to get ready. She was apparently in holiday spirits.

Something was different. As soon as I entered the interrogation room, I sensed it. This was no ordinary session. The conditions were not the same. And neither were the actors taking part in it. A man with a high falsetto voice greeted me. He had a lisp, I noticed, and could not pronounce the letter 'r'. His voice was more effeminate than the interrogator's.

'Miss Shahríyárí, is it?' he piped behind me. 'Or Mrs Sabet?'

I was sitting blindfolded as usual, facing the wall.

'I have read about your beliefs to some extent,' this unknown gentleman continued, 'and I would like us to talk about them a little.'

'Here? Under these conditions? What could there be to talk about?' I folded my arms, ready for confrontation.

'Oh no,' he interjected, hastily, sounding rather nervous. 'I don't mean a major discussion! I just wanted to raise a few points that seem a little problematic to me and ask your advice about them. After all, you are the leader of the Bahá'ís.'

'The Bahá'ís do not have leaders.'

'So what's the problem then, with our having a little chat?'

'I will not discuss any matters of belief, here, on this interrogation chair, blindfolded, facing a wall, and I will not answer any questions about my faith.'

The interrogator must have been present all this time, for he now interrupted. 'Mrs Sabet,' he said, in an oily tone. 'Relax. This is not an interrogation, do be comfortable.'

'I am not uncomfortable, but I see no point of this discussion.'

'Why not?' he retorted. 'Don't you believe in investigating the truth?'

I took a deep breath. 'Do you really think these are the appropriate conditions for investigating truth?'

'This gentleman is an expert on religious matters,' objected the interrogator.

Ah! so it was for this privileged moment that I should have been preparing my homework on the heavy tome of fake facts. It was for this meeting, this exchange with a so-called 'specialist' that I was supposed to feel grateful.

The voice of the lisping expert intervened once more. 'There are just a few questions that remain unresolved, Khánum,' he trilled. 'For example, you say that you accept the Qur'an, and yet you do not believe in the physical resurrection. How is that possible? Furthermore, there is the issue of the "Seal of the

Prophets": excuse my frankness, but how can you accept the Qur'an and disregard this explicit statement that there can be no religious revelations after Islam?'

'Gentlemen,' I replied, 'if you really care about these questions, there are better ways to find the answers than the method you have chosen.'

I knew that if I were to utter another word, I would be sucked into an absurd, hair-splitting debate, a futile exercise in angel-counting on the heads of pins they had set up beforehand. I also knew that I had a legal right to refuse to answer queries bearing no relationship to my indictment. Besides, it was abundantly clear they were not in the least bit interested in what I had to say, let alone concerned with investigating my opinion about resurrection or the relative and symbolic meanings of the term 'Seal of the Prophets.' They only wanted me to condemn myself as an apostate. At one point, as they insisted on probing me, I told them that their questions reminded me of the methods used by the Inquisition during the Middle Ages. They were not amused by the comparison. So I retreated further into silence and simply urged them to investigate other sources.

'You will definitely find replies to your questions elsewhere,' I repeated.

They persisted for almost an hour. But I remained firm. They even brought up examples of what they considered to be contradictions in the history of the Bahá'í Faith, arguing that our world-embracing beliefs were wholly inconsistent with the Qur'an. But since I refused to enter into a theological discussion, they had no alternative in the end but to leave. Just before slamming the door behind him, the interrogator sent me a parting shot.

'You've chosen not to collaborate, so whatever you suffer from now on is on you!'

As had become customary, I was left in the room after they were gone, sitting alone in the interrogation chair for another hour. No one returned to question me. No one came to take me back to my cell. And I was tired out, weary of the debris they were dumping on me day after day, the rubbish they were unloading from their landfill hour after hour, the muck they were throwing at me. I just wanted to sleep, to die, to do anything to be free of them. I wanted to shout in my huge hidden voice and be heard all over town:

What do you want from me? Why are you torturing me? Why don't you leave me alone?

But I held my peace as the light gradually faded and the day dimmed.

The old man was finally allowed to come for me. He returned me to my cell for the night and immediately poured me some tea from the big kettle he had on the wheel-tray. Then he brought me dinner in the dog bowl, which I could barely swallow.

20

THE END OF A CHAPTER

After I was left alone, I turned on the short-wave radio which had recently been placed in the grey detention centre cell. I had found it there the last time I had returned from Vakilabad. If it had not been put there by the kind old man, or abandoned by a previous detainee, then it may have been provided as a random gesture of humanity by the generous gentlemen of the Bureau, because it served so little purpose. The radio was small and red and round with only one bandwidth, and it bombarded me with music. I cannot remember when, if ever, I had intentionally listened to a radio. But during those depressing days and suffocating nights of Urdíbihisht (mid-May), in my solitary cell after the intense fatigues of interrogation, I would turn on this radio as a way of washing my brain.

A *Khurásání* song was being broadcast that evening.

Concentrate on the music. Don't think. Walk fast. Walk faster, still faster. Soak your head in the music.

But even with the music on, even while pacing back and forth, my mind was still busy. It moved faster than my legs. Before long, despite the Khurásání song, I was examining, dissecting, evaluating everything that had been said during the interrogation. Yes, I was hopelessly tenacious. A tough case even for these gentlemen. They had probably not reckoned on my being so obstinate. Too stubborn, too headstrong; what had I been called?

A dumb piece of wood.

Despite that, they allowed the 'dumb piece of wood' one more visit with her son and I was able to see my sweet Fúrúd again during that month. But just as on the first occasion, this so-called visit was brutally short, hopelessly brief, a glimpse through the car window, which was lowered a mere twenty centimetres. I cannot remember if the same three men were with me in the back seat. But I was wedged in the middle again, removed as far from the window as possible. Fúrúd and I barely exchanged a word, but I noticed that my cousin was standing beside him this time. When he took two or three steps forward and nodded a greeting to me, I was seized with anxiety. Permission had only been granted for me to see my son; how had he risked coming too? When we had to part, I noticed that Fúrúd's chin was trembling. He tried to control himself but knowing how sensitive he was, my heart filled with anguish. I was more grieved for him than I could bear. To see his unhappiness drained me even more than the interrogations.

After Urdíbihisht 25 (from mid-May onwards), I was relieved of their pressure for a few days because it appeared that the interrogator was out of town. He had gone away for at least two weeks, the old man told me. He had gone to Tehran.

'That's where you live, isn't it? Perhaps you'll see him there!' he added.

I supposed it was a joke – this unlikely prospect of meeting the interrogator out walking in the streets of Tehran when I returned home someday. I tried to laugh, to show that I appreciated his attempt to cheer me up. But it was no joking matter when the interrogator returned at the beginning of Khurdád (the end of May). I immediately sensed a difference in his attitude. He seemed particularly upset with me, and in a strange new way. He was so harsh in his demeanour, so rude and so aggressive that the hatred he had always expressed towards my beliefs felt intensely personal now. Had he lost some chance of promotion because of me? Had I caused him some kind of humiliation? It was as if he had learned something important in Tehran that gave him even more reason than before to be angry with me. Whatever the source of his frustrations, I certainly experienced the consequences.

He would lean over me from behind and suddenly bellow into my ear. He would threaten me, bully me, do everything possible – physically and psychologically – to intimidate me. I was assaulted by his breath as well as his curses. The gusts from his mouth were rancid, his words stinging. He kicked at my chair, slapped the baton of paper at my head. His fury beat down on me in tidal waves. What had happened to prompt this tempest? What had caused this new wrath? I did not dare show any reaction lest it enrage him further. But the more he yelled, the more he kicked my chair and blasted me with curses, the calmer I became, the more restrained. And the more curious.

The kinds of questions he was levelling at me now clearly indicated a change too. He no longer toyed with innuendos, as in the past; this was no carrot and stick game, no forced display of bad temper to frighten me. It was a rage arising from nervous tension in himself, the result of accumulated frustration over something which had happened in Tehran.

He dredged up many of the questions that he had already asked, which I assumed had been dealt with and set aside – Where did you go on such and such an occasion? Why did you go? Who went with you? Who did you see? What means of communication did you use while away and how many methods were available to you on your trip? And he liked me to know he already knew the answers, which seemed an even greater exercise in futility.

'So, you went on a trip to meet with members of your "justice house", did you?' he would snarl. 'Yes! Tavakkolí, Rezai and Tizfahm were with you, too, weren't they?'

But there were also new questions he had not asked before – How many people did you contact regarding the 'general amnesty' offered by the 'centre of the sect' to those who became Muslims and now wanted to return to 'apostasy'? Who collaborated with you in offering this 'amnesty' and where? Which embassies were you in touch with? What organisations paid you? Who cooperates with you in the government?

It went on and on. He did not give up easily.

I was feeling unwell. I had no wish to answer him. No, I really could not respond to such nonsense. What embassies? Which organisations? Who did he imagine paid or bothered to cooperate with us? It was all irrelevant and I was not afraid of telling him so. Several times a day, I reminded myself that the work of the Yárán-i-Iran had nothing to do with my present charges. Whenever questions were raised about the burial of a corpse in the Bahá'í cemetery, I willingly answered. Whatever distortions he brought up about general Bahá'í practices, I also readily corrected and clarified. But the work of the Yárán was another matter.

However, in order to avoid misrepresenting our activities, I went to great lengths, during the written interrogations in particular, to explain the broad principles governing the Bahá'í consultative process, for instance, or the spirit of Bahá'í elections and administration, or the objectives of unity that characterised the Bahá'í Faith. I did so with the faint, perhaps naïve hope that maybe, one day, some fair-minded reader might come across these scribblings and find them useful – not to shred and rip apart and use to torture another poor Bahá'í, but to ponder, to consider perhaps, whether such principles might be relevant and such methods could facilitate the well-being and social development of Iran.

I knew the interrogator would not read my explanations in that spirit. He was still expecting me to read the book he had given me some time ago, entitled *A Comprehensive History of Bahaism* [*Táríkh-i-Jámi'-i-Bahá'íyyat*]. Despite my refusal to debate its contents with the theological 'expert', he kept insisting that I discuss it with him.

'If you people believe in investigating the truth, then read this,' he repeated ad nauseam. 'It is a university textbook, and I want to ask you a few questions about it.'

I did not respond when he mentioned the book. I had never promised to read it and quite frankly, I found the drivel on the little red radio more enlightening. I had tried using the tome as an exercise in speed-reading for a while, but had grown tired of the tautological arguments, the strained fabrications. The book was an anthology of sorts, a compilation written by different contributors. Every chapter added more lies to the truth, more fiction to the few facts, and mixed more conjecture with reality. As a result, this supposedly unbiased text deteriorated, page after page, from exaggeration to distortion to gross misrepresentation until it finally crashed to a conclusion of vulgar insult and bare-faced slander.

The only reason I was glad to have it on hand was because it contained, here and there, quotations from the Bahá'í Writings. Whenever I came across these passages, I slowed down and read them like a thirsty creature, like someone starved. I was hungry for truth, eager to savour more than I had memorised, and grateful to meditate on these few words.

During each session, the interrogator would ask if I had finished reading the book, and my response was always negative. At that, he would once again harp on the principle of 'independent investigation of truth', saying that if I really believed in it, I should discuss the book with him. And I would answer that the book was inaccurate; it misrepresented the facts and distorted the truth. Beyond that, I refused to engage in any further discussion.

By now, the interrogations had literally become a form of torture. They seemed to go on forever. Even after a full day of cross-examination, the interrogator would give me several so-called Single Sheets to be filled at night. Like homework. He even joked about it.

'So you won't get bored in the cell,' he would say sarcastically.

These Single Sheets were yet more forms I was supposed to fill in, with personal details about other people in the Bahá'í community. A name was provided, and I was required to add further information. Many of the forms were not named at all and I was told to identify the Khádimín one by one and comment on them. I would name people the government already knew, state what was commonly known about them, and merely add neutral details. But the interrogator was rarely happy with the results. After filling in these wretched Single Sheets all night, I was harangued about them all the following day.

After reading one, he would pound into the room in a furious temper, shouting, 'What's all this rubbish? You're playing with fire, you know! Do it again! Write fifty names! You started this game, so don't complain when it gets serious! Fifty names or else watch out for the fireworks!'

It was beginning to really get me down.

* * *

The cell was airless and I could not breathe. One day I insisted that they change my room, give me a different book to read, anything. I was told with cool indifference by the Intelligence Bureau Girl that 'something would be done.' It was not. Eventually, after repeated requests, she showed up with a pamphlet containing stories in simplified language about the life of the Prophet Muhammad. It was intended for children, but considering my emotional state at that time, it was ideal reading material. I even read a couple of passages aloud for the Intelligence Bureau Girl. The young woman listened to me with respect. It was the first time she overstepped her boundaries and stayed with me longer than usual.

So I took the unprecedented risk of airing my grievances to her. I said that I had been kept in that place since early spring, with no recourse to bail, no news from my family and no air. It was getting warmer, and I had developed respiratory problems that prevented me from sleeping. The truth was, I was not feeling well at all. I had lost a lot of weight, had no appetite and was suffering from severe insomnia. The lack of light, the lack of fresh air and exercise, the prolonged solitude and rigid confinement, to say nothing of nearly three months of relentless, ruthless, rigorous interrogation, was having an effect on my health.

The Intelligence Bureau Girl must have reported all that I had told her. Despite it being the weekend, I was brought in for another interrogation the following day and told that the doctor had come to see me. The person they called a doctor, whoever she was, attended to me while I was still blindfolded. I told her that I had trouble breathing. She asked some unrelated questions, made some random remarks and prescribed some irrelevant medication that I never took.

The breathing became worse. One afternoon it was so severe that I literally collapsed. There was no open window in the room and no ventilation. No matter how often I called for the Intelligence Bureau Girl, she did not respond. So I called out for the old man:

'Háj Áqa, Háj Áqa!'

I had fallen on the ground behind the door, gasping for air from the small opening used for food, when the old man finally arrived. He helped me up and took me out to breathe. The 'fresh air outing' in the detention centre amounted to walking around a small, enclosed yard, reeking with odours from the stinking well in the middle of it. But, on the whole, I felt better for being out of doors. The old man took me back to the cell a few minutes later.

The next evening, the Intelligence Bureau Girl announced, with a restrained hint of empathy, that she would take me to a different room.

'It's not much better, but it's bigger,' she qualified, with uncharacteristic candour.

I gathered up the plastic bag containing my clothes and the single-wave radio to launder my brain and followed her, blindfolded, to another cell. It was true. The new cell was bigger, but it was also darker and dirtier, and so not much better than the old one. I had cleaned my original cell several times by then and was accustomed to its miseries. So, I spent that night in the new cell marshalling all my arguments to be taken back to the old one. But the Intelligence Bureau Girl pre-empted me. She conducted me back, unasked, the following morning, saying that perhaps I would be more 'comfortable' where I had been before.

Then, just before leaving, she turned round at the doorway with that familiar look of complacency on her face and graced me with a smirk.

'And maybe you won't be around here much longer any-way,' she simpered.

* * *

On the sixth of Khurdád (27/28 May), the Intelligence Bureau Girl opened the door of my cell with a genuine smile. She seemed as pleased with what was about to happen as she assumed I would or should be. As I followed her out, blind-folded again, I guessed this good mood must signal bad news for me.

'Where are we going?' I asked, with some apprehension.

'You will see!' she replied smugly.

I could tell she was enjoying herself from the tone of her voice. But I could also see, despite the blindfold, that she was not taking me to the usual interrogation room. The corridors were different, the corners unfamiliar. No *attar* of roses. No stuffy passageways. Something else was going on. And I dreaded what it might be.

On removing the blindfold, I discovered myself in a small room, standing before a young man who was seated behind a narrow desk. He was deliberately not looking at me.

'You're being transferred to Tehran,' he stated, with averted eyes. 'There were 130 thousand *tumans* in your handbag and we used the money for your airfare. The rest is here. Your belongings are also all here. Please wait. They will come to get you shortly.'

I was stunned. Flying home? All my weakness and fatigue vanished in a rush of joy.

'Where am I going? Where will they send me?' I asked the girl, on our way back.

'Somewhere I think you'll like,' she said. 'Evin!'

My heart skipped a beat. Evin? The dreaded prison? The place people go never to return? But I already guessed that I might go there, because Faribá and Mr Tavakkolí, who had been arrested in Mashhad some years ago, had also been transferred to Evin before their release. This might be a step towards freedom! And it was close to where we lived; I would no longer be so far from home, and my family would feel more relaxed to have me near. But most importantly, I was escaping the snare of the Mashhad Intelligence Bureau. I was more than happy about that, even if the alternative was Evin.

It is good to be ignorant but hopeful. It is best not to know the future and to struggle and rejoice in the present instead. I was glad to have my old belongings restored, but how strangely impersonal they looked when the Intelligence Bureau Girl gave them to me. My small travelling bag, my handbag depleted of money and the neighbour's black chador which no longer belonged to me. As for the dried fruits and dates my dear son had sent, I discovered there really was enough to feed an army for five years. How I wished I could have taken the food to the public prison. How sorry I was not to share it with all those hungry women and famished girls in maximum security, to whom I would now, sadly, never say goodbye.

They sent me back to my room where I cleaned the bath-room, swept the floor and folded all the blankets while I was waiting. To my surprise, the Intelligence Bureau Girl seemed sincerely happy about my departure. Maybe she was as weary of the detention centre as I was and looked forward to being freed from her duties. Maybe the job had been less of a promo-tion than she had hoped or maybe she had succeeded so well that she would now go on to bigger and better positions and guard other prisoners more worthy of her robotic arts. I said goodbye to her with genuine goodwill and wished her well in her future career.

* * *

On 31 May 2008, eighty-two days after my arrival in that city, I was taken to the Mashhad airport accompanied by two agents from the Intelligence Bureau. One of them was the man in the mustard-coloured jacket with four pockets, and the minute I saw him, I remembered I had dreamt of him the previous night. How strange – I had had no expectation of meeting him. We waited for the arrival of a female airline employee to con-duct a mandatory body search. Perhaps she thought she was in a dream, too, because she was very surprised to have to under-take the task. She only pretended to do it, complaining all the time about the absurdity of performing a body search on some-one who'd just spent three months in custody with access to nothing more dangerous than the lid of a yogurt container.

'What kind of silliness is this?' she grumbled.

By the time we passed through the special exit and arrived on the tarmac, the plane was ready for take-off. We were the last three passengers to board. I was still in a dream as I climbed the steps and sat in the front row. And when the plane shuddered and lifted off, I found myself remembering Siyávash's words when we parted, all those months ago.

What if you go and don't come back?

Well, I'm coming back now, I told him in my heart. Here I am, flying home, riding high, coming back to you. Only there was no access to the window. No glimpse of the sky, no clouds of freedom. I was flanked on each side, as in the prison car, between the two men appointed by the Mashhad Bureau of the Ministry of Intelligence, who were effectively my guards. One of them did not say a word to me the whole flight. But the man in my dream wearing the mustard-coloured jacket, was very courteous, very kind. He spoke to me with great respect. He even smiled as we conversed, as if I was a normal human being.

So I told him of my dream. 'You were wearing that same jacket you have on now.'

He looked startled. How strange, he kept repeating, how very strange!

It was indeed strange to arrive in Tehran again, after all this time. My two guards carried my belongings for me, as if I were a celebrity instead of a prisoner, and it was stranger still, and almost as good as being a VIP, when we reached the arrival hall, to find two other agents waiting to take charge of me and my baggage. They were handed a couple of envelopes by the Mashhad agents and after conferring together quietly, shook hands and parted. That was when my man with the mustard-coloured jacket came forward.

'Goodbye, Mahvash Khánum,' he murmured. 'God be with you.'

Even courtesy can be an act of courage. It was the last I ever saw of him.

21

HOPE

Emerging from the airport terminal was like being born all over again. The real world, the outside world! I gaped at the sea of cars, so many! But my 'escort' was clearly in a hurry now; one man handed me my belongings and the other raced ahead towards the car park. They both kept glancing back at me, because I lagged so far behind them, but there was no suggestion of helping me this time, no offer to carry anything.

The period of Mashhad had come to an end, and I was in Tehran at last. The land of Tá as the poets called it, the city of my heart, my hometown, the birthplace of my children, the cradle of my youth. Tehran, for me, is where the roads of real life converge with the roads of memory; it is the place of proximity and separation, of everyday reality and constant nostalgia. The weight of alienation I had been harbouring all this time lifted the minute I started walking through the rows of cars parked in Tehran airport. It was suddenly familiar, ordinary. Had three whole months really passed since I'd been dropped off here to catch the plane to Mashhad? It seemed like yesterday, when I looked at all these rows of cars. Had I really been held hostage all that time – in the qarantineh, in maximum security, in a kennel? Or had that all just been a bad dream? Unless it was a blessed one? I felt one step away from freedom. I even thought that these men might not be driving me to Evin Prison at all. I was half-waiting for them to stop somewhere along the way, turn to me and say: 'Okay lady, you're free now! Off you go!'

We came to a white sedan and one of the two men, who turned out to be the driver, opened the trunk for my bags. He was the younger member of my escort, rather nattily dressed, and spoke to me cordially. The second man, shorter in stature and taciturn, was wearing a dirty, nondescript shirt hanging out over his trousers. That did not bode well. He sat next to me in the back seat with a notebook on his knee, and did not look at me or say a single word all the way. I hardly noticed when he took out a pen and started scribbling.

Then all of a sudden, just as the engine was switched on, a third man appeared out of nowhere and took the front seat beside the driver. I do not know where he came from – perhaps he had been waiting for us among the myriad cars. He ignored me completely but the driver was courteous and curious and started chatting right from the start. He was full of questions, as if he knew nothing about me, and asked who I was, whether I was from Mashhad, why I was in Mashhad, why I had been arrested, how long ago I had been arrested, and what was going to happen to me now. Did I know?

I did not, but oh how happy I was to talk to him! How joyfully, freely, foolishly, I answered all his questions. I could see my face in his rearview mirror as I talked. I was so animated, so high-spirited, so giddy with hope that there wasn't a trace of strain on my features, not a hint of the distress I had endured over the past three months.

The driver must have noticed my light-headed exuberance. He held my gaze in the mirror for a moment, as if he was trying to steady me, recall me to my senses.

'Have you actually been freed, Mrs Sabet?' he asked quizzically.

He knew and I knew very well that I had not. But it was enough for me just to have arrived in blessed Tehran. I was over the moon to be home again and was feeling illogically free. I told him that I was, as yet, still in custody and had not, as yet, been released, and so no, I was not, as yet, technically free. He could not restrain his incredulity.

'Why are you so happy then?' he blurted.

Good question. It made me ask myself whether this joy was only related to my coming home, or whether the whole notion of 'home' was not something larger and more all-embracing than the city called Tehran. It made me wonder whether being in custody was necessarily dependent on actual captivity or whether there was some other source of inner independence, a deeper well of liberty that quenched the thirst for freedom. To be honest, I felt perfectly free sitting with those three men in the white sedan. So all the way along that busy road from the airport to the Revolutionary Court I babbled on about the Bahá'í Faith.

I don't know what came over me. It was not something I usually did. In fact Bahá'ís have learned to be extremely circumspect in Iran when it comes to their faith. It is hard to be a member of a religious minority that has been systematically persecuted for almost two centuries and not feel somewhat prudent about sharing one's beliefs, even when asked. Apart from the horror of sounding 'evangelical,' I often avoided the most commonplace enquiries lest a mere answer could be interpreted as an effort to 'convert'.

But here was this driver asking me questions about the Bahá'í Faith and how it differed from Islam. And there I was, without a care in the world, beaming at him from the back seat, with my tongue cheerfully tripping over itself and my voice dancing, telling him about the unity of mankind, the equality of men and women, the harmony between science and religion and how all faiths reflected the same essential, spiritual truths.

'It's the changeless Faith of God,' I sang, 'eternal in the past, eternal in the future. We worship the same God as you, the Lord of all religions.'

That was when I noticed that the man sitting next to me was scribbling frantically. But instead of feeling any trepidation or having any qualms, I found it almost funny. Was the poor fellow really trying to jot down every word I uttered? It couldn't be easy for him, given the rapidity of my speech and the quantity of information I was busy communicating. So from time to time, as a joke, I looked away from the driver and turned to my backseat companion with a light-hearted smile, and spoke very slowly, as if dictating for his benefit, to make sure he wouldn't miss a single word. I even found myself pitying the man. How much was he being paid to do this? Would he lose his job if he didn't fill the notebook before the drive ended? Of course nothing I was saying was particularly new, and if the gentlemen of the Ministry of Intelligence hoped to catch me saying something useful to their investigations, they would probably not depend on this medieval technique. But I did not care. I was on top of the world. Poetry poured out of my heart and mouth.

* * *

They took me to the Revolutionary Court on Mo'allem Street, and as soon as we got out of the car, all three men started walking at high speed towards the building. I had to run to keep up with them. It was well past 2 p.m. Office hours were over, and I was late again. It was only at this moment that I fully grasped reality: I had been given an appointment at the Revolutionary Court for a decision regarding my so-called 'temporary detention.'

When we reached the relevant section of the court, I saw an elderly judge wearing a long blue-grey robe standing by one of the doors. It was a moment of *déjà vu*. Like the judge in Mashhad, he was not pleased to have been kept waiting for so long.

'I was about to leave,' he said severely. 'What took you so long?'

He seated himself solemnly behind his desk, poker-faced and aloof, and left me standing throughout the proceedings. I do not know whether he was doing this to impress upon me the seriousness of the charges, or indicate their 'temporary' nature. Since the secretary was occupied elsewhere, I was alone with him, as he marched me through the usual questions.

'Name? Surname? Date of birth? Place of birth? Present address?'

He then asked me to confirm if I was a member of the committee of seven Bahá'ís, known as the 'Yárán-i-Iran.' He laid particular stress on my role in that group.

'Ah, so you are the Secretary of the Yárán, are you? Does that mean all communications with the Bahá'ís pass through you?' He insisted on knowing whether I was primarily responsible for communicating with the Universal House of Justice and if and when and how such correspondence took place. 'So you are the one who has been keeping in touch with the Bahá'í Centre in Haifa in the fake Zionist state?'

Then I knew. Then it was out and in plain sight. His questions made it clear that the charges against me had changed.

There was no reference to the dead man anymore. There was no mention of the 'unauthorised' burial in a plot for 'apostates.' The corpse could be laid to rest, at last, because the focus now was squarely on the work of the Yárán, on my specific role in it, and our communications with the Bahá'í World Centre in particular – everything I had been interrogated about so relentlessly these past weeks. In Mashhad, I had always responded with general answers – but there was no reason to do so any more. I was effectively being arraigned on these very charges.

Standing at the desk before the judge, I replied to everything in the affirmative and in writing. Yes, I was the secretary of the Yárán. Yes, I was responsible for communicating with the Universal House of Justice. And since he wished to know about our means and methods, yes, I was happy to tell him those too. I filled the form in its entirety.

Another reason why I felt free to do this, apart from the blessed absence of the dead man, was because I believed such information was fully known to the Ministry of Intelligence already. I had been told that they had questioned Mr Khánjání and Mr Tafakkolí in Mashhad, and I guessed they may have also questioned other members of the Yárán in Tehran. Indeed, during my last days in the detention centre, I had heard something on the radio which made me suspect as much.

I had been washing my mind one day with the usual drivel pouring out of the little red radio when suddenly the music programme was interrupted by a news report on the American broadcast service called 'Radio Farda'. Such programmes were invariably jammed in prison, as were all international broadcasts in the country, but between the crackles and hisses, I thought I heard the presenter saying something about the 'leaders of Bahá'ísm.' This derogatory term was exactly how the Islamic Republic referred to the Yárán-i-Iran. I could not catch who was being named, but someone somewhere was appealing for somebody's release. Release from prison? Were any of the other members of the Yárán also in custody?

I had no way of finding out, of course, and it was impossible to know if I had even heard correctly, due to the jamming. But it set me thinking about my last meeting with the interrogator. In the course of his questioning, and between his usual intimidations and innuendos, veiled threats and menaces, he had disclosed precise details about the past activities of certain members of the Yárán. His words that day echoed in my mind.

So, you went on a trip to meet with some of your 'justice house' members, did you? Yes! Tavakkolí, Rezai and Tizfahm were with you too, weren't they? Oh yes! You're playing with fire, you know. You guys started this game, so don't complain when it gets serious! Watch out for the fireworks!

Maybe he had been telling me the truth for once. Maybe those 'fireworks' were related to my dear colleagues. Perhaps several of them had been pulled in for questioning too and had been grilled on the same topics which I had refused to discuss on burial grounds. If so, no wonder he had been so frustrated with me during those last days in Mashhad! And no wonder the blue-grey judge, here in Tehran, was now hinting that matters may indeed have become serious, not only for me but for all of us.

'Do you have any news from your colleagues?' he asked abruptly.

His insinuation bristled with 'fireworks'. I had to gulp down my fear before replying.

'No. What has happened to them?'

'Nothing – for the moment!' he said, after an enigmatic pause.

I was certain, then, that something had happened and that some of my colleagues may have been detained. Due to this, and the new charges, I did not hesitate to answer the judge's questions concerning the Yárán's communications with the Universal House of Justice.

'I have sentenced you to fifteen days of temporary detention!' he announced at last, as he started gathering together his scattered papers on the desk.

Only fifteen days? Despite my fears related to the possible arrest of some of my colleagues and the interrogations they might also be facing, I was over the moon. Fifteen days would be over soon and this nightmare would end! A little over two weeks and all of us would be released! My heart dilated with joy at the thought. I was not only going to return to my beloved husband and my sweet children and my own home, but I would soon be able to see my dear colleagues again and rejoice in our freedom.

These thoughts gave me such a boost of energy that I was presumptuous enough to try to bargain with the judge.

'But Háj Áqá,' I said, smiling at him broadly, 'I've spent nearly three months in detention in Mashhad already. Why another fifteen days?'

'Well,' he replied, 'that is why I've given you such a short sentence. You might be released even sooner.'

22

DESPAIR

All the way along the road from the courthouse to Evin, my eyes caressed the city, my breath kissed every street corner, I embraced every passer-by with a smile. My happiness was indescribable. As we drove west along Shemrán Street, I gazed in wonder at the petrol station in Zafaraniyeh, the northern district of the city. Who would have thought a petrol station could elicit such emotions? How often had I refilled my car with petrol there? How often had I driven to my daughter's house along this route? I looked longingly at her road as we swept past it.

Hope can make you irrational. I found myself observing the pedestrians with fervent eagerness as they crossed the streets in front of us. I scoured the windows of passing cars to glimpse a familiar face as we drove by. Did I really imagine that somewhere among the eight and a half million people inhabiting this city, somebody I knew might cross my path just at that moment, someone who might possibly convey the news of my transfer to my family? But logic had no meaning that day. I was too thrilled at being back in Tehran. Just a few more weeks of this misery. Fifteen days would pass in a flash. I was home!

And then, suddenly, we were at the gates of Evin Prison. As we pulled up, a man leapt out of the car behind us. I had seen this tall, well-groomed individual already just before we left the judge's chambers in the Revolutionary Court. He had rushed over as I was entering the white sedan, excusing himself volubly for not being at the airport.

'I lost you,' he gushed. 'I got stuck in traffic. Please forgive me for being late.'

He introduced himself as Madáni, an official representative of the Ministry of Intelligence, and then followed us to Evin in his own car. And here he was again, marching me officiously through those infamous gates, a somewhat supernumerary escort. By now, prison registration routines were all too familiar and I certainly did not need Madáni to tell me what to do. I was registered as being in 'temporary detention' as secretary of the Yárán-i-Iran and the preliminary stages of inspection were completed rapidly. A young woman in a black chador, also tall and slim, handed me a grey blindfold and off we went.

I think this particular female guard must have recognised me from the last time I was a guest of the Islamic Republic, during my first detention in Evin three years before. Instead of holding me by the elbow, as they usually did, she clasped my hand under her chador. She even gave it a gentle squeeze as we walked along. In fact, she did so twice. And I squeezed her hand back gratefully. In the midst of all that cold officialdom, the friendly hand of this young woman gave me hope. Yes, I could surely survive; fifteen days would pass quickly. We went up a flight of stairs, walked a few paces further, then stood before what I guessed was a doorway. The buzzer shrilled piercingly, the door opened, and as we stepped through, she told me to take off the blindfold.

And there I was again. In that world again.

I recognised the women's Isolation Ward immediately. The long, narrow passageway. The darkness of it. The deathly silence of it. Not a breath from any of the cells. Not a sound. They used to say that you could hear the flap of a fly's wing in the Isolation Wards of Evin. Even the echo of footsteps was muffled to a soft shlip-shlep, because you had to wear plastic slippers in there. Shoes were not allowed. Human voices were not allowed. You had to whisper. No one else appeared as we walked past door after door towards the end of the corridor that turned left into another passageway.

Then, just as we passed by cell 112, I saw a pair of brown shoes. They were sitting side by side outside a door, as if they were waiting for me. I swear, it was as if those shoes called out to me as I passed by. My heart soared at the sight of them. And then sank. Were they Faribá's shoes? Faribá, my dear colleague, my soul sister and friend, the only other female member of the Yárán? Yes, they were! Faribá's shoes.

So she was here too? My heart caved in.

As soon as we reached cell number 215, I asked the female guard if I could go to the bathroom. I remembered that to go there, I had to pass by cell 112 again. That way, I could look at those shoes more carefully. My thoughts were in a whirl. How come I had noticed those shoes? How on earth did I even recognise them? Perhaps I was mistaken?

The guard walked me back along the passageway. Yes, they were Faribá's brown shoes. I knew immediately, from the form of her foot under the leather, that they were hers. I was engulfed by grief. Despite my earlier suspicions regarding the possible arrest of my dear colleagues, to have hers confirmed curdled my soul. She was here.

I returned to cell 215, swallowing sour tears. The female guard was kind but vigilant. She gave me a thorough body search and once again took charge of my travelling bag, handbag and watch. She also asked me to take off my bra and give her my shoes. As she was retrieving certain basic items I needed from inside the grey metal locker in the middle of the corridor, I noticed a few books and asked if I could read some, whatever they might be.

'You are not yet allowed books,' she murmured.

I reached out for a commentary on the Qur'an on one of the shelves.

'But it's surely reasonable to permit this!' I insisted irrationally.

The guard gave in and handed me the book, which was one of a set of twenty-three volumes. As the first was not on the shelf, she said she would look for it later and swap it with the one she had allowed me to have. There was a chair at the end of the corridor on which she left my large bag of dried fruits. She said they might go bad in the damp cell.

'Whenever you want some, just ask us,' she whispered.

After that she left, taking the rest of my belongings away with her. She said that she needed time to examine them.

The passage between hope and despair can be swift. The distance between my giddy joy on arrival at the airport in Tehran and this confirmation of Faribá's arrest in Evin seemed very short. Once the guard left, I plummeted into despair, now that I knew for sure I was not the only member of the Yárán in detention. I was overwhelmed by anguish at the thought of gentle Faribá also imprisoned, Faribá also in a miserable cell like this one. And I was swept up in bitter memories, heartsick recollections of the last time I was here, when the passage between hope and despair had been just as swift as on this occasion.

* * *

It was in the spring of 2005. The wedding of my darling daughter, Negár, had begun joyfully enough that beautiful day and we were all full of excitement. Flowers had been delivered to our home early in the morning and were infusing the whole house with their fragrance. Guests had arrived the day before from different parts of Iran and abroad, and just seeing everyone's faces, as radiant as the flowers, multiplied our happiness a hundredfold. The plan was to hold the Bahá'í ceremony at home at 3 p.m. in the presence of some fifty guests and then to have the celebration later in the evening in a garden on the outskirts of Tehran. Siyávash had just left with Negár to drop her off at the hairdresser early so that there would be enough time for photos and videos before the ceremony. And we were all jubilant!

But it did not last long. Just a few minutes after he left the house that morning, the doorbell rang and six officers from the Ministry of Intelligence – five men and one heavily veiled woman – invaded our home. They were there to search the house, at 6.30 a.m., and had a warrant to arrest me.

Our guests emerged from their bedrooms in hurried alarm. It was a surreal moment. Instead of breakfast laid out among the blooming wedding flowers, they were greeted by bewilderment, mayhem and disorder. Everyone was in shock as these law enforcement agents turned the whole house upside-down. They behaved ruthlessly, mercilessly. All the lockers and drawers and bookcases, all the bedrooms and storage rooms were ransacked before our disbelieving eyes. They did not even take pity on the suitcases and personal belongings of our guests, confiscating whatever they wanted, according to arbitrary criteria of their own. They rampaged through every inch of our house from early morning until noon, violating our privacy with callous efficiency, and they did not let up until three hours before the marriage ceremony of my daughter.

There were many surreal episodes over the course of that infernal morning. Our home had a split-level floor plan, with a salon ending in steps that led down towards an open kitchen area. I was restricted to the upper-level mezzanine, with no one permitted near me. However, in the middle of the upheaval, the little four-year-old daughter of a relative climbed the stairs and walked boldly up to these ruthless law enforcement agents.

'Please be kind,' she chirped. 'Remember, please, you have to be kind.'

They were visibly taken aback. They could not tell the child to shut up or go away so they just gaped at her. Her name was Leva, the Persian version of Lua, the name of that early Bahá'í whose empathy had so inspired me to clean up the filthy toilets in the qarantineh ward. All through that morning, she trailed after them, reminding them to be kind.

Another surreal moment occurred when our guests began offering hospitality to the agents. The house was filled with food for the wedding feast; the tables were laden with delicacies and set with our best crockery and cutlery. So my loving relatives began pressing sweetmeats on these intruders, inviting them to sit down and have breakfast with us. I knew that law enforcement officers were forbidden to accept such courtesies; they were not supposed to 'eat on the job'. Their discomfort was so evident that I asked my family to desist. But soon afterwards, one of the men left the house and returned carrying cups of fake hot chocolate and pre-packaged, desiccated cup-cakes in a cardboard box. Oblivious of our feelings or the circumstances, they then proceeded to sit around our dining table with cold-blooded composure, calmly eating this unappealing breakfast off our best chinaware.

I had no choice during that dishevelled morning but to sit apart from the household, physically separated from my loved ones. Since I could see all that was happening below me, I set up a crisis management headquarters on the mezzanine floor. Fortunately, the agents did not object to my doing this, so I started giving instructions to our guests from 'on high', delegating specific tasks to each person, telling everyone where to put things back in order, how to clean the house and prepare it for the wedding.

Despite our best efforts to tidy the place up, my husband faced devastation on his return. He could not believe anyone could be so heartless as to commit such a heinous act at such a time, and kept asking the agents, repeatedly, in all simplicity, to please allow us just today, just this one evening, to let us just conduct the wedding ceremony of our daughter before they arrested me. And he promised them over and over again that he would make sure that I would present myself to their offices the next morning.

But I knew the intention of these people. I had seen the date on the warrant they had shoved under my nose. It had been stamped several days before. In other words, they had waited, had intentionally delayed this arrest, and chosen to conduct it specifically on my daughter's wedding day so as to make it all the more painful, all the more bitter. They not only wanted to put pressure on me, but wished to traumatise my daughter, her fiancé, our family members as well as our friends. I told my husband that to ask favours of them would be neither effective nor befitting. These people had picked this day on purpose; they had specifically come now in order to destroy our happiness. And for that very reason, we should make sure the ceremony took place as planned, that it unfolded smoothly, impeccably, cheerfully, even more beautifully than we had hoped. In spite of them.

Towards noon, the five gentlemen and one veiled woman loaded up their vehicle with all they had confiscated, and departed. They took with them everything with Bahá'í associations and content – books, pamphlets, writings, even photographs, wall-hangings and ornaments – and just a few hours prior to the marriage ceremony of my only daughter, they arrested me and brought me here: Section 209 of the women's Isolation Ward of Evin.

* * *

Now, three years later, here I was again. Grieving for Negár, for her brother, for my husband and my dear old father, for the Bahá'í community, and above all for Faribá, locked away in this terrible place. I was crushed at the thought of her suffering so close to me and yet so far. All my energy dissolved, and I slid to the floor in a flood of tears. I suppose it was to be expected. My euphoria had been too high on leaving Mashhad and where had it led to? A dark and dirty cell next to the toilets. I had been naïvely hopeful, imagining a release in fifteen days, but was that likely to happen? I doubted now that Faribá and I were the only members of the Yárán holed up in Evin. What an impact our imprisonment must be having on the Bahá'í community. How shocked everyone must be. I wept and wept. The grief I'd been holding back all these months tore through my throat and I sobbed my heart out.

In the midst of my distress, the door suddenly opened and the guard stood there with the book she had promised to bring me. My tearful face and red eyes made it clear that I had been crying. Her face was full of compassion, and she asked softly if something was wrong.

'It's nothing,' I croaked.

She pretended she had not noticed my grief and invented reasons for me.

'Is it because of this cell?' she whispered. 'It's not one of the best, I know.'

I rose to my feet and reached out for the promised volume. It was hard to speak.

'Thank you very much for the book,' I mumbled.

Mercifully she left me alone after that and allowed me to indulge my sorrows in private. As I wept through the night, certain lines of poetry kept echoing in my mind:

All through our lives did we adore the sun,
yet when the evening came, all hope was gone;
The hardest torture was when – lost within –
each turned away from the other, one by one.[22]

23

EVIN – SECTION 209

Evin Prison is built in the foothills of Alborz, beneath the snow-capped mountains that tower above the city of Tehran. It was constructed in such a way that only a wall and its main entrance are visible from the outside. The myriad wards that comprise this notorious penitentiary are hidden behind and beneath the natural slope of the hills, buried in tunnels that stretch far underground. But none of this is evident at first sight.

After passing through the large iron entrance gate, you see a beautiful green space, filled with flowers and lush grasses, plants and fountains, with mighty trees stretching up to the sky. You are momentarily dazzled by skylarks leaping into the blue overhead; you are thrilled by the cooing of the doves among the leaves, and your first thought is 'Is this a prison or paradise?' In fact, the main compound is entirely separate from the rest of the prison complex. This is just the administrative part of Evin, its green showcase.

To arrive at the prison itself, you have to turn north and take a steep walk up the hillside in the direction of the Alborz mountains. This path leads to the iron gates of the guards' headquarters next to the principal clinic of the prison, emblazoned with the sign: *The Forty-Eight Bed Hospital of Shahíd Lájivardí.*

If you turn left at the clinic and take another short walk, you will enter a second compound – Section 4, the ward for male political prisoners held under the tightest security. There is a car park in this second compound, reserved for the exclusive use of the Intelligence officers who come here to conduct their interrogations. The prison bakery is also here, so there is always the incongruous fragrance of freshly baked *lavásh* bread floating in the air, which, despite being machine-made, is deliciously seductive. To the right and directly across from the bakery entrance, with its deceptively tempting smells, is a small iron door painted a nondescript beige colour that leads straight into Section 209.

Step through that door and you're in the heart of hell. It is as simple as that.

Section 209 contains a maze of small and large, solitary and shared confinement cells, as well as interrogation and torture rooms, along a series of connected, parallel passages. It consists of two floors above ground, with several windows overlooking the car park, and one or possibly more basement floors below. Since I was always blindfolded in these lower areas, I cannot vouch for their number. But at ground level, you see only storage rooms and administrative offices. The inspection, security and control rooms are there too, to welcome you, to identify you, to register you, to fingerprint you, and of course, to body search you. At the far end of this ground floor corridor, you will find a staircase on the left.

Seven steps up and you turn; another seven steps up and you are on the first floor. There, at the top of the stairs, you will see the wide hallway of the Isolation Ward stretching before you. It is known as the Main Corridor, and it is effectively at right angles to – and twice as long as – the ground floor corridor, below. On the right-hand side of the Main Corridor, doors branch off into narrow passageways that lead to the solitary and the shared confinement cells of the Isolation Ward. On the left are the interrogation rooms, several of which have been padded with acoustic insulation and are known by colour, as the White Room, Blue Room or Green Room. A small health centre and a few offices are also located here.

The passageways branching off to the right along the length of the Main Corridor are identified by number and known as Passage 100, Passage 200, Passage 300. The first of these leads into the women's sector of the Isolation Ward, with a green oil cloth curtain hanging in front of the door and a button that you press to be allowed entry. The bell of the Isolation Ward is guaranteed to jangle the nerves. Its harsh, piercing buzz cuts painfully through the smothering silence.

On entering what is known as '*Band-i-Sad*' or Passage 100 of Section 209, you see a row of doors along the wall to your left, which open onto a small patio, the toilet and shower room, a little storage room and all the confinement cells.

The women's sector in the Isolation Ward originally consisted of this one corridor only, with ten tiny solitary confinement cells along it numbered in the 100s. But in the year 2005 (1384), when many members of the Bahá'í community were imprisoned here, four of the interior walls between the cells were demolished and their number was reduced from ten to five, allowing for larger, shared cells instead. The wall at the far end was also broken down to create an opening between Passage 100 and Passage 200, previously used for male prisoners. When female detainees were few, a large metal locker was pulled over to block this opening but when they increased in number, the locker was pushed away, and the two parallel passages were connected. This was how the confinement cells with numbers in the 200s were absorbed into the women's sector of the Isolation Ward. Sometime later the women's sector spawned Passage 300 as well.

Evin is fertile.

The first thing you see in Passage 100 of the women's Isolation Ward is a small iron door to your right that leads down a set of steep steps to the large fresh-air yard at ground level. Here, in a courtyard which, according to my step size, is about twenty-three steps wide by twenty-seven steps long, prisoners are permitted to exercise for about twenty minutes, two or three times a week. The surrounding walls are some six metres high and a wide range CCTV camera on a five-metre pole has been fixed against a wall to the left of the entrance. Since the cells, especially the solitary ones, are very small, prisoners are often in desperate need of this yard for brisk walking and running, as well as for fresh air.

On the other side of Passage 100, opposite the door leading down to this yard, is another door leading into a small enclosure, or the little fresh-air yard. It is more like a patio than a yard, and despite its name, has something of a domestic air about it, with its washing lines overhead and its indoor plants and flowerpots standing here and there; it is used for drying laundry rather than exercise, and is furnished with a tap, a blue rubber hose and two large black plastic bins against the wall. The floor is paved with old tiles, and the roof is glassed in, with a few panes removed for ventilation purposes. Next to this patio is the white tiled toilet and shower room of Passage 100, whose single window opens onto it. The toilet is an oriental one and combined with the shower, so there is always a strong odour of drains in the patio and the passage. There is also a small storage room, situated between the toilet and shower patio, and another row of five confinement cells.

Each of the passages of the Isolation Ward for women has four shared confinement cells and one small 'punishment' or solitary cell. The larger cells, created from two smaller ones, have two doors each, only one of which is in use, but there are peepholes in both. There are also two rectangular windows facing the flat rooftop above both doors; some are covered with wire mesh, and others with a perforated metal sheet, which darkens the place depressingly. The small steel sink in each cell is often rusty, and the Western-style steel toilets in the 'punishment' or solitary cells at the end of each passage are dysfunctional.

There is a small niche, the size of a shoe box, in the middle of the ceiling of these cells, in which a low-consumption bulb shines day and night. The light is not bright enough to read by but neither does it allow for complete darkness when prisoners want to sleep. There is plenty of light outside the cell, however. Four tall windows flank the right-hand side of Passage 100, between one door leading to the fresh-air yard below and another to the guards' residential area. These fill the corridor with light and offer a thrilling view of the exercise yard below – if you are lucky enough to snatch a clandestine glance at it.

The distribution of cells is similar in all the passages, the only difference being that the toilet and shower are situated at the far end of Passage 200 and at the beginning of Passage 100. The two small solitary or 'punishment' cells of 215 and 115 are therefore liberally perfumed by malodorous drains; they are also noisier and darker than the other cells, because of the relentless rattle and throb of air-conditioning units on the roof of the guards' quarters, which block the light from the perforated windows above the doors.

There are two card-operated telephones on the left- and right-hand walls of the stairwell leading down into the large fresh-air yard. Prisoners were allowed to use these during my time in Section 209, to call certain pre-approved numbers only. There were also some telephones in a room beyond the offices on the Main Corridor, as well as in a small alcove filled with bookshelves, where the Corridor reaches an apparent dead end.

Except there is never an end to Evin. Or you may be dead before you reach it. At least one of the bookshelves in that alcove can be moved aside to reveal yet another doorway leading into yet another passage, filled with yet more cells and torture chambers…

They say that no one actually knows how many cells and wards and passageways there are in the notorious Section 209 of Evin. It seems to exist in another dimension.

* * *

Section 209 was originally created for the use of SAVAK, the late Shah's secret police, but is now under the control of the Ministry of Intelligence of the Islamic Republic. The conditions here range from the miserable to the abominable. This is where all political prisoners and prisoners of conscience are incarcerated, where a would-be anarchist, a human rights lawyer, or a girl daring to teach literacy classes are treated with equal ruthlessness, and where anyone considered a danger to the state, a threat to the regime, a risk to the stability of the government, can be interrogated, beaten, tortured and often killed, unseen.

Section 209 consists of the Public as well as the Isolation Wards, accommodating men as well as women. The pale green and off-white cell walls are etched with words of pain and longing; the narrow windows above the doors are constructed to shut out light; the floors covered by cheap beige carpeting have been trodden thin by oppression, and the atmosphere of the place is heavy in all seasons, with heat and grief, with cold and hopelessness. This is where you suffocate from want of air and are crippled by lack of space. This is where you stop eating, stop wearing your own clothes and sometimes lose your mind.

Section 209 is where the interrogator's dominance and the prisoner's subservience are absolute, where violent torturers, petty guards and haughty officials have unconditional licence over the weak, the vulnerable and the fragile – not to mention the innocent. It is a place of persecution, of forced and fake confessions, of physical and mental torture, of tricks and lies by men who, after eating a full breakfast with their families, park their cars below those windows and walk through the doors, inhaling the fragrant odours of baked bread every morning, to inflict harm on their fellow human beings until nightfall.

Section 209 is the place of paradox, where opposites live cheek by jowl: courage and cowardice, sudden screams and fathomless silence. The guards mouth their messages in here and skulk about soundlessly in plastic shoes; the entire place is suffused in a fog of stillness. But it is also the place of piercing shrieks, cries of despair and sudden shouts for help. This is a place to die or grow spiritually strong, where doubt and belief, detachment and greed are interwoven. It is a place where you can rise and fall, lose and find yourself, and where you would give up everything in the world for a little taste of steadfastness under your tongue.

Section 209 is where you reach towards your God and withdraw from all others. It is where the basest kind of behaviour serves to test the gold or alloy of your soul. It is where you learn how to sustain blows, face humiliations, defy the breaking of your will, with neither passivity nor aggression, as neither victim nor blamer. Here is where you learn to withstand duplicity and deception and suspicion and paranoia with quiet resilience and a calm trust in the truth. Section 209 is a place of transformation.

This place is a prison within the prison of Evin, a hell within a hell reflecting the worst of human nature. But it can also give you a glimpse of certitude, bring you face-to-face with the beauty and dignity of the human spirit and set you free.

24

BEGINNING AGAIN

The day after my arrival in Evin was the seventh of Khordád (27 May). I had barely slept a wink all night, listening to the rattle of the air conditioner outside the aperture above the door, so I rose with the *azán* for dawn prayers and prepared for the first interrogation. Since I expected to be summoned at an early hour, I showered quickly and asked Háj Khánum, the warden of Section 209, for my clothes. I remembered her from my previous time in Evin. She was a decent and discreet person, about sixty years old, amply built, with heavy, impassive features and a severe kind of dignity that was not wholly hostile. She had been in charge of political prisoners since the beginning of the Revolution and was now hoping to retire. But they could not find an adequate replacement for her, so, ironically enough, she was condemned to the Isolation Ward along with the rest of us.

When I walked down the passageway to the bathroom that morning, I noticed that Faribá's shoes had disappeared from in front of cell 112. Even so, I continued to see them in my mind and to imagine the shape of her dear foot in them. Maybe she was wearing boat-like plastic sandals now, like I was. Maybe the guards had removed her shoes because of my lingering looks yesterday. And this last thought confirmed my worst fears. Yes, I had better reconcile myself to the fact that I was in Section 209 of Evin Prison, where every look, every gesture, every unspoken word was under scrutiny.

The explosives were indeed waiting to go off. The 'fireworks' had really started. I could hear them, almost, in the suffocating silence of the place.

When I was imprisoned here before, we had been permitted to walk about the women's sector of the Isolation Ward without the mandatory blindfold. We even helped the head warden, Háj Khánum, with the cleaning work, sweeping and mopping away the constant accumulation of dust and plaster caused by the 'renovation' that was taking place at the time. As a result, during my imprisonment there, I had even walked as far as Passage 300 and witnessed Evin's fertility for myself, as the ward was expanded to accommodate more and more prisoners. But the situation was different now that I was holed up in the airless gloom and unrelenting stink of cell 215. There was no walking about here, except with permission to go to the shower and toilet. And no enlargement possible to contain the multiple uncertainties in my mind. The walls around me throbbed with questions, pressed in on me.

What had happened to the rest of the Yárán? Were they all in prison now? Had they been arrested after my abduction in Mashhad or at the same time? Were they in prison because of anything I had said? And how were the dear friends all over the country coping with this crisis? They must be distraught. I was dreadfully distressed for the Bahá'í community. But my greatest concern was for Iran as a whole. This regime had always persecuted the Bahá'ís; the oppression of our community was a matter of government principle and policy. But we were not the only ones being targeted now. The political climate had altered and many of our compatriots were also being denied their basic freedoms, just like us. Many ordinary Iranians were also being intimidated by the morality police, hounded by the security forces, beaten up in the streets and thrown into jail for nothing. In his book, *The Difficult Task of Supervising the Implementation of the Constitution*, Hossein Mehrpour, the head of the supervisory board of the Constitution during the presidency of Mohammad Khatami, had written:

> Under the relentless pressure of radicals and extremists, the implementation of the Constitution, especially in relation to the political, social and civil rights of people, will not only be difficult, but actually impossible to maintain.

These 'radicals and extremists' were now in power in Iran. They had already amply demonstrated their willingness to ignore their own Constitution and now their hardline policies were undermining the civil rights of all Iranians. Everyone was in danger.

So what was the responsibility of the Bahá'ís in these circumstances? How could we help our fellow Iranians? We had no power and very little means, but we did have vision and faith. Despite being throttled, the Bahá'ís had not stopped breathing. Despite being oppressed, we had refused to be victims. We had been robust in the face of blackmail, shown courage under threat and had never been supine. Most importantly, even though we knew the rule of law would not protect us, we used every legal recourse available to make ourselves heard and demand our rights, because of our cardinal belief in justice. While this infuriated the extremist elements in the government, it protected the integrity of the Faith and gave us courage to continue. Perhaps the best way to help our compatriots was by example.

These thoughts preoccupied me on that first day in cell 215 at the far end of Passage 200 in the women's Isolation Ward of Section 209. I assumed the agents of the Ministry of Intelligence must have raided my office long ago, seized the laptop, the files, everything. Perhaps they had even arrested the friends who helped me with secretarial duties. They would probably have compared all the information in their possession with the answers I had given in Mashhad. This did not bother me at all, because I had been scrupulously consistent. But I did agonise over my poor family. They had suffered so much anxiety on my account over these past three months: did they have the stamina to face the weeks ahead? They must have been hoping for my release from Mashhad from one day to the next: could they survive the new misery of knowing that I was trapped in Evin? My heart ached for them.

After tormenting myself with these worries for half the morning, I came to the conclusion that it was all was out of my hands. I could control nothing, protect no one. The only power I had, in that dark and smelly cell, was over myself. I had to be steadfast, firm. I had to stand up for the legal rights of the Bahá'í community. If I was being openly charged, not as a grave digger but as the secretary of the Yárán-i-Iran, it was the work of the Yárán that I needed to defend.

The interrogations would be different now, and my answers should be different, too.

And that raised another concern: who would my interrogator be here, in Tehran? What kind of person would I have to answer to in the suffocating interrogation rooms of Section 209? I supposed I would have to learn the tricks and techniques of a different agent of the Ministry of Intelligence, protect myself against new guiles, understand new methods and discern, from beneath the blindfold, the underlying intentions of a new gentleman.

When the cell door finally opened, I braced myself for the worst. I assumed I would be taken straight over to one of the interrogation rooms in the Main Corridor. But I was in for a surprise. A female guard appeared whom I had never seen before, with clouds of curly black hair and a startling resemblance to Homeyra, the famous Persian crooner of by-gone days. Such incongruities! She waved a hand at me, but instead of bursting into a love song as the gesture implied, or steering me towards an interrogation room as I expected, she simply took me to the health centre of the women's ward and opened a medical file for me.

A real anti-climax.

Back in my wretched cell after the medical examination, I sat hour after hour in the company of my weight of 119 pounds, my height of 5'3', my 100/10 blood pressure, and my surprisingly normal heart rate. Together we waited, my body and I, the whole day long, together we brooded. What would happen next? When would someone come for me? Who would the interrogator be? What questions would he ask? But nothing happened and no one came. Only the air conditioner kept rattling.

A second night passed in a tumult of unrest, and I felt as if I were falling down a well. Then, early the next morning, Háj Khánum opened the door. She stood there moving her lips without uttering a sound. It was only by the palpitations of my heart that I deciphered her words. Yes, I was finally being summoned. Yes, the interrogations were about to begin.

* * *

The same old routine. The same blindfold. The same sound-proofed room whose muffled, muted air I remembered from my last time in this place. And then, with a shudder of surprise, I recognised the same heavy breathing, the same voice. It was the same interrogator! I knew it was him from the first word he uttered. The familiarity was undeniable. But as he continued speaking, deepening his intonation as he did so, I had some doubts. Perhaps this was a new gentleman, after all? Or was my old nemesis trying to dupe me? For a minute I thought I was paranoid. But the thinly concealed antagonism, the deep-seated anger, the sheer hatred behind his insipid words of preliminary greeting were unmistakable.

'*Salaam*, Khánum. How are we feeling today?'

Yes, this was the same man who had interrogated me in Mashhad. Yes, he really was trying to pretend to be someone else! And then I suddenly remembered the old man's 'joke', when he informed me, out of the blue, that 'Haj Áqá' had gone to Tehran.

Perhaps you'll see him there.

So, here he was indeed, and here we were, with me blindfolded in the chair and him placing the first interrogation sheet on the armrest, just as before. He did this in exactly the same manner, leaning over my head, a little to one side. We're genetically programmed to be wary of attack from behind and above, so the movement was intimidating, guaranteed to destabilise. I focused on the handwriting on the page. It seemed more sophisticated, more legible than his usual script. But interrogators often work in teams; it was quite possible a colleague wrote these questions for him. Even this was probably intended to destabilise me.

In the course of responding to the routine personal information about my duties in the Bahá'í community, I took the opportunity to address him directly.

'I'm glad you feel better today. You were nervous the last time we met in Mashhad.'

'Why do you think I was in Mashhad?' he asked, clearing his throat extravagantly.

'From your voice and the way you move.'

He coughed and began speaking more slowly, deepening his voice more consciously. 'I'm afraid you are mistaken,' he ponderously intoned.

He had succeeded in stirring my doubts, but the more he questioned me, the more positive I became that he definitely was the interrogator from Mashhad. The similarity in the timbre of their voices could not be ignored, especially with the old man's words ringing in my ears.

Perhaps you'll see him there.

On the second interrogation sheet he gave me, the questions went straight for the jugular, addressing subjects he had probed most insistently in the past, such as my recent trip to Turkey, and my meeting there with some of the respected members of the Universal House of Justice, and other Bahá'ís. It was no longer hard for me to answer now that I knew Faribá was detained and that Mr Khánjáni and Mr Tavakkolí had probably been questioned too, on these very subjects. Since the corpse bore no further responsibility for the 'temporary extension' of my detention, I felt just as free to reply to the interrogator as I had been to answer the judge. And I did so without a moment's hesitation.

When I returned the form to him, I felt a brush of air behind me and heard a flutter of pages as he swung away from my chair abruptly. His steps were so rapid that he must have left the room at a run. The door slammed shut behind me. I guessed he had been taken completely by surprise. He had not been expecting this response from me at all.

Minutes later, he returned. He was not alone; he came with someone I did not know but whom I guessed, from his ingratiating tone, must be a man of superior rank and greater authority than himself. The interrogator's behaviour was overtly deferential towards this new arrival, who approached my chair with a steady pace and instructed me to raise my blindfold.

I had already lifted it slightly to write my answers, so I now pushed it further up my forehead until this newcomer was within my range of vision. A man of about forty-five stood before me – tall, swarthy-skinned and rather thin, bearded, with dark hair, eyes and eyebrows. He was wearing a pair of brown trousers and a patterned brown and beige shirt. It was the first time that I had ever spoken to anyone face-to-face in the interrogation room. Naturally he did not introduce himself. His words were clipped, his voice cold.

'Hello Mrs Sabet, are you well?'

'Thank you.'

'Mrs Sabet,' he continued, 'why did you not answer these questions in Mashhad?' He was holding my interrogation forms in his hand.

'Why should I have?' I responded. 'First of all, as you know, I was under no legal obligation to answer questions unrelated to my charges. Secondly, those interrogations were conducted under irregular circumstances. I'd been asked to go to Mashhad by phone and had gone in good faith. And then suddenly, without any justification, some men abducted me and others started interrogating me. I had no idea where I was at first. I was not even permitted to provide the bail the magistrate had agreed to at my first hearing.'

The interrogator, who was seated out of my line of sight, erupted furiously.

'No, Haj Áqá, that's not true!' he spat, with his old familiar bitterness. 'She knew perfectly well that she was in the Intelligence Bureau. How could she not have known?'

'How should I have known if no one told me?' I enquired.

'All the forms were stamped with its logo!'

'That proves nothing, you use that logo everywhere.'

He knew that was true. He also knew that he could no longer pretend that I did not know him. The Háj Áqá intervened at this point.

'Very well, very well,' he interrupted. 'Lower your blindfold now.'

He went out of the room then, this intelligent gentleman of the Ministry, and I was left alone with the humiliated interrogator of Mashhad, who was livid and had a hard time controlling his anger. I needed no further proof than his bad temper to be assured that he was the same person who had shouted at me and abused me for days in the detention centre of the Khorasan Razavi Intelligence Bureau.

I had caught him in a lie.

25

A QUESTION OF ANSWERS

The questions I was asked that first morning and for many days afterwards were among the most challenging I had ever faced. On and on it continued, day after day until I lost track of myself and had a hard time remembering what I had and had not said. The interrogator tried to dig every detail out of me, insisted on the minutiae of every fact, and returned again and again to the same issues, from different angles, in an attempt to trip me up. How many journeys have you made abroad? List them in chronological order and describe each one. What was the purpose of these visits? Where did you go? Dates of travel? Fellow travellers? Who did you meet? For how long? Who wrote the minutes of each meeting you conducted while abroad? And so on, and on, and on.

Were they asking the same questions of the other Yárán members? Were they interrogating them about their travels with me? And if there was any shade of difference in our answers, were they going to try to pit us against each other?

Contrary to what had taken place in Mashhad, the questions in Evin were no longer open-ended. If the contents of my home and those of my colleagues had been raided and everything had been confiscated, as I supposed, then all our files, our agendas, our reports, the minutes of our meetings, and our archives had been studied in detail. I was probably being cross-examined based on known facts and so the interrogator was testing me. Testing Faribá. Testing each of us in turn.

Had they been fair-minded, these gentlemen, had they looked at all this material with impartial eyes, they would have seen that everything in their possession proved our innocence. There was not the slightest trace in any of these documents of any political activity, any security issue, or any nefarious communication with any government of another country injurious to the interests of Iran. Everything was focused on the immediate needs of the Bahá'ís; everything was linked to the internal activities of our own community.

But they were scrutinising all this material with paranoid eyes. They had trawled through it with the aim of condemning the Yárán, of proving our activities to be illegal, and with the clear objective of turning us into a 'security threat.' So the interrogator was ripping incomplete phrases from sentences, decontextualising factoids from these materials, and was asking me to confirm, sign and fingerprint each phrase from every document in an effort to corroborate a crooked inference from the confection he had concocted. All his questions were engineered towards preconceived answers. He wanted to frame us.

For example, he would present me with the agenda of a meeting of the Yárán-i-Iran with one random item on it marked in red.

'Explain this!' he would yell.

He would then change the subject, reel in another answer arising from a different context, and then swing back and misquote my previous 'explanation' as evidence of a 'contradiction.' Or he would ask me to write a list of issues raised in the report submitted to the European Union, at its request, and would then use my answer to 'prove' that I had been 'undermining the Islamic state' to governments in Europe. Or he would quiz me on the Yárán's role in teaching the Bahá'í Faith, for which he used the ugly term 'propaganda' – a concept antithetical to the Bahá'í spirit and which I naturally denied. But all he needed was to find a chance reference in one of our minutes to somebody who happened to have shared a comment by somebody else about a third person who had made a general enquiry about the Faith, and he would use it as 'evidence' of my 'spreading corruption on the earth.'

The reports I sent to the Universal House of Justice on behalf of the Yárán were another source of creativity. He would juggle with them in this game of invented guilt.

'Did you write this?' he would shout. 'How often did you write reports like this? Who told you to write these reports? Where did you send them?'

He would then use my answers to frame me as a spy for what he called 'the Zionist oppressive fake rule'. The truth is, unless an individual happened to request elucidation about the implementation of the principle of neutrality in the Faith, the communications of the Bahá'ís with the World Centre would normally have no reason to bear any reference either to the government or to the policies of Israel. But the interrogator wanted to distort this evident truth by focusing only on the literal, physical address of the recipient: Haifa, Israel. Geography was our crime.

I suspected that the ultimate aim of this framing job was to obtain the death penalty for all seven members of the Yárán. That is what it was all leading to. These gentlemen knew what charges were needed for such a sentence under Islamic law. They also knew what proof was required for each charge. And in addition, they knew on what subjects it would be useful for them to have our signatures, so that we would appear to be confessing to our 'guilt'. Their questions were slanted to this end; they wanted us to indict ourselves.

The irony was that they only believed what they could gain by deception and duplicity – so what I said made little difference. They preferred to ensnare information by subterfuge. Whenever plain facts were provided, they always suspected that evidence was being withheld, and whatever they obtained by tortuous and underhanded means helped to stoke their suspicions. They now had access to all the facts about the functioning of the Yárán, but it did nothing to lessen their paranoia. They could not see how their fears were fuelled by their own repressive measures.

We had experienced ample proof of this already. On 29 September 1998, the Ministry of Intelligence had obtained a stash of materials in what came to be known as The Raid of 7/7/77 (29 September 1998). This 'Raid' was a break-in conducted simultaneously on several homes of Bahá'ís in Iran belonging to directors, professors and students of the Bahá'í Institute of Higher Education. The gentlemen plundered everything and confiscated every single book, pamphlet and personal notepad, as well as all the computers, files and archives related to the BIHE. They also arrested many of our organisers and teachers who resided in Iran. After careful examination of this so-called 'evidence', they were forced to acknowledge that nothing nefarious was taking place, just as we had told them again and again; nothing was going on besides straightforward academic teaching of engineering, economics, sociology, psychology, language, literature and similar university subjects, just as we had affirmed. Indeed, in 2005, during my previous sojourn in Evin, our chief interrogator, or 'Head of the Bahá'ísm Desk' as he liked to be called, admitted to me that the Raid of 7/7/77 had indeed proven that we were not 'spies or militants'. But that did not stop them from imprisoning heads of departments and administrators of the BIHE. The innocence of these people was irrelevant. Their punishment was justified simply because they were Bahá'ís.

And so, it now appeared that I was being charged on the same basis, according to the same criteria. Only I feared their intentions had become more deadly. If they had indeed arrested all seven members of the Yárán, and could extract nothing from us but the truth, there was only one recourse left: they would distort that truth to suit their own ends. When these gentlemen were determined on a death sentence, they did not trouble themselves with the inconvenient facts. When they were in a hurry to be rid of people, they would sweep aside even their own judicial procedures and kill without a qualm.

* * *

Another day, another interrogation. There were so many that I stopped counting. As I sat there with the interrogator breathing down my neck, I kept thinking about my dear colleagues who might be in precisely the same position, sitting on a chair just like this one, blindfolded just as I was, staring down at the floor with the same vertical vision. Were they being asked the same questions as I was?

That day the interrogator was intent upon accusing the Yárán-i-Iran of 'imperialist' and 'expansionist' motives, of an 'illegal extension' of our mandate.

'When the previous members of the Yárán were arrested in '66 [1987],' he said, 'they told us that they only existed to attend to the essential affairs of your community such as personal matters of marriage, divorce and burial etc. Now, for no reason at all, you people have expanded your operations. You've violated the previous agreement!'

I responded promptly that we had only been obliged to 'expand our operations,' as he put it, because the authorities had expanded the scope of their repressions against us. When Bahá'í children started being expelled from schools against the constitutional laws of the land, we had to set up classes for them in our homes. When they banned thousands of youth from university, in breach of the constitution, we had to help them complete their studies to ensure their future careers. When they dismissed Bahá'í employees from work and government offices, when they even prevented people from running personal businesses, we simply tried to create small jobs and provide domestic services for each other, based on the spiritual teachings of cooperation which he as a devout Muslim would surely understand and share. We did this, voluntarily, to compensate, to some degree, for the losses that the government had imposed upon so many of its citizens, against all moral standards, against all religious principles, and against the constitutional rights guaranteed to us in this land.

'We don't ask you for a budget, or manpower, or any other resources,' I concluded. 'We just ask that you let us help people get on with their lives.'

Of course, since he wanted to prove that helping the Bahá'ís was a crime, the interrogator always countered such statements by claiming that what we were doing was illegal. When a regime wants to repress a sector of its population, any kind of constructive activity undertaken to mitigate its inhuman policies can all too easily be defined as illegal. He was very self-righteous about it. A permit was needed if we were going to offer help to people, he fulminated. Where were our permits for the alternative services we were providing? Where were our registration certificates to prove the legality of these activities?

'But your registration certificates can only be acquired at the cost of lying or denying our beliefs,' I protested. 'You refuse to issue permits to the Bahá'ís! You disqualify all the papers we submit, all the forms we fill, and only offer us off-the-record agreements.'

As he well knew, many different kinds of permits circulated in Iran, both formal and informal. Some involved traceable paperwork, and others were mere verbal agreements, to avoid accountability. We had already been given several of these informal licences when our attempts to pursue registration processes were rejected.

'When we first let you know about the work of the Yárán,' I reminded him, 'you agreed that we could continue on this informal basis. You did not disallow our activities. You gave us your unofficial approval. You're violating your own verbal agreements with us!'

He immediately denied such an arrangement and refused to admit to any off-the-record contracts. He dodged and ducked, disowning all responsibility for the situation.

'Who offered you such a permit?' he retorted. 'I didn't do it. Who gave you that sort of informal approval? It certainly wasn't me!'

I was growing impatient with his kindergarten responses. He knew very well that official permission was systematically denied us and unofficial approval was all we *could* ask for. He knew, too, that the Bahá'í community, as the largest religious minority in the country, should be under the jurisdiction of the

Ministry of the Interior, not the Ministry of Intelligence, which refused us these permits. Furthermore, he knew that we had no contact, no reference person to give us assistance now that our activities had been redefined as a 'security issue' by the Ministry. The only name and number we had had turned out to be fake.

'We even gave you the benefit of the doubt on that score,' I protested, flushed with the injustice of it. 'We believed that you would at least provide us with a liaison person. But you have punished us for being honest with you; you have penalised us for trusting you.'

That day, the interrogator actually laughed at my defence, as if sharing a friendly joke. 'Well, in that case, you shouldn't trust us, should you?' he replied slyly.

I might have drawn blood at his words, I bit my lip so hard.

* * *

The next day, he approached the Yárán's mandate from a different angle.

'In the present climate,' he said, 'when people are thirsty for the blood of Bahá'ís, when they are sick and tired of hearing about the Bahá'ís, and when they suspect and distrust the Bahá'ís, why are you expanding your activities? Why have you started universities? Why are you creating business opportunities and helping Bahá'ís to find employment?'

Given the thick, wide blindfold over my eyes, I did not know whether the interrogator was alone with me that day or if others had joined him. But as he spoke, I felt the walls of the room expand. So I took a deep breath and summoned all those he was evoking, all my compatriots, my fellow Iranians, to bear witness to his niggardly assessment of them. And I launched into the subject as if I were addressing an imaginary audience in a vast auditorium, with the longest answer I could give, in the greatest detail possible.

First of all, I proclaimed, on what basis did he assume that the Iranian people were thirsty for our blood? That was not at all how we assessed the situation. There was a time when public prejudice against the Bahá'ís may have been more widespread due to ignorance and fanaticism. Now, however, the government's policy was far harsher towards us than the opinion of the people. Except for a narrow sector of society, who were ill-informed and easily manipulated, the majority of Iranians were much less prejudiced against the Bahá'ís than they used to be. It was the authorities who were thirsty for our blood, not the people.

'Were you to assign us our rights according to Constitutional Law,' I argued, 'the only objections to it would come from a few extremists under your control and in your pay. No one else would care. In fact, they might even support the initiative.'

I told him we had friends in all strata of Iranian society and many Muslim acquaintances and relatives across the country, in towns, schools and diverse neighbourhoods. Our evaluation was based on the actual facts not on prejudicial conjecture.

'Go to any manager who has a Bahá'í working for him today,' I concluded. 'Tell him to fire his Bahá'í employee and see what happens.'

Then I cited innumerable examples in various cities in Iran where Muslim employers had been brave enough to defend the Bahá'ís and where neighbours and friends had been willing to intervene on their behalf, regardless of the risk this involved.

'Are you going to deny these realities?' I asked.

He had no problem doing so. And although my voice rang out across the imaginary auditorium, no one else in that interrogation room was willing to vouch for me either.

* * *

The other accusation he levelled against the Yárán concerned our system of arbitration and mediation to resolve disputes that arose in the community.

'Why are you using these internal methods of arbitration?' the interrogator demanded. 'Why are you not encouraging your community to take their problems to the courts of law instead? You have set up an alternative judicial system in the country!'

Since this was yet another distortion of the truth and had been ripped out of context, I tried to provide a historical perspective again. I am not sure he took kindly to my pedagogical approach but, like him, I suffered from the limitations of my training and was a teacher by profession. So I reminded him that arbitration was an old and traditional way of settling disputes in Iran. Moreover, it was an approach that had been validated by the Qur'an itself. It had even been recommended recently by Iran's Justice Department, in an attempt to reduce the backlog of pending court cases that were clogging up the judicial system.

'Are you telling me,' I asked him, 'that an attempt to help people resolve their disputes through friendly methods of mediation is an illegal act?'

The interrogator wasn't interested in my logic. He was only throwing questions at me in an attempt to define the Bahá'í

Faith as subversive, to prove that we were trying to create a parallel system, a state within a state. He wanted to force me into saying that we had prohibited the Bahá'ís from appealing to the judicial authorities.

Apart from the charge being absurd, this was an egregious lie. The Yárán had never and would never coerce anyone into arbitration; if Bahá'ís preferred to use the court system to solve their personal problems, I assured him, no one would stand in their way.

'Bahá'ís are free to resolve these matters as they wish. No one dictates to them.'

My remark about freedom was not exactly well-timed. It infuriated the interrogator.

'No, this can't go on,' he stormed. 'Confrontation with you people is inevitable.'

Still wearing my annoying professorial cap, I suggested he might want to review the effectiveness of confrontation in the light of history. Had oppression and conflict ever yielded positive results? Had tyranny ever succeeded in crushing the human spirit at any time or anywhere in the world? Had it not, conversely, fortified peoples' defiance, encouraged their resistance? So why make the same mistake with the Bahá'í Faith?

'Why not choose a more constructive solution? Why not just accept us?'

And then I took the proverbial bull by the horns and asked him if he thought it was not equally 'contradictory' for the Christians and the Jews and followers of other world religions to accept Islam in other countries? Did these people agree with his beliefs? Probably not. But a person of his persuasion could at least hope to maintain basic rights as a citizen in other lands.

Did that settle all theological differences? Probably not. But to live in civil society, greater tolerance and forbearance was absolutely essential. Was it not?

'One day, you'll recognise us officially as citizens of this country, as patriotic Iranians who simply have different beliefs from you. It is inevitable, you know.'

I smiled beneath my blindfold at the happy thought, as he turned away from me in disgust. After he slammed his way out of the room, I sat for a few moments, staring with vertical vision at my feet in their oversize plastic slippers. How many other prisoners in Section 209 were sitting in chairs like this one, in rooms like this one, wearing oversize slippers? When would these gentlemen stop forcing us into their footwear? When would they stop hounding and haranguing and persecuting us for having feet of a different size?

* * *

One of the interrogator's bugbears was our institute programme, which he wanted to redefine as proselytising. In response, I would spell out our various activities, one by one, repeating that these only existed to alleviate, briefly, the suffering of the Bahá'í community caused by the policies of the regime. They were not motivated by anything else but need.

For example, we had established an institute for arts and crafts. Why? Because the Bahá'ís could not work, or find employment, or pursue their normal professional occupations. What did this institute do? It provided an opportunity for anyone with a skill of some kind to train other younger Bahá'ís in the same line of work. Even if that sounded fancy, the aim was simple. Apprenticeship was all we were promoting, as well as a work ethic, and encouragement to update one's vocational skills.

Another example I gave him concerned the institute for Bahá'í life, whose aim was to enable people to identify the spiritual and moral standards underlying human relationships. This institute provided marriage counselling and therapy support, because the Bahá'ís, like everyone else in Iranian society, were affected by family problems, by the erosion of relationships. The institute for youth and children was a similar attempt to give guidance to the next generation, to prepare young people to grow into civic-minded and responsible citizens. These institutes all had the same goal: society building. I asked him which of them were subversive, in his view, and how they could possibly undermine the government?

'Tell me honestly,' I asked, 'do such efforts deserve blame or praise?'

He was particularly exercised by the training institute, or so-called 'Ruhi classes,' a system of group study of the Bahá'í writings conducted worldwide.[23] Since these classes had religious content, unlike the BIHE which was purely academic and some other institutes with social, economic and artistic aims, the Yárán had officially ceased to promote them years ago to comply with the government's strictures. But the interrogator refused to believe it. He fulminated over the fact that these study groups were still being conducted, unofficially, among friends and family members in private homes. Although I tried to explain that we could hardly disband what we were no longer organising, he seemed to think that the Yárán, like clerics, could interfere and intervene in peoples' lives. I could not persuade him that we were not priests, or convince him that we respected individual freedoms.

His overall aim with these interrogations was for me to draw up an organisational chart of all the Bahá'í institutes in existence in Iran which would give the impression that we were some kind of 'fifth column' organisation, running a 'parallel government' in the country. Since this was manifestly untrue, I refused to cooperate or endorse such a ridiculous theory.

But the interrogator would not give up. He would name the institutes doggedly, one by one, and ask which were under the supervision of the Yárán and which were not. If the answer was in the affirmative, he would immediately tell me to add it to the chart. Or, he would himself say no, this institute was not under our jurisdiction.

'So who is responsible for it?' he would then snap. 'Who co-ordinates its activities?'

Finally, after this kind of back and forth for several days, he succeeded in creating a chart of our service institutes functioning in an *ad hoc* fashion, with a limited mandate, to help the Iranian Bahá'ís in dire straits. How this could be called a 'fifth column' activity by any stretch of the imagination I do not know. The worst he was able to prove was that these institutes were in fact of broad benefit to the general public as well as to the Bahá'ís. They were of considerable value to Iranians all over the country.

Then, a few days later, he began pressuring me to confess that the Bahá'í institutes had been expanded specifically to challenge the regime, and all these efforts to provide work and education and encouragement to people were actually targeting the government and against the national interests of Iran. This interpretation was so grotesque that had I not been exhausted, I might have laughed in his face. But laughing blindfolded is not easy.

I was losing my sense of humour as well as my sense of time under these pressures. Worse still, although I was in the

Isolation Ward, I knew that I was not alone in this situation. Faribá was here too, being bombarded with similar questions. How many other women behind these walls were also being interrogated? And how many hundreds and thousands of Iranian women outside them were being denied answers to the real question of their rights? You don't have to be physically blindfolded to feel such pressures.

* * *

Another subject of intense interrogation concerned the pardon offered by the Universal House of Justice towards those who had recanted their faith in the early years of the Islamic Revolution and regretted having done so. This general amnesty, to whoever desired it, was rather different to the practice in Islam, where 'recanters' were treated as hypocrites at best, and apostates at worst, the first deserving reprimand, the second, death. The policy of the Universal House of Justice was to uphold religious freedom and non-coercion, allowing an individual to enter as well as leave a community freely and at will.

The interrogator insisted on knowing who was in charge of implementing this policy, and who had corresponded with the Universal House of Justice about this pardon on behalf of those asking for it. For example, he produced a handwritten letter one day, in which those responsible for the local activities of Bahá'ís in a certain town had been asked to visit an individual there, in order to communicate news about this amnesty.

The letter included the following statement:

… in light of the extreme pressures placed on the community at the beginning of the Islamic Revolution, and the fact that some Bahá'ís, contrary to their inner feelings, may have been forced to recant their beliefs and withdraw from the Faith, such renunciations should not be a reason to deprive them of their rights. Should an individual therefore wish to have his or her membership to the Bahá'í community restored, it could be done by simply signing this letter…

The interrogator wanted to know if this letter had been composed by the Yárán itself.

'If so, state as much at the bottom of the page,' he said, 'and then sign it.'

I readily accepted responsibility. As secretary of the Yárán, I had been charged with this task. Such letters, even in the handwriting of others, were dictated by me, and all correspondence composed by others was my responsibility and written on my behalf. I was able to avoid mentioning those who assisted me in this work, because after my first detention in Evin, I had been fortunate enough to receive free counselling on the rights of accused persons. Several enlightened lawyers had informed me that according to the constitutional laws of Iran, unless an accused person was under oath in court, she was not obliged to answer questions that were not specifically asked. I gladly followed this advice to protect others.

After I had signed a statement of responsibility for the letter, the interrogator was gleeful. He thought the document in his hands proved that the Yárán had asked – indeed forced – Muslims to become Bahá'ís. Apart from being wholly untrue, the irony of this assumption seemed to have quite escaped his attention. For it was the Bahá'ís who had been placed under this very pressure when the Islamic Republic forced them to recant their faith and abjure their beliefs. I sometimes wondered whether a more robust sense of irony might not have alerted these brave gentlemen against the exposure of their own crimes.

After this particular session, I was very dispirited and began to doubt everything I had said. In order to restore myself to a sense of reality, I tried to look at facts objectively once I returned to my dismal cell. It reeked of drains rather badly that day and the pounding air conditioner blocking the little window had darkened it more than usual. But I could still see the ants marching imperturbably across the floor, under the dim light overhead.

I put the case to them, in the courtroom of my mind.

What had the relationship of the Yárán been with this government for all these decades? Had we ever fought against the regime, or opposed the authorities?

No.

Had we ever struggled for political power in this country?

No.

Had we ever, in all these years, acted aggressively towards the government?

No.

Had we been reckless, irresponsible or unwise in our leadership?

No. Or at least we had done our best not to be.

Was there anything else to be said or done for the authorities to tolerate us in Iran?

Probably not.

In that case, if they will not rest until they have annihilated us, should we bow before such tyranny, surrender ourselves and submit to their demands?

No! And no, again!

The ants marched on across the floor, undaunted, unstoppable, irrepressible.

26

WHITE TORTURE

It was another Friday afternoon, though I barely knew which one. I had been taken, blindfolded as usual, down the stairs leading towards the large yard below. And I had then been steered still further down into the basement, I suppose. I did not know how many flights of steps we descended in silence, but at the end of it, I was left sitting on a rickety bench, somewhere deep underground. On the other side of the thick walls around me, I could hear shouts and screams. Someone was obviously being interrogated nearby.

Although I knew that the underground cells and corridors of this terrible place were filled with hundreds of political prisoners and prisoners of conscience like me, it was chilling to be reminded of how many were being punished simultaneously. All the time that I had been delivering my case to the ants, someone was being tortured somewhere else.

After a while a man entered the space in which I had been told to wait. He greeted me, briefly, and asked some questions about the BIHE, not all of which I could answer. He then wanted to know which member of the Yárán oversaw the activities of the BIHE and had all the recent updates. But before I could reply, he promptly supplied the name himself.

'Oh yes, Mr Tavakkolí,' he said. 'Fine. He's the one who would know.'

And then he left. It was as if he had just come to tell me how well-informed he was. If this person was another interrogator, he was new to me. If he was merely responsible for shepherding me to an interrogation, then why didn't he do so? Why had he brought me to this basement on a Friday afternoon just to advertise what he knew about Mr Tavakkolí? Did he want me to imagine that this dear colleague of mine was shouting about the BIHE in the next room? And who was that woman screaming? Her shrieks were unbearable. I waited for a few more minutes. Then the same man returned and very respectfully invited me to please come with him. I stood up, fixed my eyes on the back of his heels with my vertical vision and followed. He was unctuously polite.

'Here, if you don't mind,' he said. 'Just a little further, if you please,' he said. 'Right, you can stop now,' he said. 'That's perfect, please wait here.'

Where on earth had he brought me? My nose was pressed up against a wall. After he left, I stepped back half a pace for the sake of comfort and waited. And waited some more. Nothing happened. The yells of the interrogator and the intermittent screams of the desperate female seemed closer than before. What did these people want from me? Why had they brought me here? And where was I? I craned my neck to listen but still could not distinguish the sounds through the wall. I hoped it was not Mr Tavakkolí who was being questioned. I felt nauseous. Why was this taking so long? Time ticked by. The stench of urine was overpowering and my nerves were fraying. It was too, too long! Then I tilted my head back to take a quick look from under the blindfold and suddenly discovered where I was standing.

The man, with his repulsive courtesies, had placed me right beside an open toilet!

Now I knew where the smell was coming from, my nausea intensified. What was going on? Why was I being forced to wait in this stinking limbo underground?

The interrogator's voice was growing louder at every moment, his insults more audible on the other side of the wall. He was using very strong language, cursing rather than talking. I gradually made out the subject matter; it appeared to be financial. Unlike the source of the screams nearby that were clearly female, the person defending himself seemed to be a man. But his voice was so low that I could not make out what he was saying exactly; he just repeatedly denied whatever he was being accused of. It was becoming unbearable. My inner clock confirmed that whoever it was must have been interrogated for at least an hour as I stood there, hearing shrieks and gagging on the stench of urine.

Just then, the interrogator on the other side of the wall let loose another volley.

'You deluded sinner, you've gone too far now, you've really eaten shit now, you good-for-nothing bastard, just you wait and see, I'll drag every last penny out of your gullet! You're going to have to tell me who else has the money, you know, you can't get away with this "sole responsibility" nonsense! Who else has access to the money?'

And it suddenly hit me, like a blow to my heart: they must be interrogating dear Mr Khánjání! He was the member of the Yárán with sole responsibility for our financial matters. It couldn't be anyone else. But however hard I tried, I still could not hear what he was saying because Mr Khánjání's voice, if it was him, was very low. Despite the interrogator's rising fury and verbal abuse, my colleague never raised his voice. He answered the questions steadily, his replies brief, his words courteous. Yes, it was definitely Mr Khánjání.

Since the Yárán did not have a high financial turnover, we had decided that Mr Khánjání should manage all the monetary matters, as he had done since 1983. This was for security purposes; it meant that if any one of us was interrogated about finances, we could really and truly say we knew nothing about the subject. We guessed that the authorities would have a hard time understanding how we could entrust all our funds to one individual. But since there was no evidence to the contrary, they had no choice but to accept it. Mr Khánjání was the only member of the Yárán who was in charge of our funds.

And that, I suddenly grasped, was why they were putting him under so much pressure now. He was protecting the rest of us. I remembered how hard the authorities had tried during the sweeping arrests in 1384 (2005) to arouse the suspicions of the Bahá'ís against Mr Khánjání on the issue of money, how they did everything to blacken his name, slander his character and sully his integrity. They wanted to sow discord among us. But it did not work, because our unity was deeply rooted. It was based on a degree of trust incomprehensible to the suspicious. Now Mr Khánjání was paying dearly for that trust.

I stood for what felt like forever with my nose against the stinking wall next to the open toilet. I lost all notion of time and space, even reality, as I listened to the interrogator's vitriol, the respectful replies of my dear colleague and the intermittent screams of that unknown female. What were they doing to her? I suppose they wanted me to imagine that if Mr Khánjání was being bullied in one room, Faribá was being abused in another. I was panic stricken at the thought.

After an eternity in that hell, my escort returned at last to take me back to the women's Isolation Ward. He no longer bothered to be courteous. He was downright rude, telling me roughly to get on with it and follow him. I had evidently put him out terribly by making him bring me to the edge of a stinking open toilet. How presumptuous of me not to fall into it despite all the hours I had been given to do so. Now, as if he had not already done enough, I was forcing him to take me all the way back to my cell. Who did I think I was?

* * *

The interrogations in Section 209 were in many ways the same as those I had endured in Mashhad. They were relentless. They were exhausting. They went on for hours. But the main difference, apart from my response to the subject matter, was that I had been truly alone in that grey-walled detention centre in the provincial north; my sense of solitude there had been absolute. Whereas here, although I was equally isolated, I was acutely aware of all the other members of the Yárán trapped in the echo chambers of Evin around me, being asked the same questions, being subjected to the same pressures. And beyond our little circle, I was painfully aware of the whole prison reverberating with suffering; thousands of prisoners were enduring harsh and intrusive questions in equally grim interrogation rooms. I spent every morning until noon on that deadly chair. As they did. And I would be called back in the afternoon for further questioning until the evening. Just like them.

Whenever I returned to my suffocating cell at night after these mind-numbing sessions, I was so tired that I could not swallow anything. In fact I had no appetite left at all during this period, and usually emptied half the food into the rubbish bin when the guard was not looking. I often wondered whether the other prisoners were also sickened by the meals and if so, what was done with the mountain of waste produced by Evin on a daily basis. The only thing I craved, once in a while, was a freshly brewed, delicately aromatic tea, preferably served in a clean, crystal glass. And the possibility of that was as remote as heaven.

I was still wearing my own clothes but had to tie the knot closer and closer on the waist of my stretch trousers. I could not believe how much weight I had lost and sometimes wondered, vaguely, whether I would just turn to skin and bone in this place, like that poor woman whose shoulder I had touched in the qarantineh ward in Mashhad.

Háj Khánum kept urging me to eat something. 'You have so many dried fruits and nuts sitting on the chair out here,' she would say. 'Let me bring some in for you before the worms get at them.'

But I was too heartsick to eat. I would decline by saying I did not want to harbour ants in the cell, and accepted nothing, refusing all but the minimum amount of food.

Other rites became a compulsion, however. When I was imprisoned in Vakilabad, my dear friends in maximum security used to refer to a custom which they cheerfully called 'the ritual bath of patience' [*ghusl-i-sabr*]. They had advised me to indulge in it too. In fact, perhaps this partly explained their addiction to shampoo. But when I asked them what the 'ritual' actually involved, and how it helped them to acquire 'patience', they laughed at me. There were no rules or rituals, they told me; they simply took a long shower, that was all.

Just stand under the water and let it come.

And so I learned to do the same. And I was lucky that the water as well as patience did come. Bahá'í prisoners had told me of the terrible conditions in Evin during the early days of the Revolution and how difficult it used to be to shower then. Limited water supplies in the 1360s (1980s) forced them to take communal showers at night, in cold water even in mid-winter. They only had a few minutes to wash themselves and their clothes. At least, I could shower every day in Evin. A luxury. Almost as good as the crust of bread in Mashhad.

Indeed, the very act of stepping into the shower was a reprieve after those exhausting interrogations. If no one else was in the bathing area or the toilet, and there was no other reason to decline the request, the female guards would allow me to take refuge there, straight after my return to the Isolation Ward. And once inside that white-tiled room, I would stand under the shower and let the water pound down on my head and run over my face. It was a way of washing off the grime of the curses and foul language, the filthy inferences and dirty suspicions of interrogation. It helped me regain my composure and was a great consolation. Immediately after my 'ritual bath of patience', I would go to sleep. It was best not to think, not to worry about the past, not to try to contemplate the future. I had no energy at that point to even imagine there was one. I could barely even think of my husband or my beloved children, let alone arouse the emotions to miss them. Fatigue had taken over my whole being. The last remaining ounce of life in me seemed to be draining away.

Whenever I showered, I also hand-washed my clothes with the bit of shampoo or soap provided by the female guards and hung them out to dry on the rope in the enclosed patio or little yard of the women's Isolation Ward, under the broken glass tiles of the ceiling, rain or shine. One day, when I brought my trousers back to my cell, I noticed something hard lodged in the hem. I fished it out through a gap in the lining and found, to my astonishment, a small heart made out of foil from the top of a fifty gram yogurt container.

Dear God! This must be Faribá's work!

She was the only one who would have recognised my clothes and the only person who would have sent me such a message. Now she knew I was near, just as I knew she was close by, in cell 115. I wanted to fly. I wanted to sing! All the blood rushed into my depleted veins with the joy of this bond with Faribá. I held the foil heart in my hand, kissed it and wept. After that, I was always on the lookout for her clothes on the drying line, and one time I was even lucky enough to loop her sleeve together with mine. I would caress her blouses and her skirts as they hung there and kiss them secretly to comfort myself. It thrilled my heart to know when she had showered and what clothes she was wearing.

* * *

To have endured solitary confinement in Mashhad only to be subjected to it again in Tehran was gruelling. Finally, from sheer loneliness, I started talking to the young female guard who had recognised me on my arrival, and had squeezed my hand so kindly under her chador. She was young and bright and told me she was writing her doctorate, and since I longed to talk about something uplifting for a change, I begged her to tell me the subject.

'It's on the divine inspiration of the Qur'an,' she murmured.

'Oh, how fascinating!' I said. 'I would love to ask you a question about that. Since you are clearly one of "those who reflect,"[24] tell me, what do you suppose might be the meaning of divine inspiration to the honeybee?'

She kept her composure remarkably well at this, and maintained her poise with a murmured reply. Her anodyne response bore little relation to my question, which she must have thought bore no relation whatsoever to her thesis. But in my bumbling manner, I was trying to suggest that inspiration could be expressed in different ways at different times and at different levels of consciousness. Inspiration for a scientist might cure a disease. Inspiration for a bee might be the instinct to build hives and make honey. Perhaps, I opined somewhat laboriously, a bee was being 'inspired' at the apian level of existence when it was guided to those flowers whose colour and odour promised sweetness. And perhaps human beings…?

She was gracious enough to let me air my heavy-handed views about how human inspiration could be intermittent sometimes, particularly for writers and poets. I had hoped to push the analogy still further and discuss the possibility that divine inspiration, unlike the random voice that whispers in a poet's ears, might be more consistent at the prophetic level. A writer might be inspired by a word here or there, but if inspiration was truly divine, might it not surge continuously in the spiritual world? Like the waves of an ocean?

'Háj Khánum, you must finish your thesis,' I urged her enthusiastically. 'Even if it is not something you want to make public, you must complete your research and examine the waves of divine inspiration that have swept through Iran too.'

It was a dangerous subject but I risked raising it again once in a while, after that. 'How's the thesis going?' I would whisper to the young woman. 'Is it completed yet?'

'Where's the time?' she would murmur with a soft laugh.

* * *

Time seemed to be running out for me even as I was losing touch with it. All through those summer days in Evin, the interrogations continued in the same manner, using the same methods. But they were gradually speeding up, as if the sessions were coming to an end, as if they had to be finished by some kind of deadline. Quickly, quickly. The gentleman was in a hurry. And what would happen after this? What would they do to me next? Despite this mounting urgency, however, the interrogator continued to play games. I suppose they were a means to flaunt his authority, intimidate his victim, play cat and mouse with his accused. But they were also the means by which his accused could play with him, could twist and turn and duck and dodge under pressure. What other games can a prisoner play?

I had the chance to play with him one afternoon when, once again, he was in a filthy temper for some reason. As most of his questions were in written form, I was supposed to scribble my answers at high speed, with no time to explain anything in detail. This time, he slammed the form onto my armrest with unusual force.

'Excuse me,' I objected. 'Why are you throwing your form at me in this manner?'

I waited a moment. He did not reply. So I wrote my answers and returned the paper to him. He immediately threw down another sheet, with such deliberate belligerence that it drifted to the ground. This time, I did not pick it up. He did not say anything either. I could hear him breathing heavily, huffing and puffing behind me in his usual fashion. But I refused to pick up the form. Finally, he was obliged to speak, which he did, too loudly.

'Are you going to reply to the question or not?' he shouted.

'I received no form from you,' I answered evenly.

He paused for a second, then yelled at the top of his lungs, 'It's under your foot. Pick it up and write!'

I waited for a few moments, taking no notice of him, and concentrated on composing myself. I wanted to remain as calm as possible. Would he say something? He didn't. And of course, he couldn't! What could he say? And what could he do, for that matter? I had effectively checkmated him. Either he would be reduced to screaming impotently and still fail to force his will on me, or he would have to bend down and pick up the form himself.

A few moments later, having made my point, I bent forward, retrieved the piece of paper from the floor and scribbled a perfunctory reply. I held it towards him, backwards. He had managed to pull himself together, and when he spoke again, it was with forced restraint.

'Perhaps you didn't notice it on the ground?' he asked, rather awkwardly.

He was trying to save face. But I did not answer. He knew, and I knew.

* * *

It was 18 Tír (9 July), and the weather was hot, the air suffocating and still. I had been sitting in the interrogation chair all morning, like on other days, answering a range of questions, like on other days. Towards the end of the morning, the interrogator placed a number of Single Sheets on the armrest of my chair again with names at the top.

'Fill these in carefully,' he ordered. 'And I mean fully. Explain the role that each of these people play in your community, and don't give me a bunch of your usual nonsense.'

He was clearly still irritated by the way I had responded to his Single Sheets in Mashhad. I used to compose a physical portrait of the person in the first few lines – approximate age, height, colour of hair and eyes – and then fill the rest of the page with an encomium to their moral and spiritual qualities. This method of subverting the Single Sheets really infuriated him. And clearly still did. A few minutes later, he snatched the page from under my hand while I was still writing; he ripped it away so fast that my pen left a long line on the still uncompleted form. He had been behaving fairly normally up till this moment.

What now?

'That's enough,' he said tersely. 'What you've written is sufficient.'

I heard him draw up a chair and sit in front of me. He had done that once or twice before. 'So!' he said. 'It's no longer in my hands now. You're on your own. The good ambassador has done his work.'

He had used this phrase before too. The thought of him as a 'good ambassador' was so absurd that I did not even try to reply. Besides, I still did not understand.

'You'll see the results of your lack of cooperation on Tuesday,' he continued. 'You realise, don't you, that you've ruined everything? Even I can't help you anymore!'

I was astonished. *Even I?* He was now posing as my advocate, my protector against all that was to come? *Anymore?* And he wanted me to think he'd been my advocate, my protector for all these months? I sat very still, assuming he would explain.

But he did not. 'Wait here,' was all he said. And then he left the room.

I waited. Minutes passed. I went on waiting. No one came. I concluded that the interrogation period was over. They must have decided to increase the pressure on me in other ways from now. They wanted me to taste the poison of fear, to destabilise me emotionally and make me feel ever more insecure. In other words, terrorise me.

Sometime later, someone *did* enter the room. He stood where I could see him with the blindfold raised and I recognised the man I had met on arrival at Tehran airport – Madáni. He placed a few of the interrogation forms I had already filled out on my armrest.

'Sign them all,' he said curtly.

He stood beside me as I did so, placing one hand over the top of the forms and flipping the pages over fast, one after another. I was obliged to sign the blank space at the bottom of the sheet at top speed because he seemed to be in a terrible rush.

'Hurry up,' he repeated again and again, 'sign quickly!'

There was only time to see the bottom of the page, so I did not know what was written above my signature. But after a minute or two, I noticed a couple of blank pages among all the others and was suddenly assailed by doubts. Why was this man asking me to sign blank pieces of paper? What was he hiding on the top of the sheet? The next time a couple of these came into view, I pulled the blank pages away from his hand.

'What are these for?' I asked, holding them up to him.

'Nothing,' he said. 'Just get on with it and sign, will you? Hurry up, it is late.'

'No!' I said firmly. 'I will not sign anything more.'

And I pulled out all the blank sheets of paper from the pile on the armrest and set down my pen. He brushed aside my challenge in a tone intended to convey that I was making a most unnecessary fuss; it was all so terribly unimportant, so very insignificant.

'Come on, just sign, will you? It doesn't matter. We haven't time for this. Hurry up!'

'No,' I repeated, stubbornly. 'I will not sign blank pages.'

He clearly had no time to lose. He grabbed the pile of paper from the armrest and left the room with his characteristic loping strides. Later on I wondered where so many sheets even came from; I didn't remember ever returning an unsigned form to the interrogator. He always insisted on a signature before I handed anything back, reminding me often not to forget to sign at the bottom of the page. So how could so many unsigned forms have piled up?

I suspect Madáni's primary aim was to have me sign blank pages to be used for false confessions. He was rushing me so that I would not notice.

* * *

Back in my cell – at the end of the same corridor where I had seen Faribá's shoes – I was restless, agitated. They had transferred me from number 215 to number 112, perhaps because it was slightly less dark and not so noisy and there was more space to walk. Or perhaps in order to deprive me of these so-called advantages later. Who knows. I was exhausted but unable to sit on the floor, covered with sweat but reluctant to take a shower. I just paced back and forth in that lonely cell, back and forth in limitless solitude, reprimanding myself, chastising myself, scolding myself over and over again for signing those blank sheets.

The thought of those pieces of paper was truly agonising. Why hadn't I first checked them? Why had I allowed myself to be forced into signing them? How many of those pages were actually blank? What were they going to use my signature for? Perhaps for something even worse than fake confessions? Perhaps for accusations against my beloved colleagues? Or perhaps it was enough to raise my suspicions that this might be their intention, so that I would worry and fret, as I was doing now. It was white torture again, the torture of solitary confinement, which does not shed a drop of blood.

I wondered a great deal that night about the definition of torture. It was not only physical harm and injury, surely, but emotional and mental damage, too. It was being confined in total isolation without any sensory stimulation, forced to sit for hours, blindfolded, through numbing interrogations, made to stand for prolonged periods, nose against a stinking wall while listening to violent screams. It was being bombarded with questions utterly irrelevant to your charges, and worst of all, subjected to menacing hints and ominous intimations. And now this: being terrorised by blank sheets of paper.

White torture.

I was in the midst of these thoughts when I remembered that the period for the 'temporary extension' of my detention, given by the magistrate at the Revolutionary Court, had long since passed. If my calculations were correct, the fifteen days had come and gone some time ago. And there was still no sign, no hint, no hope of release. Nothing I had said or done could warrant such a violation of the law. In addition to kidnapping me and keeping me hostage, placing me under arrest and holding me in custody without a proper charge, they were now detaining me here illegally. And they were probably abusing all the other members of the Yárán in the same way, just as they were mistreating Iranians all over this country, by arbitrarily repressing their rights and violating their freedoms.

Still, I had no choice but to wait. And so I waited, with the interrogator's last words booming in the silence, bouncing off the walls of the cell around me.

You'll see the results of your lack of cooperation on Tuesday.

There was nothing to do but wait for Tuesday, 28 Khordád (18 June 2008).

27

RED TORTURE

Torture has many colours, many forms, and I suspect that our particular brand in Iran, like the national flag, is unique to our culture. I had not been isolated in a white room, or made to wear white clothes, and eat white food only off a white plate, but these gentlemen knew how to inflict white torture without lifting a finger. After keeping me locked up in silence, in semi-darkness, in a suffocating cell without companionship for months on end, they only had to mouth a few hints, make a few insinuations, and my imagination did the rest. Their hands stayed 'clean' despite the verbal flogging they inflicted on me.

But torture was about to turn another colour.

Tuesday finally dawned, just an ordinary day like any other, but I was up and ready for it, waiting since the early hours. And what a busy Tuesday it was for all of us in Section 209, with alarms buzzing, doors slamming, footsteps shlipping and schlepping back and forth. Every time the ear-piercing buzzer blared, I thought it was for me. Every time I heard the schlip-schlop sound of feet, I expected them to approach my door. But they never did.

Nothing happened. For hours. Hours.

After a while, it occurred to me that the interrogator may have just thrown this day at me as an empty threat, another twist of white torture. Perhaps nothing was planned, nothing would happen and he just wanted to rattle me. And this thought gave me a kind of peace, a brief reprieve. But it did not last long. I was soon back in turmoil again. Sit up, lie down, sit up, lie down, sit up. At lunchtime, I ate more than usual, brushed my teeth, walked a few more minutes back and forth, then prayed. And then hummed a song to myself:

> When you come, I hear your footsteps
> echoing down the alleyways…[25]

For some reason, the song relaxed me. I decided to forget the whole 'waiting for Tuesday' business. Maybe this was the end of the interrogations. Maybe, after so many months, they had finally given up on me. At last.

I had spread a large camel-coloured blanket in the middle of the cell and lay down on it, resting my left arm on my forehead, the way my father did. A thin ray of light had reached the edge of the blanket, like a caress, as the sunlight fingered its way through the metal mesh of the window. I watched it dreamily. It was airless and warm in the cell, but I always welcomed the sun, no matter the season. That shaft of light was my only clock.

One of the tortures of solitary confinement is not knowing the time. Apart from my internal clock, I depended entirely on the sun, if I was lucky enough to catch a glimpse of it. In the course of my first day in this bigger cell, I had noticed the beam of sunlight falling on different spots on the walls and the floor. Each time it happened, I asked the guard for the time, and now, following the trail the sunlight traced, I could make an approximate guess.

It was about three in the afternoon.

* * *

I followed the finger of light, tracing its path across the ceiling, and thought about the interrogator. Once, when I answered a question very briefly, he had lashed out at me.

'You have become a liar!'

I was extremely upset and objected forcefully to the accusation.

'This is not a worthy attitude. I won't answer your questions anymore,' I retorted.

I was so obdurate that he could extract nothing more from me that day. He tried, failed, and was finally obliged to leave the room. After a few minutes someone else entered the room in his stead. It turned out to be the same gentleman with a frosty demeanour who had come to the interrogator's rescue at our first encounter in Tehran – the Intelligence Ministry supervisor who had allowed me to lift my blindfold and see his carefully creased trousers, his brown and beige shirt, his thin face and swarthy complexion.

'What's the problem, Mrs Sabet?' he enquired in his cold clipped way.

'The gentleman doesn't use appropriate vocabulary,' I replied indignantly. 'I'm sorry, but I cannot answer his questions if he calls me a liar. Kindly remind him of this.'

'What he probably intended to say,' said the supervisor, in a careful, propitiating tone, for he could see I was enraged, 'what he meant was that you were not telling us the whole truth. He was upset by your lack of cooperation. He doesn't mean that you're actually lying.'

The interrogator had obviously complained to him about me.

'I have never lied to him or to anyone else,' I retorted. 'I always answer the gentleman's questions succinctly, with brevity and with discretion, as might be expected in these circumstances. But

I never lie. I would not demean myself by doing such a thing, because truthfulness is a fundamental tenet of Bahá'í belief. As you well know.'

And then I added that as he doubtless also knew, a prisoner was not obliged to reveal 'the whole truth' unless she was in a court of law and under oath. So to accuse me of 'lack of cooperation' or 'lying' in this situation was utterly disingenuous.

I was reflecting on this exchange and staring at the finger of light on the ceiling above me when the buzzer suddenly shattered the stillness. This did not usually happen during the siesta hour, especially in summer when the days were long. But the minute I heard that rasping, jangling, raucous sound, I sat up at once, alert and tingling from head to toe. The footsteps of the guard approached, passed by my cell, continued to the end of the corridor, then returned and came to a stop outside my door. She opened it and mouthed the words, *Get ready*!

I was.

It took me one minute to dress. A long blouse, trousers, scarf, chador and my blue plastic men's slippers, size 11. And the blindfold.

As soon as I stepped into the Main Corridor, I sensed someone waiting for me. A man. Smelling heavily of sweat and cigarettes. He spoke in a wheedling, smarmy voice, stretching out the syllables and repeating each word as if I was mentally impaired.

'Come on!' he coaxed. 'Come on, come on, come on!'

There was something abnormal about that voice, oozing with mingled threat and ridicule. I walked behind him, my heart pounding. The backs of his old shoes were folded down beneath a pair of filthy cracked heels; his tattered grey trousers were badly wrinkled and trailed on the floor. He came to a stop in the middle of the Main Corridor and told me to turn to the left and step forward. And then he thumped both hands against my shoulder blades and shoved me with great force through an open doorway.

I lost my balance and thrust my hands forward to stop from falling, from crashing into something, someone – before regaining my equilibrium with some difficulty. Breathed in. Out. Knees shaking, heart racing. The room was warm, fusty; it stank of angry men.

The absolute darkness was terrifying. I saw no one but could feel the presence of bodies and knew instinctively that whoever was here intended to do me serious harm. The door must have been ajar because under my blindfold, I could see a pale flicker of neon seeping into the room from the Main Corridor outside. I was really frightened of that door closing. Vertical vision also gave me a glimpse of an interrogation chair by the wall nearby, so I sat on it quickly, pulled my chador forward over the blindfold and tucked the sides firmly under my armpits. But the minute I grabbed the armrests of the chair, the door was slammed shut. No more light on the floor. No glimpse of light anywhere under my blindfold. Fear and panic paralysed me as a voice thundered out of the pitch darkness.

'Who said you could sit down, *kesafat* – you piece of shit?'

Someone smelling strongly of cigarettes kicked at the chair. In spite of my 119 pounds, it jerked violently under me. I stood but could barely keep upright because of my shaking legs. Heart hammering, mouth dry, I leaned instinctively against the nearby wall to stop myself from collapsing. And then another voice roared out of the inky dark.

'She's leaning against the wall! The bitch is leaning against the damn wall!'

I moved away quickly. So far, I had distinguished the voices of three or four men. The air stank of cheap cologne, sweaty clothes and stale cigarette smoke. The room reeked of violence and bad breath. I guessed from the flat-sounding, padded air around me that I must be in one of the acoustic interrogation rooms in the Main Corridor.

So this was red torture.

The first attack was verbal. One of the men suddenly threw words at me out of nowhere, sneering, disparaging, insinuating words. Another flung an arbitrary question at me, not to answer, just to heighten the tension. A third yelled deeply offensive, boorish curses. When I attempted to respond, a fourth hurled an obscenity at me and told me to shut my mouth unless I wanted it filled… They goaded each other, inciting each other to violence.

'It's her own stupid fault, isn't it? She's asked for it.'

'She won't let things be, this one! She won't take things lying down.'

'So take her standing up then. She may be better that way!'

'That's the sort you like, bro – go for her!'

Their affronts became more and more vulgar, more and more sexually explicit. They spewed expletives, bullied me with every kind of revolting innuendo.

How can I possibly defend myself if they try to— ?

The thought filled me with terror. My impulse was to clutch my chador as tightly as I could, rip off my blindfold and scream. It was a foolish idea – my mind was too agitated to think straight – because the moment I lifted an arm towards my face, it was a signal for them. The attack immediately became physical.

They began to punch my head and slap my face and hit my arms. Then a drawling voice intervened, slurring the syllables like a drunk, 'No, bro, no, that won't do. This dame won't learn so easily. Let me show you!'

And he started to rain heavy blows on me with a whip. Beatings. Lashings. Repeated batterings at my head, my face, my eyes. I felt a stinging sensation on my neck. The pain was acute. I saw flashes in my right eye and panicked, bending forwards to protect myself. Each time my hand moved instinctively to my head, the blows became more severe.

The man doing most of the thrashing was using something like a leather belt. He whipped my sides, causing lacerating pains. Some of the blows were less severe than others but a few felt so hard that I thought I was being hammered with a rubber club of some sort.

If they start kicking me, I will buckle up and fall...

'You're gonna die, even if you aren't executed,' snarled one man.

'It's on you, lady!' wheezed the slimy voice of the one with cracked heels. 'You brought it on yourself. You'll just rot away in the corner of your cell!'

The verbal assaults continued in tandem with the physical blows – that's what made it worse. While one or two of them beat and whipped me, the others spat insults and flung imprecations. The combination was hard to bear, but frankly the physical battering was easier to cope with than the medley of obscenities, the crude sneers, the vile insinuations—

'Look at those swollen lips of hers. They'll tell you what she does for a living!'

'Are you a druggie then, lady? Come closer, will you? Show us your stuff.'

'Come on, you dirty whore, why aren't you saying anything?'

Despite my determination to stay silent, their threats were so offensive that on one occasion I could not help myself and shouted back at them with all my strength.

'I will not respond to such suggestions! I will not!'

But whose voice was that – so shrill and high pitched? My terror had turned me into a hysterical rooster and my words roused the men to a cackle of mocking echoes.

'Oh, she will not, will she? Well, well, well!'

'We know what to do with those that will not, don't we?'

'Take a load of that! She will not! Oh dearie me!'

As soon as I tried to speak, the man with the cracked heels in his folded-down shoes thrashed me hard on the head, again and again, swearing with every blow. In the penumbra of faint light that was now seeping from under the door, I saw white paper fluttering to the ground as the blows rained down; had they wrapped paper around a cudgel? How kind…

I counted their voices. Six. Six sweating, stinking, men, who were panting with their own efforts to thrash me, who could somehow see enough to do so in that pitch dark room. There was no ventilation; I was gasping for air. There was no point in screaming; the place was soundproofed, and my shrieks would probably incite more violence. So I just clutched my chador round me and held my tongue.

The blows they directed at me varied in severity, some hard, some less so. I never knew what to expect or from which direction to expect it. Was there nothing they weren't capable of? I had no idea how much time had passed either; when you undergo physical and verbal assault, you don't check the time. But I suddenly noticed I was shaking, shuddering from head to foot, trembling violently all over. I pressed my knees together to steady them. But they refused to obey. If only they would stop shaking!

Don't shake! Stop trembling!

The words were unspoken; they rose out of the darkness within me. Prayer was impossible but those words swept through me like a sacred remembrance. All I could think of was that these men should not see my weakness or my trembling. All I could hear was the absurd conversation I was having with my shuddering knees—

You represent the Bahá'í community of Iran, so you must not shake.

My ankles felt like water under me. There was nothing to hold on to but the edges of my chador tucked under my arms, but again, I addressed them in ringing inner tones—

You represent the Bahá'í community of Iran, so stop trembling.

And all of a sudden it occurred to me that whatever those men said or did, however depraved their abuses, however violent their blows, I would never fall at their feet because—

You represent the Bahá'í community of Iran.

I don't know how it happened, but a split second later, my heartbeats slowed down. A minute more and I was breathing more easily. A few deep gulps of that stale air, and I was able to control my knees and my ankles, and sensed they were no longer shaking. Even my hands, holding the edge of my chador under my chin, felt stronger. Within minutes – there I was, firm on my feet, straight as an arrow, unshaken!

I pulled in my stomach. Straightened my back. Held my head high with my chador tight under my chin. My mind was clear and could register the change: I was no longer afraid. It was as if I knew that these men had done their worst and could go no farther. Not today. They had reached their limits, at least for now. And in fact, they paused for a moment.

Maybe they were getting tired. It was as if they had noticed the change in me. Or maybe they thought I was in nervous shock, and were holding back because of it. Usually, when a person becomes catatonic with panic, the torturers stop what they are doing. But I was not in shock or catatonic. I was perfectly calm and breathing normally. After a few more desultory lashes, one of the men spoke, muttering to the others in a low voice.

'That's enough. Take her away.'

It was only when I left the room that I noticed how desperate I had been for fresh air. It was suffocating in that dreadful place. My body was hurting all over, and breathing was painful, because of the blows to my ribs, but air was what I needed most. I gulped it in deeply as I walked down the Main Corridor towards the green oil cloth curtain.

The buzzer sounded and a female guard, who was temporarily replacing Háj Khánum, let me into the women's ward. It was the one I had nicknamed Specs, because she not only wore a thick pair of glasses but had a very sharp pair of eyes behind them. As I stepped into Passage 100 and took off my blindfold and chador, she scrutinised me closely. I steeled myself under her gaze; I hated the guards to see me in grief or pain.

Specs was a pretty, plump little woman who exuded friendliness and goodwill until she lashed out at you for no reason. She used words that could be cruel and unkind. She knew very well where I had been and what had just happened to me. Her cheeks glowed a natural pink, and her eyes twinkled gleefully as she checked me out. She was evaluating my condition in order – I realised with disgust – to report it to those brave gentlemen.

As I handed my chador and my blindfold over to her, an Arabic phrase suddenly flashed into my mind. 'Child's play,' I murmured.

The woman was instantly on alert. She swung round, her pin-sharp eyes fixed on me.

'What was that?' she hissed. 'What did you say?'

'Nothing,' I replied.

But she could not let it go. She scuttled alongside me, insisting on the question.

'What did you say back there?'

'Nothing,' I repeated. 'It wasn't important.'

But it was to her. She absolutely had to know what I said. So, standing at the doorway of my cell and looking directly at her, I repeated the Arabic phrase in ringing tones so that the whole corridor could hear me.

'Child's play!' I told her triumphantly. 'Child's play!'

'What do you mean?' she gaped.

'Ask the gentlemen,' I laughed. 'They'll tell you!'

I turned it into a joke so that she could not take offence, but she knew what I meant.

* * *

Shortly after my encounter with the brave brutes and their whips, I asked for a shower and, standing under the streaming water, I began to interrogate myself.

Were you scared?

I considered the question objectively. Yes, I had truly been very scared!

How many times were you so scared in your life?

That horrific day in elementary school, when I was beaten up so badly for being a Bahá'í. The air raids in the middle of the Iraq War when a bomb exploded near our home and a poor young neighbour of ours was thrown out of her shower, dismembered, through the shattered windows. But most of all, when we fled the city in the middle of the night, with the children in the backseat of the car and missiles lighting up the sky.

And now this?

The warm water poured over my face and head as I thought of what had happened in the darkness of that room. It had been worse than the Iraqi air strikes, far worse than being kicked and beaten in school. The lashes of those sweating men, their vile words and curses had caused my knees to shake and my ankles to quiver. I felt more fear than I had ever felt before, more even than when I was hitting the dashboard in a panic as the bombs fell.

But what stopped that shaking?

What indeed? Where had that sudden calm come from? How was it that I'd found the strength to stand up straight and stop trembling?

A shining thought fluttered in my heart then, like a banner. Had I forgotten that I was not alone? Many hundreds and thousands of Bahá'ís all over the world knew by now what had happened to the Yárán. They were with me. I had not been representing the Bahá'í community by myself. Indeed, how could I have sustained that appalling experience unaided? I had been united with the whole world! Indescribable happiness surged through me and I was flooded with waves of gratitude under the shower. As the warm water cascaded over my battered head, I felt, almost palpably, the torrent of love and unity that had penetrated the torture chamber and strengthened me.

But it did not blind me to what had happened to my body. I was covered with painful welts and huge bruises. It was clear there would be no further interrogations from now on, no questions, no answers, no forms to fill out – only physical assaults. They wanted to break my bones, crush my limbs, destroy me. I remembered what the interrogator called out when leaving the room one time, as if offering the prognosis of a fatal disease.

You've chosen not to collaborate, so whatever you suffer now will be on you!

I remembered what one of the foul-mouthed men had spat at me in the darkness. *You're gonna die, even if you aren't executed. It's on you, lady!*

It was clear: they even wanted to blame us for the torture they inflicted on us; it was our own fault that we were being flogged to death!

* * *

Another week went by in silence and solitude. I waited for Tuesday, full of apprehension. The sun was tracing the same corner on the blanket when I heard the buzzer. The long, loud screech of a blunt finger on the button outside the door of the women's Isolation Ward. It was him. I listened carefully for the footsteps of the guard. Yes, she was approaching my door. She stopped. She opened it. No word, no gesture.

This time, I knew where I was going. And I knew what to expect.

I had been suffering badly from headaches and assumed it might be because of the blows to my head. Just prior to my arrest, I had had laser surgery on my eyes and wondered whether the headaches were something to do with it. In either case, I tried to ask the men please not to hit my head so hard. Although I held up a hand to protect myself from their blows, the only result was that my fingers were now badly injured too.

My loutish, bad-mouthed conductor led me to the same insulated room on the Main Corridor. He stood outside as he had done before, waiting for me to go in ahead of him. I did so – slowly, nervously – expecting the worst, but he did not thump me between the shoulders this time. That was almost worse because it took an eternity to enter the room.

After a few hesitant steps, I reached the same corner where I had stopped before. The stale air was the same. The rank smell and voices were the same. But they had not yet closed the door when the light fell on a clump of curly black hair clotted with dried blood at the base of the wall before me. I immediately thought of my colleagues. Which of them had hair like that? And then I was overcome with shame. What difference did it make whose hair this was? Someone had been tortured here. A man, a woman, another human being. Another poor suffering wretched innocent human being had been horribly beaten and abused here!

When they launched their attack on me, I was not in the chair, but standing. I was not leaning against the wall either, but was trying to cover my head with my hands to prevent the blows raining down too hard. They started beating me violently, hurling invective.

'I just had an eye operation,' I pleaded.

They began to laugh, and the abuse and ridicule swelled from all sides.

'She's had an eye operation!'

'The hell she did! Who gave her the right to have an eye operation?'

'How dare she! Why did you do it, stupid? You'll regret it!'

'For her funeral, that's why she did it!'

They shut the door. I was plunged into darkness as a coarse voice bellowed, 'Let's finish the old cow off today – the piece of filth!'

Fear shot a bolt of lightning through my heart. I was shocked by their words, as a woman, as a mother. Why would these men subject a woman old enough to be their mother to such abuse? I do not know why motherhood came over me so strongly at that moment, but I kept thinking that I was probably the age of these men's mothers. Would they treat their own mothers in this manner – even if she believed in a different religion?

The blows continued. The man I thought of as Bad Mouth because of all the curses that poured through his lips was hammering at me so hard that the side of my body closest to him was becoming acutely painful. Did he have a family, this man? Did he have a wife, children? Did he beat his wife like this? What did his children think of their father? Haj Áqá, man of God, faithful follower of Imam Ali, believer in the martyr Imam Husayn, pious Muslim working in Section 209 of Evin Prison. Were they proud of him? How did the rest of these men behave with their wives and families? Were they all just as violent and abusive out of this place as they were in it, or were they entirely different people at home?

My unspoken questions were probably not ones they had ever bothered to ask themselves. Their questions to me were equally incomprehensible and their curses intolerable. I did not respond to either. But my silence was an excuse for them to mock me all the more, to jeer at me with crass insinuations and goad me with repulsive innuendos.

'Where did you spend the night in Kerman, lady, hey?'

'Who did you happen to sleep with while you were there?'

They were referring, I suppose, to a trip that Mr Khánjání and I had made together, to meet with the Khadémin in the provinces. So the interrogator had fuelled them with certain facts to distort? I was so revolted by their words that I reacted vehemently, this once.

'Gentlemen, do you know whom you are talking about and talking to?'

I noticed with surprise that my voice was firm, if still a little high-pitched. But it merely solicited more scorn. Someone across the room exploded in a loud guffaw.

'Whoa, take a load of *that*!' he yelled. 'Who the fuck *are* we talking to?'

'Watch out,' another sneered. 'Don't go too far with this one, or you'll be in trouble.

'This lady's studied in the Ruhi classes, you know; you cannot accuse her of being naughty!'

I kept quiet, but they did not. They all had something to say, some indecency to throw at me, some coarse obscenity. Bad Mouth started to ask me questions – absurd and profane, bizarre and blasphemous questions – related to random, irrelevant issues. I told him that I had already answered; I had already written down everything for the interrogator.

'We have torn up your answers and thrown them down the toilet, lady,' he drawled. 'Everything starts all over again in here!'

Not for the first time, I wondered if they were drunk or on drugs; their vitriol was slurred and out of control. In fact, I had the impression they did not always know what they were say-ing. Their actions and words seemed almost mechanical.

During this second torture session, they kept shutting and opening the door. It was such a relief whenever they opened it that most of my attention was drawn to the little light that seeped into the room. Although I could not see the men, I was begin-ning to distinguish their voices and guess which of them was beating me. I also noticed, when the door was open, that I could count their feet; that way I could gauge their distance from me and better prepare myself to withstand their blows. While most of them taunted and insulted me or swore and cursed me, there were always one or two who would keep up the beating.

That day, while I stood in the ink black room filled with the stench of these six callous men, I was not shivering or shaking, despite my beating heart and dry mouth. As they continued expending their breath on futile blows and foul language, I drifted right out of that place, floated far, far away and left those people hammering away at a figment of their own imag-inations. I may have been a prisoner, but at that particular moment, I was free of them.

Whenever they paused in their whipping, a surge of energy would rush through my veins. I knew they could never truly hurt me. Even if they reduced me to pulp on the ground, they could not humiliate me. I was neither their victim nor their scapegoat. I refused to be demoralised by men who could demean themselves before a woman old enough to be their mother, who had sunk so low as to break her body in this bes-tial fashion. I felt sorry for them.

An hour later, after the man with the flexible ruler or cable returned me to my cell, I remembered why, today of all days, I had been so aware of my own motherhood. It was my son's birthday tomorrow! He had given me one of the most beautiful experiences of my life when he made a mother of me. And with that thought, my heart went out once more to the mothers of these men who had been beating me up. I mourned for them, grieved for them. Those women too had once held innocent sons in their arms, had suffered and sacrificed for them, had believed and planned for their futures. That it should come to this – ?

* * *

Later that afternoon, I asked for soap to have a shower. They usually divided a Golnar soap bar in half, but that day, Háj Khánum gave me a full bar. I eyed it laconically.

Ha! She knows you're going to be their guest for quite some time.

In the shower I discovered the horizontal welts all over my body were even deeper this time: red, swollen cuts and painful open wounds. My arms, my sides and my right thigh were all raw and stinging and the fingers of one hand were also severely injured. I was standing under the shower with the water searing these lesions and blood staining the tiles when Háj Khánum suddenly opened the door. I yelped in protest and quickly squatted on the floor. But she had been told to inspect my body, to see if there were any signs of injury.

First they hurt you; then they pretend to do something about it.

That same afternoon, I was taken to the health centre in the Main Corridor. The very pious doctor did not actually examine me; he did not even deign to look at me in the eye. I wasn't blindfolded that time, but he might as well have been. Since he dared not touch me, he asked Háj Khánum to bend my neck forward and bend it back again, to pull my right arm up from the shoulder and down again. And then, with astonishing complacence, he announced that stress was also known to cause cuts and bruises. He offered to inject me with some serum to help absorb the blood and suggested some painkillers for the pain. I accepted neither.

That day, I prepared myself for the possibility that I might never leave Section 209. Tyranny would continue as long as the enemies of justice and tolerance were in power. It was the immemorial pattern. And I was not alone in having experienced it.

Red torture followed white, and green was still to come.

28

MR. KHÁNJÁNÍ

Another week passed, and all through it I read the commentary on the Qur'an the guard had given me. Although its interpretations were superficial, simplistic and, to my mind, deficient, I kept reading until I finally reached the story of Job.

I understood Job better now. It had always seemed terribly unfair to me that God should inflict so much hardship on the poor man, so much pain and misery on one of his most faithful servants. I had always asked myself why Job had to suffer and how he had endured it. He had done nothing wrong. What was the meaning of it? Now I was beginning to see…

> Were it not for the cold, how would the heat of Thy words prevail,
> O Expounder of the worlds?
> Were it not for calamity, how would the sun of Thy patience shine,
> O Light of the worlds?[26]

This paradox meant more to me than ever before. I had never grasped how abasement and tribulation might lead to happiness, how anguish and pain could brighten to joy. But I would not have bartered them now for all the comforts in the world.

During those days of red torture, I was in an extraordinary state of emotional and spiritual exaltation. It seems implausible, but I felt both realistic and optimistic at the same time, both connected to this harsh treatment and also utterly detached from it. On the one hand, I was ready to believe that the next sound of the buzzer could bring tidings of my unconditional release from prison. On the other, I was fully prepared to die when I heard it. Had Háj Khánum opened the door and handed me my death sentence instead of a blindfold, I would have been quite ready for it.

But whether I came out of this ordeal alive or not, I felt a growing solidarity with the martyrs of the Bahá'í Faith, the tens of thousands of men and women who had given their lives for this Cause from its inception until now. For the first time, I was beginning to see a glimmering of what had sustained them. I was becoming convinced too, that I might be destined to die at the hands of this regime. And I was completely resigned to it.

It was a Thursday. The following Tuesday would come soon enough but I still had the weekend ahead of me to recuperate. Weekends and holidays were unbearable in Section 209. The sound of the buzzer and the coming and going of feet schlepping past my cell were greatly reduced. Interrogations and torture sessions were fewer. The silence was stifling.

What a dichotomy! In solitary confinement, and especially when it is prolonged, you wait for these interruptions with a kind of impatience, a certain excitement. I had already experienced this paradox in Mashhad and was conscious of it again in Evin. Interrogation is a form of communication. It is a debate. It poses a problem that you must resolve and since it can ultimately be a test of strength, a battle of wits, it stimulates curiosity, about yourself and your interrogator, it explores your limits.

And I was discovering that torture was the same. If you could manage to win one round in this physical and spiritual combat, you become eager to step back into the arena and accomplish another. This is how the warrior spirit within you goes beyond resistance and becomes resilient; this is how your sense of self revives after being battered and brought low.

The sound of the buzzer echoing down the Main Corridor should not have been for me that day. But I recognised the unremitting, incessant, uninterrupted sound; it was Bad Mouth's way of pressing the button. So soon? I had been tortured that same Tuesday. Surely he was not coming back for me already on Thursday afternoon? But the footsteps of the guard stopping in front of my door quashed all my calculations.

A few minutes later, wrapped in the chador and muffled by the blindfold, I was walking behind that vile man again, with a fluttering inside my stomach. We passed the health centre; we passed the interrogation rooms; we passed the Green and White acoustic rooms, both heavily insulated. We passed an office, and the desk along the wall of the Main Corridor where one or two men were usually seated – I had seen them on occasions when I risked tilting my head to peep from under the blindfold – and then we reached a dead end.

Although I had never been this far down the Main Corridor since my arrival from Mashhad, I remembered the small alcove located here from my last imprisonment in Evin: a wider space furnished with a card-operated wall phone, two metal filing cabinets and a bookcase full of books. Now I noticed from under the blindfold that they had moved one of the filing cabinets aside to reveal a small door in the wall behind it.

Bad Mouth stepped through the door and I followed. I was immediately hit by the smell of construction work – fresh paint and plaster and, incongruously, petrol fumes. I had no idea where I was being taken. The passageway beyond the hidden door seemed very narrow. I sensed that two people could not walk through it side by side. After taking several paces forward, my guide turned to the left and entered another space. A room, a cell? A wider passage? From beneath the blindfold, I saw the feet of several men standing around.

I counted their shoes and the hems of their trousers; there were at least four or five of them. Clean and polished shoes, neatly ironed trousers. So! Not the same type of torturers as before. Who were these men? What were *they* going to do to me?

Courage is not the absence of fear. It is simply the ability to keep going while frightened. That could also define obstinacy, of course, but I was suspended between terror and the ability to overcome it. As usual, my internal interrogation had already begun.

If this is your execution, are you ready for it?
I think so.
What if your voice shakes, or your hand trembles?
It won't.
How can you be sure?
Because I won't let them see my weakness.
And what if this leads to your release?
Now that *is* a sign of weakness! What would be the use of release?
You never know…
Such absurd capacities for optimism.

At that moment my freedom meant nothing to me. The freedom of the Bahá'í community was what mattered, the freedom of children to go to school and youth to study at university and people to engage in their professions and earn their livings with dignity. The freedom of the women of Iran to have equal rights and not be snuffed out like second class citizens, and the freedom of all Iranians to be free to distinguish between the truth and falsehood, at last. In brief, the freedom and well-being of every human being, here and the world over, was all that counted for me at that moment.

These thoughts were racing through my mind when Bad Mouth suddenly stopped. I barely avoided treading on his calloused heels and stopped one pace behind him. My exalted thoughts quavered in the stratosphere for a second and then came crashing down.

A voice called out. 'Look here!' It was one of the unseen gentlemen standing round me, 'You refused to cooperate, so you had to be punished. Now, Khánjání is being punished because he won't cooperate either. He will be executed at dawn. And you, you will be executed on Saturday.'

Silence. Total silence. A silence mingled sickeningly with the smell of plaster and petrol. A tide of turbulent thoughts rushed in on me as I stood God knows where, surrounded by God knows who. Mr Khánjání, tortured? Mr Khánjání executed? So, it *was* finished. It was over. They were not going to allow him to leave this place alive. Nor me, for that matter. And I suddenly remembered the words of the interrogator one day, the unfinished question he had left hanging over my head like the sword of Damocles as he walked through the door:

If we choose one of you two to be executed…?

So they had chosen; it was only a matter of which of us died first.

'Now you can see Khánjání for the last time,' Bad Mouth wheezed.

He directed me from that passageway into a different room which he entered before me. I waited at the threshold, sensing all the men gathered behind and around me. At the order of one among them, I lifted my blindfold for a few moments. And saw —

A cell, stark, without windows. A high, narrow, iron bed in the middle of the cell. A chair in the corner. And Mr Khánjání's slippers, placed neatly beneath it, side by side.

Dear Mr Khánjání was lying face down on the bed. His ankles and toes had been bound together and were pointing towards me. His head was turned to one side at an odd uncomfortable angle. The soles of his feet were dusty, perhaps because he had walked barefoot from the chair to the bed. Both were painfully red and swollen.

A man was standing at the foot of the torture bed with his back to me. He was tall and slim, I guessed quite young, and was wearing elegant light grey trousers. I could see his hair was glossy and black; he was holding a whip in his hand. It appeared to be made of leather with a delicately woven handle and a few thick leather straps dangling at the end.

'Mahvash!'

My heart jumped to my mouth. Bad Mouth was calling my name, but I did not reply. The man with the whip suddenly lifted his arm high and brought the leather down with a stinging blow on Mr Khánjání's feet.

A soft sigh escaped the lips of my dear colleague, a deep exhalation. That was all. But it cut through me like a knife. Bad Mouth called me again—

'Mahvash!'

And the young man raised his arm high a second time and inflicted another blow, callous and uncaring, on the flaming soles of dear Mr Khánjání. He sighed softly again.

I couldn't bear it. 'Yes,' I croaked. 'Yes.' Like a crow.

'So you're here then?' the young man asked, with his back towards me.

'Yes.' I didn't recognise my voice.

I could not see the face of the torturer either. He had taken up a position that made it impossible for his features to be observed. But I wonder whether he felt my eyes boring into the back of his head, because he suddenly told me to lower my blindfold and leave the cell.

Bad Mouth ordered me to follow him out. The passageway was empty. All those feet and elegant shoes that had witnessed this demonstration of human cruelty were gone. I was paralysed, stupefied, unable to think or move. Each step I took was hoofed in lead.

'Come on, come on,' drawled Bad Mouth.

He dragged out the words as his trousers trailed along the floor ahead of me. He was walking faster and faster, and I was following more and more slowly, two or three steps behind, partly to keep my balance and stop myself from falling and partly to avoid breathing in the foul mixture of cigarette smoke and cheap cologne on his soiled clothes. He did not stop on the way but headed straight for the curtain in front of the women's Isolation Ward.

'They'll give you a sheet of paper,' he growled, 'so you can write your will, or any other nonsense you want.' Then he rang the buzzer and mumbled, 'Get in there.'

Before the guard had even pulled back the curtain, he had already turned on his cracked heels and disappeared.

* * *

As soon as I stepped inside the women's ward, I asked to use the shower. The ritual bath of patience. Water. Dear God, give me water. Let me weep in the shower at least, where no one will notice. But I could not. I stood there dry-eyed while the water poured over me, as if the fountainhead of all my tears had turned to dust, as if I had become stone.

And under the torrent of water, the whole history of the Bahá'í Faith in Iran unfurled before my staring eyes. It was like watching a film – one that has not yet been made, that no one has yet seen – and the speed with which the images passed before me was incredible. I saw it all unfold, from the very distant past to now. From the village of Niyala where Bahá'u'lláh was bastinadoed and made to run, to the foul Black Pit from which he was finally banished, never to return. From the fields of Badasht where Ṭáhirih was unveiled to emancipate men from the past, to the town of Barfurúsh where Quddús was butchered by a mob's blood thirst. I saw starving souls under siege in Fort Tabarsi, heads of the betrayed held high in Nayríz, captive women and children of Shiráz, riding to their deaths under the blazing sun. All the heroes and heroines of Bahá'í history who had suffered persecution and been killed for their beliefs were paraded before me – and now Mr Khánjání was about to join these thousands gone before us. It seemed to me that he was running to meet the gentle figure of 'Abdu'l-Bahá, in an ecstasy of gladness, his arms open wide.

Did they want to humiliate Mr Khánjání? Did they imagine they could bully him, coerce him, terrorise him? Did they think that this inhumane show they had put on for me to see would undermine his faith, or mine? Did they hope to break our spirits by beating us?

Take heed, O you whose hearts are turning black!
Plead pardon, you with hoary temples turning white.[27]

Spiritual resilience is a story that has been told from time immemorial. And it will always need to be told anew, in every age, because it is rooted in a very simple truth about the human psyche. We resist coercion; we respond to attraction. We reject force and are attracted to love. Although intimidation, suppression, accusation and lies may appear to hold sway for a time, they are doomed to fail in the end. And that is why the story of resilience has to be recalled and repeated, again and again, and in our times more than ever.

All I could think of in the shower was the urgency of telling it. These memories, these experiences and the stories of these incredible people, like Mr Khánjání, Faribá and the other members of the Yárán must be remembered and live on. If I survived all this, if I had the chance, I promised myself I would write all this down. I would tell the story of these days. I wanted history to remember a little of what we were going through, in our own words. I wanted Iran to know our story. It may be difficult to believe, but even then, under the streaming water, sentences were forming urgently in my mind.

But it looked as if I would not survive. What if I could not write this story before we were all snuffed out? How I wished I had the means of writing then and there, in the shower, even if the paper turned to pulp and the ink washed down the drain. And with that thought, I saw how foolish I was. Even if I did not write it, others would. Even if I could not see this story published, others would make sure that it would be. This was not our story only: it belonged to everyone. It was a story embedded in our collective consciousness.

The 'ritual bath of patience' had its salutary effect. My heart was reassured. I even felt guilty about how calm I felt, how composed and serene in spirit. I was neither worried nor afraid. Tonight, this very night, our dear Mr Khánjání was going to be executed, and yet I was not perturbed or agitated. I just felt grateful and closely connected to him. For a while I thought of those clean brown leather shoes and crisply ironed trousers standing behind me as he was being whipped. To find such people in a torture chamber was shocking to me. They were not the same sort of men who had tortured me, dressed in filthy clothes with dirty feet in cheap plastic sandals. They seemed of a different order and class entirely. Were they gentlemen of the Intelligence Ministry, who had gathered to hear some exculpatory 'evidence' forced out of Mr Khánjání *in extremis*? Or were they members of the judiciary, perhaps, there to witness legal matters, to sign death warrants? What were they feeling now, after having witnessed that shameful scene? How would they sleep tonight?

I came back to my cell in a strangely disembodied state. I did not feel like praying. I did not feel like eating either. I pulled the commentary book on the Qur'an close to me on the blanket, but I did not feel like reading. Perhaps my eyes grazed the pages but instead of seeing the words I began to conduct another internal interrogation, in my usual way.

What is this curious state of detachment?
I don't know.
Are you in shock, perhaps?
No.
You're probably in denial then?
No.
Is it quite simply disbelief?
Well, yes and no.

* * *

Sleep was banished for me that night as I lay there in Evin thinking of dear Khánjání's execution. If it had not taken place as soon as I left his torture chamber, I assumed it would take place at daybreak. So I fixed my eyes on the mesh of the window to watch the sky light up. And as dawn broke, I could see in my imagination the event unfolding, step by step. I accompanied my dear colleague to the foot of the gallows. I stood next to him until the noose was tried around his neck. I watched the footstool being pulled from under his feet. I even saw his feet dancing in the air and bore those terrible imaginings to the last unbearable moment, to the final jerks of life, to the closing stillness. And then I gave way to my sense of loss and hid my head under the blanket to cry in secret, to suffocate my sobs and scrape the tears off my face so the guards would have nothing to report.

Friday was my funeral. I was buried at daybreak beneath the dust thrown over dear Mr Khánjání. How much we would miss him, this man of faith, of certitude and integrity, this noble man of shining steadfastness, murdered for no reason. I was haunted by his family's grief, by the anguish that would sweep through the Bahá'í community when they heard the news. I could not bear the thought of the sadness that would overwhelm everyone. So to counteract it, I started imagining all the Bahá'ís in different towns who would arise to strengthen and encourage the friends up and down the land. I conjured their faces, evoked scenes, was assailed by a myriad of images.

The morning passed, and around noon I suddenly remembered myself.

So what about you? What did they say? That you would be executed – when?

I could not remember. The day of my execution would have to be Saturday, because Friday's dawn belonged to Mr

Khánjání and that had already come and gone. I was surprised, in retrospect, that they carried out executions on a Friday in the Islamic Republic of Iran. When would they inform my family of my death on Saturday? How would my dear ones react? I imagined the faces of Negár and Fúrúd, their grief, their sense of abandonment. And then, with a fierce intensity that was frankly incomprehensible to me even then, I managed to push these emotions aside and told myself: they are not the only children who have lost a mother in this world. They will not mourn for me all through their lives.

No one has ever died of grief over a dead mother.

I convinced myself that they would get over it and determined not to dwell on their grief so as to overcome my own. If I became sentimental over my children, it was all over for me. I knew myself too well. And the same went for my beloved husband, Siyávash, my dear father and sister – no, there was no time for mawkishness, no time for love letters now. And then I remembered there was no sheet of paper either, which should have been given to me for the purpose of writing a will or 'any other nonsense'.

But there was no point in following that up. What nonsense could I write, anyway? One last note to my loved ones, with no certainty that it would ever reach them? One more affirmation of my faith which the gentlemen could use as 'evidence' to justify their actions? There was nothing left but to await my imminent execution. How would they proceed? Where would they take me? I was getting curious, as the minutes of my life ticked by.

Nothing happened. There was no change in the afternoon's routine. I called for the guard once, just to examine her facial expression, but there was nothing to see. I was sure she would have been informed of my fate, but she gave no sign of it.

I spent another sleepless night, until the call to prayer unrolled across the city. A new dawn and still no news. The door opened and a tray of tea, unaccompanied by words, was pushed through by Mask, a female guard whom I had named for the covering she always wore over her mouth. I never knew whether it was not to infect me, or because she feared I would contaminate her. To communicate in whispers was already difficult; to understand someone who hid her lips, impossible. But even that seemed unremarkable today. There was something banal about the silence of this last breakfast. After my cup of unsweetened tea, some thin *lavash* bread and a bite of cheese, it was just another day like all the rest.

I felt the better for eating and arranged the blankets for more comfort. Then I opened the commentary on the Qur'an and sat down before the open page.

What will you do, if this is your last day alive?

I prepared a list of activities: prayers, reading, exercise, shower. Then if I am still alive, lunch, midday rest, more reading, on the spot jogging. Then if I am not yet dead, dinner, and perhaps reading my quota of comments on the cell walls. This last activity I had been eking out carefully since I had been in solitary confinement to make it last as long as possible. Reading those 'wallwritings' was my only contact with humanity, my invisible link to others who had occupied this cell before me. Year after year, women prisoners had rolled the tin foil cover of yogurt containers into a tight point, like the nib of a pen, and used it to scratch their grief and longing into the paint, engrave their prayers and piteous cries for help into the unrelenting plaster:

Oh God, have mercy on me!
I miss my children!

How can I go on like this?
When will it end?

There were howls of rage too, and shouts of exasperation and frustration and desperation cut into the walls:

To hell with you all!
The eleventh interrogation!
Please God don't let me break down, don't let me give in!
Death to X – !
Death to Y – !

Also rows and rows of parallel lines for the days, the weeks, the months, possibly years passed in this cell before I inhabited it.

These tiny, crabbed markings covered the walls from floor to ceiling; some must have been scribbled lying flat on the floor because you had to lie on the ground to read them. I don't know how the others were written so high. But they were all meditations on human suffering, reflections on human endurance, contemplations on human hope, prayers and poems. I allowed myself to read just a few of these to help endure the hours. And then it would be another Saturday over. And if it was to be the last, well, so be it…

My daily prayers and reading took a long time that day. The atmosphere in the cell was heavy and hot, sultry and slow. The only source of cool air was in the corridor, where there was an outlet to the air conditioner, but it did not reach me. And slowest and heaviest and hottest of all was the passage of time. I refolded one blanket as a carpet, refolded another as a cushion to sit on, and refolded a third to use as a table. I tried to study the commentary on the Qur'an but could not concentrate. I tried to exercise, then lie down, then sit up, then lie down, sit up, lie down, sit up. Too hot. I listened, I watched, I waited. Breathless for the buzzer. For some news. For any contact with a human being, an interrogation, an execution even, anything except this limbo of grief and suspense. I kept telling myself, calm down, nothing has happened to you yet, and no matter what does happen, you cannot lose…

I was busy with my internal dialogue when the door suddenly opened. There had been no buzzer but the guard hissed the familiar words through her mask:

'Get ready!'

29

GREEN TORTURE

Bad Mouth was standing outside the women's ward.

'Come on, come on,' he drawled, dragging out the words in his predictable way.

I cannot explain why I was so happy to hear his sleazy voice; was it the sheer relief of communication or the imminence of death, at last? Even if he was taking me to my place of execution, I was happy to follow his filthy cracked heels there, all the way down the Main Corridor. Even if I could not see him, I was grateful to hear him grunting as he pushed the bookcase aside in the little alcove at the very end. Then, as we stepped through the same low door into the same narrow passageway, my relief congealed to fear. He turned to the left at that same corner smelling of plaster and petrol, and entered a room. I followed him, ready to breathe my last. I guessed it was the same cell in which I had witnessed the lashing of dear Mr Khánjání, the torture or death chamber with the high, narrow iron bed on which he might have been killed. I was trembling in spite of myself. And now it was my turn.

Bad Mouth told me to sit on the same chair beneath which I had seen Mr Khánjání's slippers. I did so, carefully putting my feet where they had been placed, side by side.

Please God, whatever happens, let me be as brave as he was.

'If you don't collaborate,' hissed Bad Mouth, 'you'll face Khánjání's fate. The same thing will happened to you as happened to him. Right here.'

The blood galloped in my veins. I did not speak. What did he mean by *collaborate*?

'So?' he said gruffly. 'Will you or won't you?'

I did not utter a word. There were none in my head. Except –

Collaborate?

He began to curse me, to yell and swear at me. 'Are you deaf, woman? Can't you hear me, you stupid cow? Why aren't you answering?'

My brain had seized up. The strange word tumbled over my dry lips incoherently. 'I have no collaboration,' I whispered. It was the most bizarre thing to say, not even correct in a grammatical sense, the result of pent-up terror, perhaps, the anticipation of the final blow he would give to my head and end me. What a way to go, not even knowing what I meant.

My response just provoked more roars of rage. But Bad Mouth did not touch me.

'You have no collaboration?' he repeated. 'What the hell d'you mean? I'll give you no collaboration! Look here, lady, I'll be straight with you. You have to write something for me today, d'you understand? You have to write something, get it?'

I cringed away from his breath, wincing under the blindfold in expectation of another beating. None of this made sense. Wasn't I going to die?

'What should I write?'

'That's your problem! You have to cough up something that you've never written before. Get it? Get it?' he repeated.

I was utterly taken aback. Write instead of die? But did that mean that they had chosen to execute Mr Khánjání instead of me? I was filled with horror at the thought. Better die than live instead of Mr Khánjání, and write – what was I supposed to write?

'But…' I began again.

He did not let me finish. 'Something you haven't spoken about to anyone else,' he yelled. 'Anything at all, you stupid woman. And you must damn well do it today!'

I was shaken by the sheer force of his fury. How could I defuse the situation, deflect the anger of this savage, unpredictable, confrontational man? I took a deep breath.

'Very well. I'll be glad to write for you. But may I think about it?'

He gave a grunt, and his tone shifted down a notch. 'That's more like it,' he growled.

'I need a little time,' I continued. 'But I'll find something special for you.'

And then to my astonishment, his bluster evaporated as suddenly as it had erupted. 'I knew you'd finally come round,' he said, mollified. 'So how long will you need?'

'Until tomorrow?' I hazarded. Was I really bargaining to stay alive another day?

'Right. One day. And that's all you'll get, understand?' Then he started talking to me as if I were a wayward child. 'Go and think about it, okay? Think well. You'd better remember everything, so you can write it for me, okay? You'll be ready tomorrow, okay?'

I promised, stunned as much by his bizarre request as his abrupt mood swings. I followed him out of the room, half-unnerved, half-bemused, and as we started walking back the way we had come, I wondered if Bad Mouth was mentally unstable. How could this man be sane? Or was he just trying to confuse me with these weird demands and sudden shifts? Was he trying to get me to cooperate before I died or was this strange request a means of delaying my death just so that I would be tortured by the terrible idea that Mr Khánjání had been executed instead of me? Or perhaps the gentlemen with their polished shoes and neatly ironed trousers were threatening him for reasons I would never know, and he needed to prove himself to them? There were wheels within wheels of torture in this place.

Well, you might as well make your peace with Bad Mouth before you die.

As I was thinking this, he suddenly stopped in front of a wall phone in the little alcove.

'All right now, come on, come on,' he drawled, 'let's make a phone call, shall we?'

I was bewildered. There I was thinking of death and forgiveness and here he was bribing me with phone calls! Why was this man, who had expended so much physical energy in thrashing and beating me, and had wasted so much verbal vigour in attacking and abusing me, now offering me a phone call? To buy my 'collaboration'? To trick me into a false confession? It had occurred to me, over the past few days, that all this talk of execution might be a charade. I was beginning to wonder if it was just part of the game they were playing, just another twist of the knife. Another twist. And another, and another...

Green torture. The kind that spreads its tentacles in your brain.

From under my blindfold, I could see him searching in his pockets for a phone card. I was jolted back to reality. After all these weeks and months, would I really be able to talk to my loved ones – for the last time? I stood beside him hardly daring to breathe. A phone call was vital for two reasons. First, to confirm Mr Khánjání's death. Next, to hear the voices of my loved ones, to let them know that I was – well, still alive – at least for now.

The bubble burst. Bad Mouth stopped fiddling in his pockets.

'Sorry lady, you're not in luck today,' he wheezed. 'I don't have a phone card on me after all. But tomorrow, when you've written your stuff, you'll get your call.'

* * *

Once back in my cell, I slumped on the ground, exhausted. I did not feel like doing anything. I had absolutely no desire to write even if I had something to write about or with, which I didn't. It was all mind games. I had not anticipated the lengths to which green torture could go. Perhaps those men standing around, watching Mr Khánjání being whipped, had only come there to watch me being tortured by that sight. How many ways could these gentlemen torment us? What crops of cruelty could they still come up with, what harvests of spite? Was an entire bureau of the government dedicated to these evergreen torments of uncertainty? If so, its budget alone must be enormous. If one were to evaluate the importance of the Bahá'í Faith according to how much money was spent by the government on this sort of vindictiveness, we must be worth billions to the Islamic Republic of Iran.

I was beginning to suspect either that Mr Khánjání's execution might be another bluff or that mine was. Maybe neither of us would be killed – yet. For they had played similar tricks on other Bahá'ís in the past. In 1983, we learned that the members of our last, disbanded National Spiritual Assembly had been taken on several occasions to the foot of the gallows where the executioners would hang one person and return the rest to their cells. One day, as they were standing there, forced to watch a colleague die, one of the members had turned to another, who later survived to tell the tale, and said, with a wistful smile –

'I never thought it would be so easy!'

When his turn finally came, that dear man welcomed death with ease because he had been preparing for it for so long. Indeed, hundreds of thousands of Iranian men and women have had death dangled before their eyes over the past four decades and have been forced to prepare for it. Perhaps this never-ending, self-propagating torture was a form of preparation, and I should be grateful for it. Green torture made death easier in the end.

Was Bad Mouth trying to make it 'easy' for me? Or was I now in a position to make it 'difficult' for him? The more I thought of it, the more convinced I became that if he wanted my 'collaboration' so badly, it was probably for his own sake too. Perhaps I was a bargaining chip for this man, a chance for promotion, payment, survival. And I could deny it to him. At my own cost, of course. Lose-lose. Some games are that simple.

But what 'collaboration' could I possibly offer the man? Bad Mouth's style was not exactly investigatory; it was based on force rather than information. Unlike the gentlemen of the Intelligence Ministry, he and his cronies had no interest in the Bahá'ís. They probably never asked themselves why they should beat or bully or kill us. They did not give a damn about our beliefs or our behaviour. They just wanted to stay employed.

For several hours, after that strange episode, I had no idea what I could write for Bad Mouth that had not already been submitted to the interrogators innumerable times. Nothing came to mind. And then I had an idea. Since there was nothing left to tell, why not tell Bad Mouth precisely nothing, and do so as if it were something of great significance?

When the buzzer sounded again a day or two later, I was prepared, though feeling a fluttering of fear lest this man should see through my bluff. He led me down the same passageway to the same room, suffused by the same ominous smell of chalk and petrol. This time I had graduated from the door to the chair, and now from the chair to the bed itself. A dubious elevation. I had to take off my shoes and sit on the edge of the bed now, with my bare feet dangling over the side. The fluttering of fear rose and beat in my throat.

Bad Mouth started playing the interrogator. 'Did you think well?' he breathed.

'Oh yes,' I replied. 'I thought really hard but why don't you tell me what subjects you want to know about. Why don't *you* ask me questions.'

I was calling *his* bluff; he had no questions. But I had not reckoned with his smut.

'I didn't want to force you to lie down,' he said darkly, 'but you're making me!'

I shuddered. After seeing Mr Khánjání in this room I had imagined being in his position. It was bad enough for a man, but far worse for a woman to lie on her stomach on this torture bed, her head twisted to one side, her toes and ankles tied together with this ghoul hovering over her. I did not know how far Bad Mouth would go, but his insinuations were as repulsive as ever and I shrank away as he drew closer to me.

'Shall we just get it over with, lady?' he wheezed.

After a few more seconds of hesitation and fear, I could not hold out any further. And I blurted out my little idea.

'Actually, I don't think they know about our medical committees,' I said.

'Medical committees?' he replied, pulling back in surprise.

I feared he would recognise my 'nothing' the minute I offered it, but he was ready to jump on anything. I could hear it, in his wheedling, cajoling voice.

'Spit it out!' he said. 'Go ahead, lady. Spit it out, about these medical committees!'

'Well,' I began, taking a deep breath, 'we appoint two or three individuals, you see, to extend medical assistance to needy patients in regional towns far from the capital…'

And then I explained all the banal details of the Yárán's system of medical assistance. When a sick person came to Tehran for specialised treatment, I told him how this medical team could be contacted, how they would make appointments for the person, how they would accompany him or her to these appointments, and if the sick person had to be hospitalised, how they would arrange for friends to stay with the patient, and so on. I was sure that these subjects were of absolutely no significance, but I was taking a gamble. And to my amazement, Bad Mouth swallowed my 'nothing' whole.

'Very good,' he said approvingly, 'here's pen and paper. Now start writing!'

I slipped off the bed, groped my way to the chair and turned my back to him as instructed before writing a couple of lines under the heading of 'medical assistance.' All he needed was to glance over my shoulder and see the scribble filling the page and after a few more lines, he patted me on the back. As if I had been a good, obedient dog.

'That's better!' he said patronisingly. 'Get up now, put on your shoes.'

It was such a charade that I wondered again whether he was quite sane and if he could even read. Or was this just a little power game he was playing with me for his own diversion? And what did it mean that I had agreed to play with him in order to save my own skin at the cost of Mr Khánjání's death? He shambled quickly out of the room after I gave him the scribbled form, and I followed at his heels, like the dog he was right to assume I was.

When he reached the phone alcove, he slowed down. I sensed him fumbling for a phone card in his pocket. Time for payment.

'The number?' he muttered. 'Who d'you want to call?'

I gave him my husband's number, trembling with anticipation and hope. He dialled, waited, then handed the receiver over to me. Other than the one-minute telephone call I had been granted almost five months ago, on 2 Farvardín (22 March), this would be the second time only that I'd heard my dear Siyávash's voice.

He picked up. He did not recognise my voice at first, just as before, but as soon as I greeted him again, his voice bloomed with excitement. Just as before. He kept repeating the tired old clichés – *How are you? Where are you? What are you doing?* – which nevertheless sounded fresh in his dear mouth. But although it was a relief not to have his voice echoing through a loudspeaker and heard by half a dozen gentlemen of the Ministry, it was impossible to ask him about Mr Khánjání with Bad Mouth breathing over me; it was still difficult to have a real conversation.

'I'm well,' I said. 'How are you?'

'Is it over yet?' he asked.

'Not yet, my dear.'

I felt, almost, that I might even be speaking about my life. Not over. Yet. There was an awkward pause which I rushed to fill.

'How are the children?'

'They're well.'

'And how are you? How are your spirits?'

He did not answer. I stopped breathing. He did not mention Mr Khánjání. Was he holding back the news that had already spread through the community? Did he want to protect me from knowing what I already knew? I panicked and tried to fill the silence with repetitions. A minute or two passed, one or two more banalities were exchanged, and then –

'Hang up!' muttered my nemesis.

My heart ached. So little time, so few words, so much left unsaid. I begged him to let me call my daughter as well. But my collaboration value had clearly expired. Bad Mouth had turned away and was already wading down the Main Corridor. I followed his cracked heels.

'Come on, come on,' he drawled back at me, in his usual smarmy way.

He pressed the buzzer outside the women's Isolation Ward, and then just before the door opened, to my complete surprise, he turned and spoke to me.

'Keep well!' he murmured unexpectedly before shuffling away.

I returned to my cell in a state of shock. They were the first humane words this man had ever said to me. It suddenly hit me that perhaps Bad Mouth had not needed my 'collaboration' at all. Perhaps he had gone through this little charade just to allow me a phone call, just because he felt sorry for me. Or ashamed. Or maybe it was pure human compassion because he knew I had not long to live.

Had I fallen for his bluff?

* * *

A few days later, when I was almost convinced that there must have been a choice, as the interrogator hinted there might be, and Mr Khánjání *had* been executed instead of me, I heard the buzzer once more. A smooth voice was speaking to Háj Khánum. It was Madání who had come for me this time. He took me to the end of the Main Corridor once more, and through the dreaded small door, and led me back to that same horrible torture chamber. I felt dizzy and almost fell as I was engulfed by the same sickening smell of plaster and petrol.

Dear God, will this never end? Or is it the end at last?

Then just as I was expecting imminent death, yet again, he ordered me to remove the blindfold, and I almost lost my mind. For there was Mr Khánjání himself – alive! Dear Mr Khánjání – not executed, not hanged – but lying in the same position as before, on the torture bed, with the same thin man standing over him, holding the same deadly whip.

I was dazed. How I had mourned his death. How I rejoiced now at seeing him alive! I wanted to fly and simultaneously to cry out loud at finding him in these circumstances again. Had they revived my hopes just to make me watch him suffer under the lash once more? Or worse still, were they going to execute him before my very eyes? This was green torture truly. These duplicitous gentlemen were willing to twist the knife over and over again in our very souls, just to reach their ends.

'Mr Khánjání,' said Madání, 'where is the report of the European Union?'

The question came out of the blue, unaccompanied by the lash, and Mr Khánjání replied without any hesitation. His voice was gravelly and rose out of the very depths of his throat. I wondered how long he had been lying there, with his head twisted to one side.

'This one, at least, should be in Mrs Sabet's possession,' he said hoarsely.

I was taken aback by the question and even more so by his answer.

This one, at least, should be in Mrs Sabet's possession?

The report of the meeting we had had with several representatives from the European Union was no secret. I had already been asked about it several times; I had already provided all the details to the interrogator. Why were they trying to force this information out of Mr Khánjání again? But what did he mean by saying this one was in my possession? The report *had* been in my possession when the files and documents and archives were in our home, before I left for Mashhad. But I assumed these had all been confiscated when I was arrested and the house was ransacked, as had happened at my daughter's wedding. I was baffled.

Maybe Madání just wanted to see my reaction, because soon after this enigmatic exchange, he hustled me, blindfolded, out of the room again. I had no idea where he was taking me but it was well beyond the acrid-smelling passageway and even further away from the Main Corridor. I was in a daze as I followed him, haunted by the sight of Mr Khánjání, torn between relief and indignation, gripped by the dread of what might happen next. Madání led me around several corners and at the end of the labyrinth sat me down in a room that seemed like a large salon, filled with tables and chairs. As I was trying to catch my breath, he placed a form on my armrest, once more, in his usual haste.

'What did you write in the report of the European Union?' he said. 'Write it down again, exactly as before. Word for word. Quickly! Quickly!'

I was stupefied. I wanted to think about Mr Khánjání, I wanted to ponder his words. The last thing I felt capable of doing at that moment was to dredge up, all over again, the points raised in an outdated report. When the team from the European Union had visited Iran some years before, the Bahá'ís had been asked to list the multiple discriminations suffered by our community under the current regime. How many times did I have to summarise that list?

'But why? I've written all this for the interrogator already!' I told Madáni, somewhat reproachfully. 'You have all my various attempts to remember it, as well as the original.'

He did not utter a word. And in his silence, Mr Khánjání's words acquired a new resonance. *This one, at least, should be in Mrs Sabet's possession.* Had my dear colleague been trying to tell me something? Was he letting me know that our home had not been raided when I was arrested? Perhaps all the records of the Yárán were indeed still in our possession – including the original report to the European Union; perhaps everything had been removed *before* the house had been ransacked a second time. I had no way of knowing, and Madáni certainly wasn't going to tell me. But if Mr Khánjání's words did mean that the Intelligence services had come too late to find those documents, it occurred to me that this young man, who was always gushing and rushing everywhere, might be as frustrated by the error as by the futility of his current demand. No wonder he had nothing to say for once.

Like all agents of the Intelligence Ministry, Madání was characterised by deceit. I had always wondered whether these good gentlemen even believed what they said about the Bahá'ís. Did they really think we were spies, fifth columnists, foreign agents? Were they truly convinced of all they accused us of doing? I was genuinely mystified.

'Mr Madání,' I asked with a sigh, as I steeled myself to dredge up what had been in the report yet again, 'I know you work for the Intelligence Ministry and regard all matters from the perspective of security. But when you accuse us of nefarious activities, surely you know, deep down, that the charges are false? Or do you truly believe what you are saying?'

'Obviously we believe,' he retorted. 'Now, do please hurry up…'

'But you *surely* know it's all pure fabrication, Mr Madání,' I persisted. 'You know and I know and no one else is around, so why not just admit it?'

But candour was impossible for the man. All he could do was insist that I hurry up. I told him that he was not being very efficient with his valuable time. Our community was not complex; we were not a secret cult, harbouring hidden agendas. He could acquaint himself with the facts very quickly and easily if he wanted; they were all out in the open.

'Once you look squarely at who we are and what we are doing,' I urged, 'it should be obvious to you that your accusations are completely baseless.'

But he could neither admit nor deny the truth of my assertion, and even refused to say why he needed yet another iteration of the European Union report. He had probably never seen the original. Perhaps he had even lost my previous summaries. Maybe, at the end of the day, the real reason I was obliged to undergo this futile exercise was his sheer incompetence. He spun a cocoon of opacity around me to no real end, with a repetition of hurry, hurry, get on with it and write everything up, for the umpteenth time.

As I completed the form with my blindfold lifted, I heard footsteps behind me, and two other men entered the salon. They sat close by, at one of the other tables. I did not need to look at their polished shoes and the crisp folds of their trousers to guess that they too may have been in the torture room. Since I could not stop thinking of Mr Khánjání, I spoke to them in Madáni's hearing, as I signed off with a flourish.

'Do you know how old Mr Khánjání is?' I asked. 'Can you really allow yourselves to treat such a respectable man of his age in this inhuman manner?'

I sensed they were slightly abashed by my question, these two young men of the Ministry, semi-bearded and probably in training. But Madáni immediately intervened.

'Khánjání is a valuable asset for us!' he said defensively.

You don't know half his worth. I handed the form to him in silence.

'He's a treasure for the Revolution!' he added, as he took the paper from me.

Well, you certainly cannot steal that treasure by whipping the soles of his feet. I pulled down my blindfold, so as to look at him no longer.

Madáni did not say another word. Within minutes, I was scurrying after his long, loping steps towards the women's Isolation Ward. I had never been so relieved to pass through the green curtain so that I might distance myself from that ambiguous man, nor so grateful to take refuge from his futile rushing and gushing in the silence of my cell. For the next several hours, I could only ponder the words of Mr Khánjání and give praise with all my heart for the treasure locked away but still alive, somewhere in the labyrinths of Evin.

30

THE OTHER WOMAN

My solitary confinement had become interminable. It was almost mid-August, and I had been effectively locked away, cut off and kept in isolation for six agonising months. I had been separated so permanently from the world that I might as well have died. With vital stimuli reduced to a minimum, with no colour, no natural light, no beauty, no horizon before my eyes and a minimum of sound in my ears, I sometimes wondered if I was still Mahvash or had become someone else entirely. It is easy to lose sight of yourself when the world around you shrinks to a pinhole, when you are either snuffed out by a blindfold or see nothing but blank walls within five feet all around you. The only voice you hear apart from your own is that of your interrogator, your torturer, the absolute sovereign of this unreal world, who uses every means of sensory deprivation – sight, sound, smell, touch and even taste – to intimidate and terrorise you.

But although the conditions of my confinement were hard to bear during that seemingly endless summer of silence and unrelieved solitude, I was given a brief and perhaps accidental reprieve on a few occasions in the course of the month of Murdád (late July to early August). These momentary encounters with other people somehow kept me alive.

One deadly hot day, when I was unexpectedly called back to the interrogation room, I heard a familiar voice as I stood waiting at the door. Someone I immediately recognised was telling me to take off my blindfold, and there was Mr Ghadimí before me, the gentleman who had interrogated me briefly in 1384 (2005) when I was first detained in Evin. He had been friendly then and greeted me cordially now. He had always prided himself on being a reformist, on conducting interrogations with affability and wit. Even when telling me his name, he had done so with a wink and a nod, implying that it might not be his real one. It went without saying that all gentlemen of the Ministry used pseudonyms.

'So,' he said, 'first you were in Mashhad, and now you are here. Well, well, well! It seems that Mahvash Khánum is not so lucky!'

'Why not, Haj Áqá?' I parried light-heartedly. 'I do not feel unlucky.'

'So how's it going anyway?' he said, smiling. 'How're you doing this time round?'

'As well as might be expected,' I replied. 'How should a normal person "do" in a place like this?'

He laughed volubly, as if it were hilarious for me to consider myself a normal person. Then he told me that he now lived in Switzerland with his wife, who was a doctor there. He had apparently feathered his nest nicely, travelling to foreign lands for his government, using a visa he had acquired through marriage. I noticed how smartly he was dressed, what fine Swiss shoes he was wearing. He had been lucky in his life, by all accounts.

'God willing, your life will work out too,' he said in response to my congratulations. 'But it seems you've been unlucky so far,' he insisted. 'Such a pity, Mahvash Khánum.'

Since he evidently enjoyed dwelling on my misfortunes, I did not deny him this little pleasure and bid him farewell with good humour, hoping we might soon meet again. A few days later, when I was summoned to the green curtain at the entrance of the women's ward, I found someone waiting for me there, who was also dressed, as I glimpsed under the blindfold, in neat, clean shoes and elegant trousers. I followed him down the Main Corridor, thinking it was Ghadimí. Such elegant Swiss shoes, such classy Swiss trousers.

'Is that you, Haj Áqá?' I asked, following his swift steps.

He replied rapidly, over his shoulder, in the affirmative. Then, at the threshold of one of the acoustic interrogation rooms, he paused, indicating that I should go in before him. Since I had always been interrogated without my blindfold with Mr Ghadimí, I lifted it to greet him as I walked in. I had barely turned my head before he began berating me angrily.

'Lower your blindfold! Turn around, turn around!'

I obeyed, in bewilderment. I had seen him now: a man of medium height, grey hair, and one drooping eyelid. Certainly not Ghadimí. Why had he acknowledged my greeting?

'I apologise, sir,' I said, hurried. 'I thought we were acquainted. I did ask and you did say you were Háj Áqá.'

'Everyone here is a Háj Áqá!' he retorted haughtily.

It was true. Whether all these Háj Áqas and Háj Khánums in the pay of the regime had really gone on a *haj* or pilgrimage was moot, but they all masqueraded under that label of piety. I was afraid of another barrage of anger from this possible pilgrim but nothing happened. His rage subsided like a freak storm: thunder, lightning, but no rain. No punishment, no penance. Instead, incongruously enough, my presumption was rewarded.

'Go ahead,' he said shortly afterwards. 'Go and make a phone call.'

I was astonished, overjoyed, and asked if I could call my father. He checked if I had the correct number and since I did, he took me to the phone alcove. I could hardly believe my luck. My father was so excited that I was worried he might have a heart attack at the sound of my voice. My own heart was turning somersaults. That day, I called Negár and Fúrúd, too – very briefly – but just to hear them talking was sufficient to lift my spirits. Just to be in touch with the real world was enough to restore my sense of self. At least for a while. I was immensely grateful to the man with the drooping eyelid who was not Mr Ghadimí.

Soon after this blessed contact with my family, I was directed to a room in the same area and brought before a table at which a young man was sitting. He gave me yet another form to fill out, and as I was doing so, I noticed a book about Islamic history on his desk, translated by the Shi'a scholar Ali Daváni, which I knew to contain several descriptions of unmitigated savagery and extreme violence.

'Oh, please don't read that!' I begged him with a smile.

'Why not?' he asked.

I laughed. 'It'll make you even crueller than you already are.'

'Come on,' he teased. 'What's so especially cruel about us? You guys were part of Islamic history yourselves up until the time of your grandfathers.'

'Well, that was a while ago, and we've reformed since.'

We both laughed then, and exchanged a few thoughts on the phenomenon of human violence and the possibility of behavioural reform. It surprised me that this young man was brave enough to talk to a high-security prisoner so freely, and seemingly without prejudice.

I signed the form. The young man asked if I knew my way back to the women's ward. I said that I did and left the room. It was the first time I had walked alone down the Main Corridor, without a blindfold. It was the first time I had pressed the buzzer of the Isolation Ward on my own and passed through the green curtain independently. And so I entered Passage 100 in the full blaze of that summer's day in a state of dazzling autonomy.

These were hopeful events, for me. I had seen that Mr Khánjání was alive; I was not being tortured; I had called my father and my children; I had spoken to the young man with ease; and now I had walked all the way down the Main Corridor to my cell without anyone controlling my movements. For a brief moment, I felt almost normal.

There was one other time, too, in the course of that long and lonely month, when I was allowed out of the cell to phone my family and experienced a moment of normality. In the phone registration room, I found a few men idling around, doing nothing. It was easy to chat with them because they were bored. So we spoke together for a while. They knew very well that I was a Bahá'í. I expressed the opinion that these walls of fear and prejudice between us were unnecessary. We were fellow human beings, after all; we were compatriots.

'But we have an issue with Israel,' said one, 'whereas you people are on good terms with that government.'

I raised a quizzical eyebrow. 'I ought to be grateful you didn't call us "agents" and you know, we try to be on good terms with all governments, even our own.'

'There's no way we would ever befriend Israel,' another added.

'Quite so,' I said. 'That's what you say today. But, tomorrow, when our governments reconcile to their mutual advantage, you will be friends and brothers. Just as with Iraq.'

And I reminded them of the terrible war of the 1980s, before they were even born, of the thousands of young men who died when Iraq attacked Iran, of the many homes destroyed, of the thousands of lives ruined. 'Thirty years ago, those people were considered our enemies and now we call them "Iraqi brethren." Maybe one day, the same will happen with Israel. There are no permanent friends or enemies,' I said, 'just permanent interests.'

'By the way,' another of them asked, 'what *is* your exact relationship with Israel?'

I told him that the Bahá'ís had no political ties with Israel, that the founder of our Faith had been exiled from Persia by the Shah and sent to Palestine as a prisoner of the Sultan in the nineteenth century. So our spiritual centre in that region was a historical accident.

'It's all the fault of the Qajars and the Ottomans,' I said wryly. 'We're still paying for the follies of these two empires. Why did they have to plot together to banish the founder of the Bahá'í Faith to a place that would change its name eighty years later?'

We all laughed then, and when I asked them whether they did not think it somewhat demeaning to have their decisions controlled by the political expediencies committed by a Shah and a Sultan over a century ago, they looked rather sheepish.

And that ended the discussion.

I do not remember having had any other conversations with anyone else that summer, except occasionally with one of the female guards who dared to exchange a few words with me when no one else was near. These brief encounters of quasi-human interaction were my only anchors to myself. An entire archive might have been accumulating in Evin, filled with endless forms signed by somebody called Mahvash, but I was disappearing. It was clear that not only was my body suffering from all the beatings, but my mind too was being affected. Apart from all the joint pains, I was experiencing memory gaps and attention loss. My heart rate was irregular and sleep deprivation had become endemic.

During one of my sleepless nights, while I was pacing back and forth inside my cell in the semi-darkness, the door quietly opened behind me. One of the female guards had noticed me walking around at 3 a.m. and had come to check on me. She was a big-boned woman, whom I'd nicknamed Braces on account of the orthodontic wires on her teeth. She came as close as she dared into the cell, peering at me with concern.

'Are you in pain?' she whispered.

'No.'

'Are you worried?'

'No.'

'So why aren't you sleeping?'

'I don't know.'

She stood there on the threshold for a few minutes, talking to me quietly, telling me about her life. She spoke gently, and with a kindness that I had never experienced from her before. I was deeply touched and close to tears by the time she bade me goodnight.

'Whenever you cannot sleep,' whispered Braces, 'I will come back so we can talk.'

These few minutes of communication with a compassionate human being helped me sleep better that night than I had been able to do for months. But the next night, I was back to pacing the cell and my condition began to deteriorate seriously.

* * *

Although I had no trust in the health centre of Section 209, or the doctors in it, I was forced to receive medical attention there at Háj Khánum's insistence, on several occasions. One of the doctors enquired about my charges one day and then asked me about my beliefs in the presence of Háj Khánum herself. She listened very respectfully and even suggested that I come back so that we might talk again. I do not believe this was a trick; I think she understood that I had really reached my limits.

This same doctor kindly prescribed a blood test for me and the following morning, Háj Khánum took me to the laboratory in the main clinic, outside Section 209. I had never been there before. We took a lift down to the basement where the lab was situated, and returned a day or so later to complete some administrative work before taking the lift back up to the fourth floor. And that was when something very strange happened.

In the lift.

It was the only lift in the clinic and a very basic one at that – just a metal box suspended rather precariously on rusty cables – but there was a large mirror in it. A few seconds after it jerked and clattered into motion, I looked up and saw a woman in the mirror. A thin, pale woman standing next to Háj Khánum. A woman with silver hair showing from under her scarf and chador, which she had folded under her arm. A woman with both arms crossed, holding her elbows in two bony hands. I was surprised. Who was this? I thought there were only two of us getting into the lift, Háj Khánum and myself. How did this other woman get in here? She had apparently joined us without my noticing. I looked round to see her. But she had vanished! There were indeed only two of us there. I was confused.

Then it hit me.

Is this other woman really you?

There was no other explanation. After a minute or two, I had to accept that this pallid, grey creature in the glass really was Mahvash. It may sound strange, but I waved at myself, moved my hand a little and literally waved, to double check reality against reflection. I will never forget that moment. Only a few short months had passed since I had seen myself in the mirror of the cream-coloured sedan at Tehran airport on arrival from Mashhad. What had happened to me since then to make me doubt my own appearance and render me incapable of recognising my own face? When papers and records were signed and we stepped back into the lift to go down to the ground floor, I drew closer to the mirror and examined this new self more carefully.

My features were not so thin as to be completely unrecognisable, especially those prominent cheeks of mine. But I had become another woman entirely. The radical weight loss, the pale drawn face, the un-plucked eyebrows, the silver hair showing from beneath the scarf and the gaunt body wrapped in a navy-blue chador with small white flowers – none of it was who I thought I was. I had seen those same sorrowful eyes and that same lost gaze on the faces of the women in the high security prison of Vakilabad.

Solitary confinement had stolen me from my self.

Many have written about the effects of solitary confinement on the psyche. Many have analysed its consequences. But now it had touched me personally, I was shocked. I had felt perfectly fine in the privacy of my own thoughts; I knew who I was in my heart and did not feel in the least unstable or distressed about my spiritual identity. But I was alienated from my body and as a result, something fundamental about my being had been lost.

In solitary confinement, everything you think you know is stripped away. You have no idea where you are, let alone who you are. You have no idea who your interrogator is or why you are being questioned like this. You do not know the actual names of the guards – these veiled moths who flutter up and down the corridor in silence, uttering the fewest words in the lowest possible tone when no one is near. You do not know how many cells there are, or who else is locked away inside them. You hear no external voices, unless you are being harangued and attacked, physically and verbally. Trapped in this delusional world, marooned in this desolation, your identity is gradually eroded. You fade away.

Solitary confinement was making me physically ill; there was no doubt about it. But its poison also seemed to be seeping into my spirit. The brain needs sensory stimuli to remain healthy. It is deeply damaging to paralyse the five senses in addition to severing all personal relations. So was my soul diminishing even as my body suffered from these privations? Did self-alienation only wound the psyche, or did it bruise the spirit too? Was I actually alive?

The anticipation of death had made me ask myself how well I had lived my life. But perhaps it was already too late. That 'other woman' in the lift made me realise that I might lose myself before I ever found out what kind of life Mahvash had lived. I had become the husk of a human being. Was anyone left inside the shell that had once been me?

31

FARIBÁ

The next few weeks were among the worst of my life. I had never sunk so low nor felt so utterly down. Although I paced endlessly back and forth, back and forth in my cell like a caged animal, I was feeling increasingly ill, wretchedly unwell, with no physical or spiritual stamina left. And with each passing day, I became more desperate to see Faribá. I was praying to see Faribá. I felt that if I did not see her soon I would break; I would not be able to bear it much longer. On a couple of occasions during an interrogation I asked to please, please be allowed to see her. The interrogator never answered me.

After that first day, I did not see her dear shoes again, but I saw her clothes from time to time on the laundry line in the small yard. After finding the small heart of foil she had slipped into the lining of my trousers, I thought my own heart would burst with longing for her. I wished I could send her a message, convey my affection to her, let her know how much I missed her and thought about her. But there was no way to do it.

At the beginning of Sháhrivár (late August), I could stand it no longer. I was so determined to see Faribá at whatever cost that I think I became a little mad. I stood beside the door near the flap of the peep hole where I would not be seen by the guards and spent the whole day watching the prisoners walk past my cell on their way to the bathroom. I did not know any of them, but waited hour after hour to catch a glimpse of Faribá among them.

Then one day, during those difficult weeks, a very pretty young girl brought her face close to the top flap in the door and quickly glanced inside the cell.

'Who's there?' she whispered, then vanished.

Her face was etched in my mind and now I kept looking for her as well as Faribá. She was tall with curly hair tied at the back of her head; sometimes her beautiful hair was braided, so I nicknamed her Curly Head. Another girl with straight, shiny hair, whom I named Raven Black, would also pass by from time to time and of course many prisoners came and went, but not Faribá, never Faribá. Some days I panicked. Had she died? Or had they moved her elsewhere so I would never see her again? Other times I felt certain she was still in the same corridor because her clothes would appear on the line. We only had two sets of clothes, so I even knew what she was wearing on any given day. But I still had not seen her.

Unfortunately, some of the guards started to notice me hovering by the door at all hours, peeping out of the top opening. Both apertures in the cell door were generally closed, the square one with bars at eye level, and the narrow rectangular one at the bottom for food. And when the guards wanted to exert their power, they opened the flaps of these apertures for 'good behaviour' only to slam them shut for 'bad.' For they could always keep an eye on us through the spyhole above the top one. I knew I would soon be reprimanded if I kept looking out of the top opening. The flap would be shut in my face and then I would really go mad.

Since the weather was warm that summer, they had opened both flaps in the doors for the air to circulate. So I decided to kneel at floor level and watch the legs passing by of everyone going to the toilet. I tried to remember the trousers they were wearing and then listened for the click of the toilet door that signalled their return. I had calculated the distance between my cell and the toilet to be five or six steps and knew I had around thirty seconds from the time the door clicked shut until the person passed by my cell. Of course, some women walked faster and some slower, but I would count the seconds, then stand up quickly, just at the right moment to catch a glimpse of their faces through the bars. My calculations were nearly always correct, but I still had not seen Faribá!

I repeated this movement so many times that I began to develop knee problems after several days. All I did, day in and day out, was kneel, listen, stand up rapidly, peek through the flap and then quickly flatten myself to the side of the door so the guards would not see me. I had seen everyone come and go in Passage 100. I had even memorised their faces. Several of them had also seen me when I stood up. But where was Faribá?

Then one day I was determined.

I will see her today, I will! I must!

I was so fixated on seeing her that I was willing to break my knees to make it happen.

And I shall not miss a single person passing by.

I knew that Faribá was wearing her black trousers that day, but even so, I was not going to risk only looking for black trousers. I leapt to my feet to peek at the passing faces, no matter what colour the trousers were. Then I noticed that someone was walking towards my cell with incredible rapidity. She was walking by my door so fast that I could barely get to my feet in time to catch a glimpse of her face. It must be Faribá!

And there she was! Wearing her red and black checked shirt with her black trousers, flying past my cell with the speed of an arrow. She did not even glance in my direction, but I saw her profile for a split second – and was seized with uncertainty.

Was that really our Faribá? So thin? So pale? It could not be. But it had to be. Why else would she be wearing Faribá's clothes? Ah! How miserable I was then. I slid down the wall and slumped onto the floor, murmuring and whispering to myself –

What has happened to you, my darling Faribá? What have they done to you?

Had Faribá endured days of disdainful interrogations too, hours of beating and battering at the hands of those foul-mouthed men in that dark room? Had it been her voice in the basement that day, her terrible screams I heard when I was left standing by the toilet? You do not hear screams as shrill as that even in childbirth. I knew how strong she was. My sweet Faribá was a mountain of strength, but if God forbid she had ever screamed, would she have sounded like that? And at such thoughts, I began to weep as I had wept when I saw her shoes.

Barely a few minutes later, Háj Khánum opened the door. Did these people have ears attuned to the sound of sobbing? I was still slumped against the wall.

'I have good news for you,' she said softly.

I scrambled to my feet, bleary-eyed. Good news? I could not utter a word.

'I'm going to bring you to your sister,' she smiled.

Impossible to speak. Impossible to breathe, almost. Not just a passing glance, but an actual visit with Faribá? I could hardly contain my happiness. Was such joy even conceivable? I would know how she was at last, hear her news, learn what had happened to the Bahá'ís after my abduction. Perhaps I could even stay in her company for a little while. Perhaps the worst of our hardship was over and these tortures and interrogations would end. Hope and wonder flashed through me like repeated strokes of lightning. I felt so energised that I was ready to believe that my own perseverance had conjured this miracle.

And perhaps it had.

At any rate, the moment Háj Khánum stepped aside from the door, I pushed through the few inches she allowed me and flew out of my cell. I had guessed Faribá to be in cell 113 at the end of Passage 100. I had even used the excuse of needing a bar of soap from the guards' station to go that far once or twice, raising my voice as much as I dared, at the risk of punishment, in the hope that Faribá would hear me and look through the bars. So I knew where she was, and now, on that bright new morning, with the doors of both our cells finally open, I ran down the passage with the speed of light. Háj Khánum caught up with me as I hovered on the threshold of cell 113, and we entered together.

Faribá was standing by the sink and turned around as soon as I reached her. I flung my arms around her and we hugged each other, weeping and laughing, laughing and weeping. Faribá, my friend, my sister, my colleague, my co-prisoner! I still remember that after a few moments I had to control the force of my embrace in case I might actually break her bones and hurt my dear sweet Faribá! I could not believe I was with her.

Háj Khánum did not interrupt us immediately. An experienced prison warden, domineering but at the same time humane, she gave us time. Perhaps this sixty-year-old woman, who had studied in a seminary and worked in this terrible place since the beginning of the Revolution, had witnessed enough cruelty over the years to have grown tired of punishment.

Perhaps she simply enjoyed seeing our reunion, appreciating our mutual affection. She paused for a while before speaking, allowing us to indulge our joy.

'So?' she enquired, with a faint smile. 'What would you like to do now? Which of the two suites would you prefer to occupy?'

We were incredulous. Were we really going to be allowed to stay together from now on? Would we actually be permitted to share a cell? Our happiness was unbounded. We could barely contain our excitement and asked for a few moments to consult about it. I examined Faribá's cell, and she examined mine. Mine had ants, and since it was so close to the toilet, it smelled worse than hers. So I gathered together my few belongings and blankets and moved into Faribá's domain, feeling like a queen.

* * *

12 Sháhrivár (2 September), the day I joined Faribá in Evin, will forever count as one of the best days of my life. It was the first day of the month of Ramadán so no lunch was served, but we had each other, and since we had saved our breakfasts, we could share our midday meal together. But I cannot recall eating anything; our excitement was too great. We talked non-stop, all that day and all that night and all the following day and night too. Without pause.

We began with the news of my arrest, the precautionary steps that had been immediately taken by the Yárán, how my family had reacted. And then I heard about the Yárán, how and when and where they had been arrested, and what had happened to the other members, as far as could be guessed. We only stopped talking to cry, to laugh, and then to cry again. I asked her why she had walked past my door so fast, when no one else did.

'I didn't want the guards to get suspicious!' she admitted. 'But they probably did.'

We spoke for forty-eight hours straight. Our need to share our experiences was bottomless. I told her about the interrogations in Mashhad; she told me about those in Tehran. We compared our tortures, white, red and green, and I discovered that Faribá had not been deprived either of the bounties delivered by those generous men in the dark room. She said that she had distinguished five voices during this same torture, but I think I had the benefit of an extra one. She added that she too had been taken to see dear Mr Khánjání while his feet were being bastinadoed. And she reassured me that the voice I had heard, those blood-curdling screams of the woman in the basement, had not been hers. It seemed that one of the refined techniques these brave brutes employed to terrorise female prisoners in particular was to expose them in this way to the recordings of women being raped.

What amazed us both was the similarity of our reactions and replies to the interrogators. It was astonishing to discover how alike we were in our interpretations, how parallel our thinking, how similar our reactions. We had both come to the same conclusions about the aims of the gentlemen. We had also both avoided mentioning the Bahá'í Faith to others but had then discovered that everyone knew why we were in prison.

I told Faribá how the female guard who had kindly given me the damp, clean uniform to wear for the court hearing had accompanied me to the car park when I was leaving Mashhad and had asked me what the Bahá'ís believed. When I enquired, in surprise, how she knew that I was a Bahá'í, she had showed me the transfer form, on which I read, in the section labelled 'charges,' the word 'Bahá'í' written clearly for all to see. That was the first time I had seen official proof that our crime was simply to be Bahá'ís.

Faribá told me that the authorities had stormed the homes of the six other members of the Yárán simultaneously on the morning of 25 Ordíbehesht 1387 (6 May 2008). All correspondence and everything related to our work had been taken – all our books, our records, our archives, our laptops and whatever had the slightest connection to the Bahá'í Faith had been appropriated. But she also confirmed that I had interpreted Mr Khánjání's enigmatic remark correctly, because contrary to all expectations, my home had *not* been raided when they first arrested me. Our documents had *not* been confiscated from there but had indeed all been saved. Was this because my charges at that time concerned burial issues rather than the activities of the Yárán? If so, the poor dead man may even have shielded our home for a while, as well as keeping me company in my solitude.

Faribá and I had each lost over forty pounds and our clothes hung loose on our bodies when we met. We were both resigned to imminent execution and ready for death, but it was remarkable how soon we found our appetites once we were together. We consumed all the fruits and nuts that I had not been able to swallow before. We also discovered that we could buy food in Evin, and gradually began preparing little meals for ourselves with fresh fruit and salad when it was available. We created a routine of shower times and laundry times, exercise times and reading times. We took turns cleaning the cell, recited our morning devotions together, and in the evenings spread out our blankets next to one another so we could whisper through the night. And what poems we chanted, what prayers of thanksgiving!

Whatever you have committed to memory is a precious treasure in prison. And in solitary confinement, it becomes an elixir of life itself. With the two of us together, this resource was doubled. We slaked our thirst on passages we knew from the Bahá'í writings, on Rumi's blessed Mathnavi, and on as many verses and odes of Persian poetry as possible. Soon after, my family were allowed to send me a copy of the *Divan-i-Hafez* and this great poet became our constant companion too. We also borrowed other books whenever allowed. On one occasion, we asked Braces, who claimed to be a reader, to bring us something to read. To my surprise, all she could offer was a copy of the prophecies of Nostradamus!

The memory of our Bahá'í friends provided another source of comfort and solace. Sometimes we would sit quietly, side by side, playing the Khádimín Game, which consisted of mind-travelling from city to city all over Iran, and from one neighbourhood to another in every town and village, recalling the names of the friends who lived there. And wherever we travelled in our imaginations, we would gladly share stories about the Bahá'ís of that place and recount whatever we could about them. My great good fortune was that this game was not the least bit competitive, for otherwise, Faribá would have always won. She had an excellent memory for names and places.

And so the weeks passed. As summer turned towards autumn, we gradually grew calmer and more tranquil, but although our excitement was reduced to normal levels over time, our gratitude for being together never diminished.

* * *

Since we were now in a shared cell rather than in solitary confinement, conditions had changed slightly, and during that last month of summer, several 'guests' joined us. After being in unrelenting isolation for months on end, company is usually a cause for happiness in Section 209, a blessed reprieve, but since we had to share the cell with others so soon after we had just been reunited, Faribá and I were not so happy about it. We would have preferred not to be obliged to 'host' anyone just yet.

The first 'guest' they brought us was none other than Raven Black, the same young girl with the straight black hair I had already noticed through the bars. She introduced herself with quiet indifference: Shirin Alam Houli was her name and she was Kurdish. Faribá and I were both initially apprehensive; we suspected she might have been sent to spy on us, to report on us to the gentlemen of the Intelligence Ministry. But within a short span of time, it became clear this girl was not 'that sort' either. She did not play dirty games.

Shirin was from the mountain town of Maku in the far north of the country, and after a few days with us, she began sharing interesting stories about the people of her region and their beliefs. They performed acts of worship on the high crags above her hometown, because over a hundred years ago, she told us solemnly, a holy man had lived there. He had fallen down one day, and when his blood spilled on the rocks, the place became sacred. And so the people of Maku believed their wishes could be granted in that spot. We were much taken by this tale because in 1848, the herald of our Faith, the Báb, had been imprisoned for nine months in Maku, in a citadel built high into the escarpment. How strange that the local inhabitants might still recall this fact after so long, and might have embroidered fanciful superstitions around it because of its lingering importance to them.

Shirin told us that even today people still climbed all the way up that mountain in memory of this mysterious 'holy man' and called on him to bear witness to their vows.

'My mother and other relations have also pledged in that spot,' she said simply.

We gradually became good friends with this guileless girl, who was very steadfast in the path she had chosen, and was ardently committed to her cause. She asked us, please, if we ever went to Maku, to find her home and visit her mother. Shirin was a political activist, and knew she would not leave the prison alive. She was with us for about two weeks before they took her away for good. We gave her a pack of dried dates and never saw her again.

One night soon after she left, an Armenian woman was brought to our cell. Silva had emigrated a few years before and then returned to Iran to do research and training in the field of women's health on behalf of an American organisation named IREX. Her area of speciality was the care of mothers and newborn babies, especially those with AIDS. Now, she had been arrested together with three others, including Dr Arash Ala'i and his brother Dr Kamyar Ala'i, two well-known Iranian physicians and promoters of AIDS control.

Silva was the second person with whom we became closely acquainted in Section 209. Even a short time spent with someone under such perilous conditions draws hearts and minds together, and we learned a great deal about human nobility during the first night we spent with this young woman. A deep and abiding friendship developed between us and we were sad when she left our cell the following day. But soon afterwards, a woman named Leila replaced her and we had to readjust once more to another 'guest'.

This newcomer had barely settled in the cell before the guard opened the door and pointed to me.

'Pick up your things and follow me,' she ordered with a peremptory hiss.

'Where to?' I breathed in surprise.

'You have to go somewhere else,' she said.

I was devastated. I had expected never to be separated from Faribá again. But now it appeared, to my great distress, that I had no choice. Two women had been released from solitary confinement, and since the prison authorities did not want *them* to share a cell, they were transferring me so one of them could take my place with Faribá.

Cell number 112, to which I was assigned, was right next to Faribá and Leila. And when I stepped through the door, I discovered with delight that it was occupied by our new Armenian friend, Silva. She leapt to her feet, overjoyed to see me, and I greeted her with equal relief, and so our friendship was re-kindled. Warm-hearted and sociable, Silva suffered severely from claustrophobia and had been traumatised by solitude, so she desperately needed companionship. For my own part, although I grieved being parted from Faribá, I felt great sympathy for this sincere and idealistic young woman. In that sense, I gained something from my loss for one of my mantras was to try to turn stumbling blocks into stepping stones and view calamity as providence. It was the only way to survive.

Silva had decorated her cell beautifully and given it a flavour all her own. Since this was a double confinement cell with two doors, she had spread a shawl of beautiful *termeh*, a traditional embroidered cloth, behind the second closed door, on which she had placed some very exotic objects – a bottle of foreign olive oil, a packet of Turkish coffee, a large jar of Nescafé, some sugar in a disposable plastic cup and a couple of candles. She had made these special purchases through the interrogator, she said, because as a 'foreign prisoner' she was given preferential treatment or, effectively, bribes. There was also a large plastic bag in the corner filled with chocolates and biscuits her inter-rogator had purchased for her. But Silva refused to touch them. After ten tormented days in solitary confinement, she had been forced into signing a fake confession and the poor woman could not forgive herself.

I had never lived with a practising Christian before, so I was not familiar with her customs and observances. She, too, had never met any Bahá'ís and knew nothing about the Faith. As a result, we had some deep conversations together and talked for hours. I was relieved to find that despite her piety, she was not fanatical but very open-minded.

Silva would light candles whenever she prayed. She would cover her head with a clean, white shawl. I think she may have also burned incense. Aside from these external details, our belief in prayer concurred and our spirits were united. Silva would pray in her own language, and I would chant what I knew by heart. Our devotions were full of fervour.

But sometimes this dear young woman became very low-spirited. She would rest her head in my lap and I would stroke her hair as she cried. She was about thirty-three years old and needed to talk about her memories, her country, her town, her home, her mother, her job, the love of her life. And so that the exchange would be an equal one, I told her about my family, about the Bahá'í community and the history of its persecution. I do not know why but I was even moved to tell her the story of my daughter's wedding and what had happened that day. It seemed to open the floodgates of Silva's grief. It was as though she too had been holding back oceans of sorrow behind a dam of self-control, and she sobbed aloud for Negár.

She felt a deep affection for my daughter without even knowing her; she asked about her repeatedly while we were together. And although she knew little about it, she respected my commitment to the Bahá'í Faith too, and the reasons I was ready to stand by my principles. One week after I moved into her cell, Faribá joined us, and after that our joy was complete. We had the ants, we had the smell, but the three of us were together again.

It was a miracle.

32

FRESH AIR

When you are in prison, you become highly susceptible to miracles. You look for them everywhere and see them nowhere. You despair of ever experiencing them and yet believe they will happen at any minute, despite the odds. And some may occur, dramatically, in a flash, leaving you dubious of their reality, while others are not recognised as miracles at all, except in retrospect, when it is too late, perhaps. But Faribá and I experienced one miracle in Evin that stunned us both with its pure simplicity.

We were supposed to have fresh-air outings three times a week in the large yard, but this relief was often denied. Apart from being vital for health, twenty minutes out of doors was also a routine, a regular pattern, a kind of rhythm that was absolutely essential for well-being. When we were arbitrarily deprived of going out, it was something of a blow: not quite as bad as abduction or torture or the mind games of interrogators, but disappointing nonetheless. In the beginning, we used to have to wear the chador over our clothes when we went out but later this stricture was waived. And then whenever we had the chance for an outing, we dropped whatever we were doing and ran out as we were.

One day, I was cleaning the cell, which was my duty on Fridays, and was busy washing the sink, scrubbing the carpet and picking up strands of loose hair from the blankets with a wet cloth. I enjoyed these simple tasks because they were physically tiring and kept me in touch with myself. But when the door suddenly opened and Háj Khánum gave us the signal, I stopped what I was doing immediately. It was the moment for a fresh-air outing. Everything else was of secondary importance and we were ready to leave within minutes.

What a relief it was to run out into the large yard and breathe the fresh air at last. We walked briskly, we walked fast, because this was the only advantage the place offered. Twenty-three by twenty-seven steps around the enclosed area and then twenty-seven by twenty-three steps back. I walked in a figure eight, and Faribá walked round and round the rectangular space from wall to wall. But in the middle of our energetic exercise, we heard a sudden jangle of keys and the grind of the door being unlocked. How strange. Was someone else coming into the large yard already? So soon? How brief this outing had been; we had barely filled our lungs. Our spirits drooped with disappointment.

And then I suddenly heard Faribá calling out in surprise – 'Mahvash!'

I was on the far side of the fresh air yard when she called, and she was closer to the door. I turned round and was confronted by the most astonishing sight. There was dear Mr Khánjání standing in the fresh air yard, without his blindfold! His attention had been caught by Faribá's voice, and he was glancing up in great surprise when I turned to him. A frown knotted his brows and then he saw us. We flew towards him just as some other prisoners were stepping through the beige painted door behind him. They were Mr Khánjání's wardmates, men from his cell who had come for exercise, with their guard.

Before we came any closer, Mr Khánjání had already turned around, placed his hand gently on the chest of the first man, and pushed him back through the door. And then with perfect composure, he shut the door in the prisoner's face. It remained closed. And then he turned back round to face us, just as we reached him.

Our dear Mr Khánjání opened wide his arms, and within seconds, both of us, like lost children who had found their father on a lonely path, were leaning our heads against his chest, weeping with joy. He hugged me with his right arm and Faribá with his left and it was as if all the power and might of the world was gathered in those arms of his. They were so strong, so powerful; it was incredible. I guessed the closed-circuit camera above our heads had never witnessed such a scene; it was surely the most dramatic moment of the day for the guards watching their multiple monitors. Our three heads were close together and all I could do was whisper, *'Fadaye shoma, fadaye shoma*... May my life be ransomed for you.'

For I was truly ready to sacrifice myself for this dear man. I was ready to give up my life for all he had gone through on behalf of all of us.

Seconds later, he opened his mighty embrace, and we both took a step back and gazed at him in wonder, our tears glisten- ing in the light of his. We would have stood there for hours, saying all that could not be said through that look, washing away all the anguish of our last encounter through our tears. But this unexpected encounter had to be brief.

With the same gentleness, the same calm, he turned round and opened the door. Although it had been unlocked all this time, his wardmates had not attempted to press through and were still standing there, waiting patiently. No one had complained. No one had resisted. All the men, and even their guard, had stayed inside. Our guard also arrived just at that moment to escort us back to the cell. And the men had their turn in the yard.

Our cell could barely contain our excitement; the four walls around us were absolutely no impediment. We were flying, soaring with rapture. It was astonishing. We had actually met one of our beloved colleagues, and he was healthy, well and strong as ever, with his ability to think fast, to act swiftly and respond with confident wisdom undiminished and undeterred. What an incredible coincidence! How had this been possible? The fresh air schedule was strictly controlled because the large yard was common to all prisoners in Section 209, male and female, and for that reason as well as others, great care was taken to prevent any meetings between them. Yet we had suddenly found ourselves standing there together with Mr Khánjání, without any impediment, without any barriers.

As we marvelled over it, we calculated the thousand ways it might not have happened – another prisoner might have come into the yard before him; any one of his cell mates might have grown impatient and tried to push the door open or at least protest; the guard himself, escorting these prisoners, should have technically raised a hue and cry – but didn't. Instead, we had been granted this sublime gift of being briefly in the fresh air with our colleague.

It seemed to Faribá and I that we were breathing far more than fresh air after our meeting with Mr Khánjání in the large yard. We were punch drunk for days, ready for anything. We found ourselves more alive than before, more conscious of living. For if being really alive meant we should be prepared to

die, it was not a problem. If it meant we might have to live the
rest of our days in prison, we were content. We were ready for
either. The sheer wonder of what had happened felt like a rec-
ompense for all the beatings, a reward after all that solitude; it
was like breathing fresh air in the suffocating corridors of Evin.

A miracle.

* * *

In fact, the most remarkable miracle in Evin was also directly
linked to fresh air behind those high, forbidding walls. But
unlike our sudden meeting with Mr Khánjání, it was a slow
miracle. It evolved gradually. It began invisibly and emerged
silently, like the very movement of air through those labyrin-
thine passageways. And the first signs of it may even have
seemed ominous and unpropitious. Fresh air can be a shock to
the system. It is not always welcome to all alike. Changes in
the atmosphere, like sudden gusts of cold, can provoke cries of
protest, indignation, fear – particularly among the insulated
and cloistered. And such reactions had occurred in Iran long
before Evin was ever built.

Decades before the Islamic Revolution came into being, the
message of spiritual renewal at the heart of the Bahá'í Faith
had elicited all those same reactions – of protest, of indignation
and of fear. The principles of social change of this Faith, which
questioned the ingrained prejudices of people, had already provoked reaction and rejection in the past. The early Bahá'í community had been denigrated for ideals that are taken for
granted by many today. Their adherence to gender equality
was slandered as 'prostitution'; their belief in education was
defined as 'spreading corruption on earth'; and their faith in the

progressive nature of religious truth was defined as 'apostasy' and 'heresy'. And now, under the present regime, we were being accused of colluding with 'enemy powers', were considered 'foreign agents', 'spies', and 'fifth columnists'; we were called 'political activists'.

What made this particularly ironic was that many of our enlightened friends in Iran had been deriding the Bahá'ís for decades for not being more political. Even as the regime accused us of 'political subversion,' we were disparaged by fellow Iranians for our non-involvement in political protest, disdained for our lack of political engagement, reproached for our political passivity. And this disapproval was echoed inside Evin. For irony of ironies, under the Islamic Republic of Iran, the Bahá'ís found themselves in prison with 'political activists,' sharing cells with the 'politically engaged', eating, sleeping, talking and listening to some of the most vociferous 'political' opponents of the current regime, men and women who also happened to be among the best educated and well-informed of our compatriots, concerned with issues of justice, equality and human rights in civic society. It was the greatest opportunity for us in the world, to learn, to think, to discover, to open our minds... No wonder Evin has been called the best university in Iran!

But certain friends who were a source of our enlightenment, stimulation and even education nevertheless still criticised us for what they saw as our 'apathy' when it came to engagement in partisan politics. Many could not understand why we were happy to sing patriotic songs such as 'Ey Iran' or 'Yár-i-Dabistání'[28] but refrained from chanting political slogans. They found this pusillanimous.

'You're just self-serving fence-sitters!' they would scoff. 'You talk about the discrimination against Bahá'ís but how can that change if you're not politically engaged? How can a just society be established through people like you?'

And our cell mates who rejected religion entirely were particularly irritated with us.

'Oh, come on,' they complained, 'here we are trying to liberate the country from antediluvian notions of "God", and you're still promoting this rubbish. We want people to break free from the old yoke of religion, and you're trying to convert them to a new one!'

They dismissed our attempts to redefine words like 'God' and 'religion'. They thought us naïve to suggest that the Bahá'í model of society-building could heal secular as well as spiritual ills. They argued vociferously for the separation of 'church and state,' and were much surprised, though incurious, when we whole-heartedly agreed with them. But their political engagement did not always resolve the differences between themselves. Since political activists were frequently supporters of contrary and sometimes violent ideologies, their discussions often grew contentious and disruptive. Opposing camps were easily formed within the prison walls. Our disparities reflected the diversity of Iran, after all.

But while people outside these walls can exist in separate worlds, if necessary, we prisoners have no escape from one another; we live cheek by jowl. Like the Fatimihs and the Zahrás and Maryam and Naneh, we are obliged to share our food, use the same toilets and resolve our problems together if we are to endure these appalling conditions. So we have to listen to each other and come to a consensus. We have to consult together respectfully and maintain our unity. If not, the prison authorities will exploit these tensions to our common disadvantage. They will divide us so that they can rule us with impunity.

Discovering this reality in pursuit of simple, practical goals meant that abstention from partisanship was finally perceived by our cell mates not as cowardice, nor as indifference, nor as a lack of patriotism, nor as an absence of will, but as a deliberate refusal to be polarised, as a conscious decision on the part of Bahá'ís to desist from fuelling conflict and provoking strife. And when – slowly and irresistibly – that principle began to demonstrate its effectiveness as a tool for community building, even in this microcosm of the prison, our friends started asking questions…

One day we looked at each other, Faribá and I, and noticed that something strange was happening in Evin. Fresh air was blowing through the corridors of the prison; clean air was wafting through these stuffy cells. Very gradually, the age-old prejudices between us and our dear compatriots were quietly dissolving. The bigotries that had stood between us for almost two centuries were crumbling away. Despite the high walls around us, these inner barriers were finally falling. When we registered this miracle, it was even more astounding than our unexpected meeting with dear Mr Khánjání, vibrant on the other side of death.

We knew it was just the beginning. It would take decades more for this fresh air to be recognised as essential to the future of Iran. But time was on our side.

The purest air human beings can breathe comes from recognition of our oneness, acceptance of our essential unity. The gates of the heart open wide when we see how little distinguishes us from others in the world. There is no difference between the millions who have braved tyranny in the past and those who are enduring injustice right now, between the Bahá'ís of Iran today and everyone else in our suffering country – the Kurds of Kurdistan, the Lurs of Lorestan, the people of Azerbaijan or Baluchestan, of Khorasan, Gilan, Mazandaran or Kerman, those from the southern Gulf region in Bandari, from Fars, Isfahan, Abadih and Marvdasht, from Vilashahr, Shahinshahr and Najafabad. All the peoples of this beautiful land deserve the right to breathe the fresh and unpolluted air of oneness.

And that consciousness is beginning to blow all over the crying world. It cannot be denied. The oneness of humanity is no longer a dream; it is the only solution for the planet's survival. However diverse our cultures and beliefs, however varied our opinions and identities, our only true distinction, as long as we live and die on this same earth, is to become a source of fresh air to others. And that air of oneness will surely blow through and revive our country too, when the doors of our hearts in Iran will open wide.

> Kiss the hand of your would-be assassin!
> Dance your way to the Friend's abode!
> How blessed that hour, how sweet the instant
> When the inmost spirit surrenders and
> The embodiment of faith takes flight
> Towards those evanescent heights.[29]

POSTSCRIPT AND THE
YÁRÁN OF IRAN

When Mahvash was reunited with Faribá Kamalábádí in the late summer of 2008, her months of solitude in prison finally came to an end. And their unexpected reunion with Mr Khánjání, in the fresh air yard, marked a turning point in her incarceration. From that time on, although she had to endure untold hardships and deprivation over the next decade, Mahvash's experience in prison was collective rather than individual, communal rather than solitary.

But while her suffering was shared, her writing became passionately personal in prison. Mahvash had always loved poetry and like many Iranians, knew scores of the classics by heart: the poems of Sa'adi and Hafez, the tales of Ferdowsi. She had always written poems too and offered them as gifts to individuals and members of her family. But in prison, they demanded to be heard. Initially, she simply repeated them to herself and tried to recite them over the phone to her family members, through the glass, during their sparse visiting hours. But this was not sufficient; they were bubbling up with ever greater urgency and needed to be written down. After the miraculous discovery of a pen tucked under the sink in her cell, she began to scribble her poems on spliced pieces of tissue paper and hide these fragile treasures in books, under blankets and even inside her clothes. Finally, she was able to smuggle them out of prison on the backs of her courageous cell mates. Three volumes of her poems appeared in Persian, and the English translation of the first, *Prison Poems*, won her recognition as International Writer of Courage by the Belfast poet Michael Longley at the PEN Pinter Prize ceremony in 2017. This initial selection was subsequently translated into Norwegian, Spanish, Italian, German and French, and Mahvash has since become an honorary member of Danish, Austrian and English PEN.

Poetry became her private source of fresh air.

All through her months of solitary confinement, the interrogator had repeatedly ordered her to write. Indeed, the injunction 'Write! Write!' hurled at her head, which had been intended as a punishment, proved a source of release, of relief and freedom instead. Encouraged, inspired and motivated by her fellow prisoners in Evin, several of whom are among the most erudite, cultured and heroic women of her generation, Mahvash began to write in earnest during the years that followed. From 2011 on, she started to record her past experiences and daily challenges, filling the notebooks that became the basis of this book.

Just before her release in September 2017, Mahvash underwent a final interrogation by the gentlemen of the Ministry of Intelligence. When asked what she would do with her time when free, she responded, with a flash of humour, that she certainly had no intention of spending it in her kitchen! But, she enquired, would they *really* release her? For her twenty-year sentence had been commuted to ten and back again several times; she had no idea if she would leave Evin 'horizontally or vertically,' as one of the gentlemen had mocked. While fully expecting to be detained at the last minute, she nevertheless planned the escape of her notebooks, for she was determined that her words would reach the world. And so once again, with the help of others, she was able to send her memoirs over the prison walls.

Mahvash's third arrest occurred five years later and just two months before the brutal murder of a young Kurdish woman, Mahsa Amini, which sparked the *Woman, Life, Freedom* movement in Iran. As result, Mahvash's prison cell was soon crammed with dozens of women, young and old, indicted for their protests against the mandatory hijab. Since then, government policy has also hardened towards the Bahá'ís, and there has been a rapid rise in the detention of women in particular over the past three years. Numbers have multiplied even more in recent months. The charges against the Bahá'ís are the same as ever; the accusations are as false as before. The only difference now is that many more Iranians share their plight.

This has been particularly true since the so-called '12 Day War' provided the regime with a pretext to arrest hundreds of Iranians as alleged Israeli spies. Paradoxically, it was the political prisoners who bore the brunt of the repression after the conflict culminated in the bombing of Evin. Many died in this ambiguous attack – visitors, guards and inmates all meeting a common fate – and the place was, for several months, a ruin. But the spirit of Evin unfortunately lives on. The male prisoners were rapidly distributed to various provincial prisons up and down the land and the women of Section 209 were sent to the insalubrious female penitentiary of Qarchak, south of the capital. Mahvash and Faribá had already experienced the horrors of this repurposed livestock farm in the middle of the desert. They had already endured the filth, the pollution, the open sewers, the saline water and murderous meals during their first ten-year prison sentence as members of the

Yárán-i-Iran. Indeed, conditions in this notorious prison are so bad that Faribá is reported to have said that it would have been better to die under the bombs than return there. But Mahvash was not in Evin when the bombs fell. She was recuperating from major heart surgery at home and has been living under a sword of Damocles ever since. Subjected, like more than ninety million of her compatriots, to the price rises, the food shortages and eighteen-hour water and power cuts, she is also at the mercy of a 'committee of medical experts' who will decide when she is well enough to be re-incarcerated.

At this time of writing, she is expecting to receive the order at any moment. She is waiting with her bag packed, ready to be summoned back to prison from one day to the next. She is serene, unperturbed and perfectly prepared. For it is precisely during such dark moments that the human spirit shines brightest. The challenges confronting Iranian prisoners and people alike are immense at this time. So is their vision, which must transcend disunity and prejudice if it is to meet those challenges. But a nation that has played so critical a role in past conflicts in the region surely has the potential to bring peace, prosperity and well-being to its own citizens and to those beyond its borders in the future. However uncertain the present circumstances and however precarious her personal plight, Mahvash's memoir opens the doors of hope to that future. It offers an affirmation to all who share her compassion for humanity that freedom of conscience and justice shall ultimately prevail, in Iran and in the world.

The Yárán-i-Iran

Although this book is based on the solitary months of Mahvash Sabet's imprisonment, there was not a moment during this period when she was not thinking of the six other members of the Yárán-i-Iran. She feared for her dearly loved colleagues from the minute she was arrested. She agonised over the pressure they might be under due to her detention, and she guessed, in the end, that they were suffering just as she was.

It seems appropriate to end this book by acknowledging each briefly, by name.

Mahvash's closest companion in prison was the only other woman in the group, Faribá Kamalábádí. Born in Tehran on 12 September 1962, Faribá is no stranger to persecution. In her youth, she witnessed her father's imprisonment and torture when he was fired from the government health service in the 1980s and, after graduating from high school with honours, she too was debarred from university because she was a Bahá'í. In her mid-thirties, she embarked on eight years of informal study culminating in an advanced degree in developmental psychology from the Bahá'í Institute of Higher Education (BIHE). One son and one daughter left Iran to live and work abroad, but her youngest daughter was still in school at the time of her arrest. Faribá was deprived of attending her daughter's wedding as well as the birth of her first grandchild. She too was arrested again in July 2022, and condemned to another ten years imprisonment, with Mahvash.

Many of the prisoners who met these two women during their first ten years in Evin were profoundly affected by them. The American journalist Roxana Saberi, who shared a cell with them, stated in an interview: 'Faribá and Mahvash were two of the women prisoners I met in Evin who inspired me the most… They showed me what it means to be selfless, to care more about one's community and beliefs than about oneself.'

The third person mentioned in these pages is the most senior member of the Yárán, Jamaloddin Khánjání. Born 27 July 1933 in the city of Sangsar, Mr Khánjání grew up on a dairy farm in Semnán province and never obtained more than a high school education. Yet his dynamic personality soon led to a successful career and the brick-making factory he established was the first of its kind in Iran, employing several hundred people. In the early 1980s, he was forced to shut it down and the factory was later confiscated by the government. Mr Khánjání was a member of the third National Spiritual Assembly of the Bahá'ís of Iran that was disbanded in 1983, and which, one year later, saw four of its nine members executed by the government. Arrested three times before his sentencing as a member of the Yárán in 2008, Mr Khánjání was once again imprisoned in August 2023, along with his daughter. Over ninety years old and in fragile health, he was released after paying an exorbitant bail.

A fourth member of the now-disbanded Yárán, also on furlough from prison at this time due to ill-health, is Afíf Naemí. Born on 6 September 1961 in Yazd, and raised after his father's death by his uncles in Jordan, he learned Arabic in elementary school but was unable to pursue his dream of becoming a doctor when he returned to Iran. Denied access to a university education as a Bahá'í, he diverted his attention to business, taking over his father-in-law's textile factory in the early 1980s. Like Mahvash and Faribá, Mr Naemí was arrested again in July 2022 and condemned to a second ten-year sentence.

The fifth member of the Yárán is Behrouz Tavakkolí. Born on 1 June 1951 in Mashhad, Mr Tavakkolí studied psychology at university and then completed two years in the army, where he was a lieutenant. After his marriage, he undertook additional training to specialise in the care of the physically and mentally impaired, holding a government position as a social worker until he was fired due to his faith in the early 1980s. Prior to his imprisonment in 2008, he had already experienced intermittent detainment and frequent harassment and was jailed for four months without charge in 2005, spending most of that time in solitary confinement. To support himself and his family, Mr Tavakkolí established a small carpentry shop in Gonbad where he also conducted classes in Bahá'í studies for adults and young people. His two sons were educated through the BIHE and he himself had served on several Bahá'í institutions before these were banned in the 1980s. Like Mr Khánjání, he was a member of the Yárán from the late 1980s until the group was disbanded.

The sixth member of the Yárán was Saeíd Rezáíe, an agricultural engineer known for his scholarship and poetry. The author of several books on Bahá'í topics, he inspired Mahvash to start writing poems by slipping a tiny verse into her hand when they met briefly during the visiting hours in prison. Born in Abádán on 27 September 1957, Mr Rezáíe spent his childhood in Shiráz, and after completing high school with honours, obtained a degree in agricultural engineering from Pahlavi University in that city. After his marriage in 1981, he became a farm manager at a time when persecution of Bahá'ís was particularly intense, and opened an agricultural equipment company in Fars Province in 1985 that won wide respect in the region before being forcibly closed down. He later moved to Kermán, working as a carpenter and doing other odd jobs as the Bahá'ís faced increasing economic strangulation. Before his arrest as a member of the Yárán, he had already experienced detention in 2006 and forty days in solitary confinement. His two daughters were among fifty-four Bahá'ís arrested in Shiráz in May 2006 while engaged in a project for underprivileged youth.

Finally, the youngest member of the Yárán, Vahíd Tizfahm, was born 16 May 1973 in Urmia, in Iranian Azerbaijan. After receiving a high school diploma in mathematics, he became an optician in Tabriz, where he later owned an optical shop and studied sociology. He was married at the age of twenty-three and had one son, who was only nine years old at the time of his arrest in 2008. Mr Tizfahm served the Bahá'í community enthusiastically before all Bahá'í institutions were disbanded. At one time he was an eager, fervent member of the Bahá'í National Youth Committee and later was appointed to the Auxiliary Board, an advisory group at the regional level. He also taught local Bahá'í children's classes before being appointed to the Yárán in 2006.

Since the dissolution of the Yárán in 2008, the persecution of the Iranian Bahá'í community has continued unabated. But in spite of all the false charges against them, they have responded with a quiet dignity and a refusal to be victimised. Nor has their determination to work for the progress of their country diminished. In an open letter addressed to the Iranian Bahá'ís in August 2022, the Universal House of Justice defined the high standard of behaviour they have been called upon to character-ise, ideals which – as her memoir attests – have surely inspired Mahvash Sabet:

> The Bahá'ís seek justice and long for fairness and equity, but never pursue retaliation and revenge... They are driven out of their homes, but are a shelter and refuge to others... They are wronged, but are the well-wishers of those that wrong them... Beloved friends! ...bring hope to your countrymen's hearts. Be a source of consolation to every burdened soul and of confidence to every weary heart. Care sincerely for everyone and bring solace to every helpless one. Heal the pains of others and thereby

ease your own pain. And before Almighty God ask forgiveness for those who commit iniquity against you, and
pray fervently that the dross of prejudice and ignorance
may be cleansed from their hearts.[30]

FURTHER READING

'Abdu'l-Bahá. *Memorials of the Faithful*. Wilmette, IL: Bahá'í Publishing Trust, 1971.

— *The Will and Testament*. Wilmette, IL: Bahá'í Publishing Trust, 1945.

Amanat, Abbas. *Resurrection and Renewal: The Making of the Bábi Movement in Iran, 1844–1850*. Ithaca, NY: Cornell University Press, 1989.

— *Pivot of the Universe, Nasir al-Din Shah Qaja 1831–1896*. Washington DC: Mage, 1997.

Avery, Peter. *Modern Iran*. London: Praeger, 1965.

Balyuzi, Hasan M. *The Báb*, Oxford: George Ronald, 1973.

— *Bahá'u'lláh*. Oxford: George Ronald, 1980.

Banani, Amin. *Tahirih: A Portrait in Poetry*. Los Angeles: Kalimat Press, 2004.

Browne, Edward G. *A Year Among the Persians*, reprint from the 1893 edition. Belgium: Time-Life Books, 1983.

Cheyne, Thomas K. *The Reconciliation of Races and Religions*. London: Adam & Charles Black, 1914.

Curzon, George N. *Persia and the Persian Question*, London: Longmans Green, 1892.

Effendi, Shoghi. *God Passes By*. Wilmette, IL: Bahá'í Publishing Trust, 1944.

Mehrpour, Hossein. *The Hard Responsibility of Monitoring the Execution of the Constitution: A Collection of Letter and Legal Advice from the Committee for Monitoring the Execution of the Constitution, 1997–2005*. Saless publishing, 2005.

Milani, Abbas. *Lost Wisdom: Rethinking Modernity in Iran*. Washington, DC: Mage, 2004.

Milani, Farzaneh. *Veils and Words: The Emerging Voices of Iranian Women Writers*. Syracuse, NY: Syracuse University Press, 1992.

Mohammadi, Narges. *White Torture: Interviews with Iranian Women Prisoners*. London: Oneworld Publications, 2023.

Momen, Moojan. *The Bábi and Bahá'í Religions, 1844–1944*. Oxford: George Ronald, 1981.

Nabil-i-A'zam. *The Dawn-Breakers: Nabil's Narrative of the Early Days of the Bahá'í Revelation*. London: Bahá'í Publishing Trust, 1953.

Saberi, Roxana. *Between Two Worlds: My Life and Captivity in Iran*. New York: HarperCollins, 2010.

ACKNOWLEDGEMENTS

Before her third arrest, Mahvash appointed two long-standing friends to look after her literary estate and entrusted her poems and notebooks to two others to be translated and edited. But this book would not exist without the help of many more who made its publication possible. We would therefore like to thank a token few, on Mahvash's behalf.

Her courageous husband, Síyávash Sabet, deserves the greatest gratitude for his loving support, as do her son Fúrúd and her daughter Negár who was her mother's liaison when she went back to prison. She would doubtless wish to also acknowledge the other members of Yárán, and Faribá Kamalábádí in particular, who helped her to read and correct her records, as well as those brilliant Iranian women – Faezeh Rafsanjani, Narges Mohammadi and Nasrin Sotoudeh, in particular – who befriended and encouraged her to write while in prison. She would surely want to offer thanks to several unnamed fellow prisoners too, through whose courage her poems and notebooks escaped Evin. And special gratitude is also due to her literary agent, Kathleen Anderson, who offered her whole-hearted commitment to represent Mahvash, sight unseen, as well as to May Hofman of George Ronald, for having the vision to publish Mahvash's poetry when she was quite unknown and still in prison.

In addition, great appreciation is due to Rida Vaquas and Mary Victoria for their editing skills, and Amir Soltani and Marie-Catherine Vacher for their invaluable insights. Many other readers have also kindly commented on the manuscript and should be acknowledged, including Annie Latimier, Farzaneh Milani, Jan Fredrickson, Fionnuala McManamon, Jill Munro Husser, Mark Neville, Martine Caillard, Sarah Vincent Mar, Rob Weinberg and Ruth Goodwin.

Mahvash would surely want to thank you all.

ABOUT THE TRANSLATORS

Azita Mottahedeh was born in Iran and educated in the UK, where she attended the universities of Canterbury and Reading at both undergraduate and graduate levels. A seasoned translator from Persian to English, she has specialised in works about the Bahá'í Faith for more than thirty years. Her translations include articles and talks, memoirs and poetry, as well as lengthy books of philosophy, history and theology, including *175 Years of Persecution: A History of the Bábís and Bahá'ís of Iran* by Dr F. Vahman. Other works she has translated include *The Life of Anís Zunúzí* by R. Mehrabkhani, *The Kingdom of Existence* by Dr Ali-Murád Dávúdí, and Volumes I & II of *Radio Talks* by I I. Fatheazam. Several of her translations are in the process of publication. Azita Mottahedeh currently lives in Spain.

Bahiyyih Nakhjavani was born in Iran, raised in Uganda and educated in the UK, where she received a BA and BPhil from the University of York before receiving a doctorate from UMass in the US. She was also awarded an honorary doctorate by the University of Liège in 2007. In addition to teaching English literature and creative writing for four decades, she is the author of four novels about Iran and Iranians – *The Saddlebag, Paper, The Woman Who Read Too Much* and *Us & Them* – in addition to essays about the Bahá'í Faith such as

When We Grow Up, *Response*, *Four on an Island* and *Asking Questions*. She has also collaborated on the translation and adaptation into English of Persian poetry by Forough Farrokhzad and Mahvash Sabet. Bahiyyih Nakhjavani currently lives in France.

NOTES

1 https://www.bic.org/news/european-parliament-urges-unconditional-release-bahai-prisoner-conscience-mahvash-sabet

2 This institution later merged with another to become the University of Tehran.

3 'The Islamic Republic has disqualified us Bahá'ís from existence': letter of Mahvash Sabet, Evin Prison, Ábán 1402 (November 2023). https://iranpresswatch.org/post/24255/mahosh-sabets-letter-from-evin-islamic-republic-disqualified-bahais-for-life/

4 The Iranian calendar is a solar one, the first three months corresponding with spring, the second three months with summer, the third with autumn and the last with winter. The first day of the week in Iran is a Saturday so Fridays mark the beginning of the 'weekend.' https://sites.la.utexas.edu/persian_online_resources/numbers-1/calendar/

5 The city of Mashhad in Khorásán Razavi province, northeast of Tehran, has traditionally been the stronghold of the extreme right wing faction of the government of the Islamic Republic. The provincial branch of the Ministry of Intelligence in that city controls a detention centre near the public prison of Vakilábád, where political prisoners and prisoners of conscience are regularly detained and interrogated. Mahvash had to guess where she was. https://www.amnesty.org/en/documents/mde13/5206/2022/en/

6 The Persian word 'qarantineh' does not have the medical associations of its English counterpart. It is the designation used for the holding ward in Iranian prisons where those unable to pay bail are kept on remand. The sanitary conditions in such places are notorious and infectious diseases abound. There is no health care for the sick apart from drug substitutes.

7 Siyávash's offices, before being appropriated by the government, used to be in 'Doosti Alley', or Friendship Lane.

8 Erosion of civil liberties was on the rise immediately after the election of Ahmadinejad and after 2006, government control by the hardliners in Iran led to an increase in human rights violations: https://2001-2009.state.gov/g/drl/rls/83185.htm; https://www.cfr.org/backgrounder/irans-waning-human-rights

9 The Bahá'í calendar is made up of nineteen months consisting of nineteen days each, with four or five (on leap years) Intercalary Days taking place just before the month of fasting. This period of voluntary abstinence starts from 30 Esfand or 1 Farvardín (1 or 2 March) and culminates in the celebration of Naw-Rúz or New Year, on 20 or 21 March. https://www.bahai.org/beliefs/life-spirit/devotion/fasting

10 Lua Getsinger was an early American Bahá'í who had overcome prejudice through action. https://en.wikipedia.org/wiki/Lua_Getsinger

11 A precursor of the 'Woman, Life, Freedom' movement of 2022, the 'One Million Signatures' campaign, launched as a peaceful protest in 2006, aimed at changing the Iranian laws that discriminated against women. Activists such Nasrin Sotoudeh were attacked, jailed and underwent hunger strikes. https://en.wikipedia.org/wiki/One_Million_Signatures; https://learningpartnership.org/sites/default/files/resources/pdfs/One-Million-Signatures-Campaign-English_0.pdf.

12 An honorific term commonly used in Persian: "Khánúm" means Madam and "Áqá" means Sir; the addition of "Háj" or "Háji" infers piety and the performance of pilgrimage to Mecca.

13 'God is the Most Glorious' is a Bahá'í greeting.

14 From 'Song of the Greatest Wish' by the Persian poet Ahmad Shamlou, re-translated into English by A. Mottahedeh and B. Nakhjavani.

15 'Scarlet Wednesday' or *Chaharshambeh Suri* is an Iranian fire dance festival of Zoroastrian origin. It is the first festivity of the Iranian New Year, or Naw-Rúz. https://en.wikipedia.org/wiki/Chaharshanbe_Suri

16 The addict is calling on a variety of saintly figures associated with the history of Islam. Abul'Fadl is a title given to Abbas ibn-e Ali, the son of the fourth Sunni caliph, who is revered in Shi'a Islam for sacrificing his life to bring Imam Husayn, the Prophet's grandson, and his family water at the Battle of Karbala. Fatima Zahrá was the daughter of the Prophet Muhammad, the symbol of faith, chastity, purity, charity and kindness to the poor and the deprived. Imam Husayn is the third Imam and martyr of Shi'a Islam, whose shrine is the object of pilgrimage in Karbala. The Imam Reza/Rida was buried in Mashhad and therefore made the city holy.

17 The historical facts Mahvash evokes in this passage relate to the persecution and incarceration in the summer of 1852 of the founder of the Bahá'í Faith, Bahá'u'lláh, in the pestilential dungeon beneath the palace of the Qajars known as the Black Pit (Siyah Chal). This story and others related to the early history of the Bábi and Bahá'í Faith have been recorded in *The Dawn-Breakers* by the chronicler Nabil, chapter XXVI, pp. 631–2 and *God Passes By* by Shoghi Effendi. See Bibliography. https://www.bahai.org/bahaullah/life-bahaullah

18 The anthem sung by the condemned Bábís under the palace of Nasiru'd-Din Shah during the massacres of 1852. https://bahaistories.com/subject/prison-bab

19 The rice used in the prisons of Iran is notorious for its poor quality and sickening odour.
https://iran-hrm.com/2019/06/08/qarchak-prison-irans-worst-for-women/; https://irannewsupdate.com/news/women/leaked-reports-highlight-harassment-of-female-inmates-at-isfahans-

womens-prison/;   https://www.ncbi.nlm.nih.gov/pmc/articles/
PMC6270224/

20 The concept of 'impurity' or '*nejásat*' in Shi'ia Islam has been
    used against Jews, Zoroastrians and Bahá'ís. Also dogs. Bahá'ís
    are regarded as *najes* or untouchable by Iran's most fanatical
    clerics because they accept a revelation after that of Muhammad.
    The anti-Bahá'í rants on the radio of a particularly virulent
    cleric called Falsafi incited considerable violence and caused
    sporadic attacks against Bahá'í all over Iran in the early sixties.
    https://www.almahdi.edu/workshop/purity

21 The oldest member of the Yárán and a highly respected
    member of the community, Mr Khánjání had also been
    elected to the last National Spiritual Assembly of the Bahá'ís
    of Iran before it was disbanded in 1983.

22 The fourteenth-century Persian poet, Shafí'í Kad-kaní,
    translated by A. Mottahedeh and B. Nakhjavani.

23 The Bahá'í institute process is an educational framework of
    study designed to enhance Bahá'í individual and community
    life.   https://www.bahai.org/action/response-call-bahaullah/
    training-institute_

24 A possible reference to Sura An-Nahl (The Bee) in the Qur'an:
    'And your Lord inspired the bees... From their bellies comes
    forth liquid of varying colours, in which there is healing for
    people. Surely in this is a sign for those who reflect.'

25 The opening lyrics to the folk song 'Soghati' (souvenir gift)
    performed by the famous singer Hayedeh, much loved by
    Iranians all over the world, who left the country shortly
    before the Revolution, in 1978, and died in 1990 in California
    at the age of 47.

26 *The Fire Tablet* by Bahá'u'lláh. https://en.wikipedia.org/wiki/
    Fire_Tablet

27 Words of the twelfth-century mystic poet, Saná'í, addressed
    to all oppressors, on the dangers of pride, passion and greed.

28 An anthem sung by demonstrators on the streets, student
    protesters, and even at expatriate rallies, this revolution-era
    classic epitomises the country's struggle for freedom. Like Joan

Baez's version of 'We Shall Overcome' it has become part of popular culture. https://www.pbs.org/wgbh/pages/frontline/tehranbureau/2009/11/my-grade-school-friend.html

29 Adapted from the Bahá'í Writings.

30 The authorised translation from the Persian of this letter can be found on the following site: https://payamha-iran.org/en/document/365